D0789085

On Trust

On Trust

Art and the Temptations of Suspicion

Gabriel Josipovici

Yale University Press

New Haven and London

Copyright © 1999 by Gabriel Josipovici

All rights reserved. This book may not be reproduced in whole or in part, in any form (beyond that copying permitted by Sections 107 and 108 of the U.S. Copyright Law and except by reviewers for the public press) without written permission from the publishers.

Set in Walbaum MT by Best-set Typesetter Ltd, Hong Kong
Printed in Great Britain by St Edmundsbury Press

Library of Congress Cataloging-in-Publication Data

Josipovici, Gabriel, 1940–
    On trust: art and the temptations of suspicion/Gabriel
Josipovici.
    Includes bibliographical references and index.
    ISBN 0–300–07991–5 (alk. paper)
    1. Trust.   2. Literature—Philosophy.   3. Authorship—Moral and
ethical aspects.   4. Authority.   I. Title.
PN56.T77J67   1999
801—dc21   99–16233
                                                              CIP

The illustrations on pages 179 and 194 are Charity, Envy and Injustice from Giotto's *The Virtues and Vices* from the Arena Chapel, Padua (photographs: Scala).

A catalogue record for this book is available from the British Library.

10 9 8 7 6 5 4 3 2 1

In memory of my mother

A Winter's Tale

Mamillius: 'A sad tale's best for winter.'

Why a sad tale Mamillius?
Rather a tale of trust.
When buds, unfurled
to meet the lengthening days,
have flared with autumn's flame,
and when that flame is spent
the stark reality of trees
penned on a parchment sky
in bold calligraphy
foretells the spring:

life has gone underground;
the dead Hermione
shall come alive again;
Perdita is not lost,
she will raise up a son,
new crops will rise,
and even you, the ear of corn
cut down before its time,
is it not you
who tell this winter's tale?

Sacha Rabinovitch

Contents

Preface

Though the problems which this book explores have been with me for a long time, the impetus to examine them head on came with the invitation from the University of Oxford to take up the George Weidenfeld Chair of Comparative Literature for the year 1996–97. I am grateful to my old university for showing such trust in me and to all the friends and colleagues who made my stay there so enjoyable and stimulating. Jon Stallworthy, Malcolm Bowie, Rachel Trickett and, above all, Tony Nuttall, through their encouragement and critical acumen, gave me the confidence to persevere in the exploration of what at times seemed like a nebulous and even non-existent project. To them, my thanks. At St Anne's the Principal, Ruth Deech, and the Fellows were warm and welcoming; I doubt if I would have made the progress I did in developing my argument had I found myself in a less friendly atmosphere. My thanks too to

George Weidenfeld, whose ebulliance and generosity made me realise that the great age of patronage does not necessarily belong to the past.

I took several of the lectures I delivered at Oxford to Princeton, where the Council of Humanities and the English Department had invited me to be a Whitney Oakes Fellow in April 1997. I would like to thank all those involved, and in particular Maria diBattista, Alexander Nehamas and especially Michael Wood for making my stay in Princeton so pleasant. I learned much from them and have taken away fond memories of a lively and friendly intellectual environment.

I cannot remember when I first started discussing the theme of trust and suspicion with Brian Cummings, but it was a long time ago, and it was he who, when I wondered whether the subject might not be one which was better left alone, urged me to have a go at it and then responded in his wonderfully generous way to the chapters I showed him. As I was writing I discussed each chapter in detail with Bernard Harrison. We have been arguing about books, ideas and life for so long that it is difficult to know by now whose insights and formulations are whose. But he knows as well as I do that this book would not have been what it is had it not been for those exchanges. I almost feel like saying: what is good in this book belongs to him; the rest, I am afraid, to me.

I am grateful to Stephen Michelmore for his help in chasing up references; he has been more than generous with his time. Judith Ravenscroft was an ideal copy-editor: careful, patient, persuasive. As ever the staff at Yale have been exemplary in their efforts to ensure that demanding authors are thoroughly satisfied. To all of them, and especially to Candida Brazil, my thanks.

The book took shape in the aftermath of the death of my mother, Sacha Rabinovitch, and her generous and alert spirit lies behind much of what I have to say. I would like to think that this is, in the end, a book that would have given her pleasure.

Introduction

This book is an attempt to make sense to myself of problems which have been present to me, in a half-conscious sort of way, for all my writing life. Put very simply, this has to do with feeling on the one hand the need to write as something almost physical, like the need to breathe; and on the other hand that it is somehow no longer possible to treat writing as a *craft* and thus often being reduced to feeling it as an *indulgence*.

A craft implies a tradition into which you are inducted by a master; in which you serve your apprenticeship; and in which you in turn become a master. It implies that what you are doing when you practise your craft is, if not necessary to society, at least sanctioned by society. Weaving carpets if you are a female member of a nomadic tribe in Eastern Turkey is a craft tradition; your teacher is your mother, who, as well as passing on her skills to you, inducts you into a whole range of motifs, from which you will never depart, even though no two carpets you make will be precisely the same as hers or even exactly like each other. Being a violinist in a symphony orchestra in the West is to belong to a craft tradition, albeit a more conscious and highly organised one; the day is fast approaching when our society will feel it no longer has any need for symphony orchestras, but we are not quite there yet.

Being a writer is utterly different. Society may pay you for what you produce, but the laws of the marketplace are not the laws of the music academy: there is no sense that all are agreed on what is good and that such agreement rests on a common view of tradition.

Once, of course, writers were called makers, and making poetry, like painting pictures and composing music, *was* a craft tradition. We may pretend that that has not changed by having juries adjudicate literary awards and introducing creative writing courses into the university curriculum, but we are fooling ourselves. It is not just that my view of the best novel of the year is unlikely to coincide with that of the Goncourt or Booker Prize juries; it is that we would probably not even agree on what it was we were looking for. The issue rises to the surface every now and again when attacks are made on 'the London literary mafia' by those who feel themselves to be outside it. These attacks are often dismissed as sour grapes, and that is what they often are; but they point to a deeper problem than that of insiders and outsiders; they point to the fact that judgements in the arts are felt to be dictated by social, not artistic factors, and this is precisely because no-one knows what purely artistic factors would be any more.

I believe we have to be deeply suspicious of any claims to be representing tradition, in art as in politics. But at the same time I feel just as strongly that the notion that we are now free to plunder *all* traditions, selecting what we want and dismissing the rest, which in art and philosophy goes by the name of post-Modernism, is equally misguided. I believe that the spirit of suspicion has at some point to yield to the spirit of trust – trust in the material, trust in our abilities, trust in the act of making itself. The problem is how to keep suspicion from turning into cynicism and trust from turning into facileness. Trust without suspicion is the recipe for a false and meretricious art; but suspicion without trust is the recipe for a shallow and empty art.

But this is too abstract, too theoretical. I am not talking about large metaphyiscal issues but about everyday practical problems (the two are of course connected). I am talking about what happens when the need to write forces you to sit down in front of a blank sheet of paper, and the sense of not belonging to any craft tradition frustrates that need.

Here is what I am talking about: listen to these five different versions of a tiny piece of dialogue:

1) – Shall we go then?
    – Well . . . All right.
2) – Shall we go then? said Jack.
    – Well . . . All right, said Jim.
3) – Shall we go then? asked Jack.
    – Well . . . All right, answered Jim.
4) – Shall we go then? asked Jack hesitantly.
      Jim was tight-lipped. – Well . . . All right, he said at last.
5) – Shall we go then? asked Jack, letting a note of hesitation creep into his voice.
      Jim was tight-lipped. His face remained expressionless. – Well . . . His voice trailed away. Then, pulling himself together, he said firmly: – All right.

You see how many choices are involved, even in a simple exchange like that. And you see how different is the feel of the narrative in each case. And that is to leave to one side the problem of the purely visual feel of the dashes which I have chosen instead of the more usual inverted commas. In my own work I have always favoured the dash, but to explain why is not easy. Is it because it is the more normal convention in French? Because Joyce uses them? But that would not be enough to make me fly in the face of the English convention. Is it then because I feel that they somehow correspond better to what I am after? That must be it, but why is that – which is in effect to ask: what am I after? As we read novels we are mostly unaware of the writer's having to make choices, but if you're the writer you can't help but be.

Now if I can write a tiny fragment of dialogue in so many different ways, how am I going to decide which is the right way? If each decision depends on how I feel on the day I'm writing, or how I imagine novels ought to be written, or, which amounts to the same thing, on which books I've read, then what happened to my need to speak? For that was something intensely personal and urgent, something which seemed to have nothing to do with books and to be too deeply rooted to be dependent on daily fluctuations of mood.

There are no large or global answers to this question. There are only temporary and local accommodations. Each time I begin a new work it plagues me afresh. The solutions of other writers cannot help you, for, as Eliot put it,

> last year's words belong to last year's language
> And next year's words await another voice.

At the same time the discovery that other writers have faced similar problems to your own gives you the confidence to keep going. For though each of us has to find his own solutions, and though each work brings its own problems, the sense that one is not alone in one's confusions is a profound relief. It is more: it is a source of strength in the moments of dejection.

If the sense of a craft tradition has indeed gone for good in the arts then at least it may be possible to put together a sort of tradition of those who have faced this situation in all its implications. It is with this tradition that I will be dealing in the latter part of this book. I will be exploring the dangerous but necessary journey every post-Romantic artist has to make, without maps or guides, into the unknown, a journey which will never get under way so long as the artist imagines that he can rely on past traditions, but which will founder if he lacks the trust to go where the forms of language and his instincts take him.

In order to understand this situation properly, though, we need to go behind it, to earlier artists and their relation to the world and to their own craft traditions, so as to grasp what was lost when those traditions were no longer felt to be viable. This is what chapters 2, 3, and 4, and the excursuses to chapters 2 and 4 will attempt to do.

To begin with, though, it will be necessary to focus on the present age, the age which has aptly been called The Age of Suspicion.

1 The age of suspicion

My whole body puts me on my guard against each word; each word, before letting itself be put down, has to look round on every side; the phrases positively fall apart in my hands, I see what they are like inside and then I have to stop quickly.

Franz Kafka

In 1950 the Russian-born novelist, Nathalie Sarraute, published an essay in *Les Temps Modernes* entitled 'L' Ère du Soupçon', The Age of Suspicion. It was a typical novelist's essay, dealing with a problem of great concern to her, how to depict character in fiction, under the guise of exploring a general *malaise*. Nevertheless, its title was prophetic, for in the almost half-century since its publication it has become abundantly clear that there is no better way to describe the culture of our era than as the age of suspicion.

1950 was not of course an arbitrary date. A year later Theodor Adorno published in Germany the little book of aphorisms and reflections he had written in exile in America as the war was drawing to a close and news of the Nazi atrocities was beginning to emerge. Section 5 of Part I of *Minima Moralia* begins: 'There is nothing innocuous left ... Even the blossoming tree lies the

moment its bloom is seen without the shadow of terror.' 'Mistrust',
he insists, 'is called for in face of all spontaneity, impetuosity, all
letting oneself go, for [spontaneity] implies pliancy towards the
superior might of the existent.'

For Adorno exile and the news coming out of Europe had sharp-
ened the sense of how apparently benign emotions can lead to
horror: 'The caring hand that even now tends the little garden . . .
but fearfully wards off the unknown intruder, is already that which
denies the political refugee asylum.' And, in a characteristically
oversimple but nonetheless suggestive comment: 'There is a straight
line of development between the gospel of happiness and the construction of camps of extermination so far off in Poland that each
of our own countrymen can convince himself that he cannot hear
the screams of pain.'

This must surely strike a chord in all of us. It is summed up in
Adorno's famous remark that after Auschwitz lyrical poetry is no
longer possible. It is no longer possible because what it leaves out
casts too dark a shadow over what is included and raises questions
about the very impulse which gave rise to lyric poetry in the first
place. Yet it is important to realise that the attitude of suspicion
not just towards the words and deeds of others but even more
towards our own is not simply the result of the awareness of the
atrocities of the camps. Sarraute, after all, took her title from
a remark of Stendhal's, made in 1832: 'Le génie du soupçon est
venue au monde.' (The spirit of suspicion has entered the world.)
And Keats was already struggling with a similar feeling when he
wrote on 8 October 1817 to Benjamin Bailey: 'Health and Spirits
can only belong unalloyed to the selfish Man – the Man who thinks
much of his fellows can never be in Spirits.' Yet Keats felt, equally
strongly, equally instinctively, that poetry *should* celebrate happiness
– and that contradiction at the very heart of his enterprise was
of course to be the subject of his greatest poems and most
moving letters.

Adorno himself was later to write of Hölderlin's poetry that 'it attacked, with good reason, the type of subjective lyric that had become the norm since Goethe's early work'. Hölderlin, he argues, struggling with the perception that there is no unified self to express and no adequate language with which to express, forges a style that constantly draws attention to the fact that the very notion of style is now in question. If this is the case then he stands, along with Sterne and Kleist, as one of the precursors of those nineteenth-century thinkers who prided themselves on writing 'against the times', to quote the subtitle of one of Nietzsche's books, and who have been described by Paul Ricoeur as the 'masters of suspicion'.

What does Ricoeur mean by this and by the equally striking phrase he used to describe the work of Marx, Nietzsche and Freud, 'the hermeneutics of suspicion'? What characterises all three men, he suggests, is that they revealed that what we had taken to be natural, a 'given', was in fact man-made, the result of choices and decisions made by individuals and communities. Thus Marx laid bare the workings of capital, Nietzsche the workings of morality, Freud the workings of sexuality. Where the Enlightenment had seen all men as essentially one, and human nature as unchanging, the nineteenth-century masters of suspicion set about exploring the *genealogies*, the secret histories, of morals and social institutions, with the aim of freeing men from bonds to which they did not even know they were subject.

To understand the radical nature of the hermeneutics of suspicion we need to look at one of two examples of it at work. In one of his earliest essays, 'The Use and Abuse of History', Nietzsche raises the simple but devastating question: why history? 'Consider the cattle', he begins, 'grazing as they pass you by: they do not know what is meant by yesterday or today, they leap about, eat, rest, digest . . . , neither melancholy nor bored. This is a hard sight for man to see; for, though he thinks himself better than the animals because he is human, he cannot help envying them their happiness . . . But he also wonders at himself, that he cannot learn to forget but clings relentlessly to the past.' The nineteenth-century passion for history – we might think of our own culture's passion for biography and travel-writing – is, he suggests, not something neutral, innocent; it is profoundly pathological. It is akin to sleeplessness, an inability to lay the past to rest. Our civilisation is in danger of breaking down through this lack of sleep, this compulsive need to know the past.

Nietzsche prefaces his essay by quoting Goethe: 'I hate every thing that merely instructs me without augmenting or directly invigorating my activity.' And he returns to Goethe at the climax of one of his last books, *The Twilight of the Idols*. What he admires in Goethe, he says there, is his 'limited perspective', his ability to set himself a host of strictly limited and practical goals. Goethe is an ideal for Nietzsche not because he is one large vague thing, a 'genius', but because of the many distinct things he turned his mind to and mastered: writing poems and plays; running a theatre; study-ing the ways plants grow and how we perceive colour; advising rulers. He undertakes nothing for the mere sake of instruction, but always 'for the sake of life and action'. By contrast, what Nietzsche finds so horrendous about the modern passion for history is that we indulge in it as in a compulsive activity, not asking ourselves if it is good for us or if it invigorates our activity but as though know-ledge about the past were a good in itself. In fact we are more like men who stuff themselves with food simply because they don't know how to stop, with the result that there is a disaster waiting to happen to us.

In another of his late works, *The Genealogy of Morals*, Nietzsche returns to the attack on the age's need for history, its use of history as a drug, but this time he sees it as part of a larger problem which affects *all* enquiry. Many of his contemporaries, he says, have accepted that the Christian God is a myth, but they nevertheless still persist in acting and thinking as though there were a God, for they still believe that the world has a meaning: 'These men are a long way from being *free* spirits, because they still believe in truth.' That is, for all their scepticism about Christianity, they believe that all the little grains of scholarship and scientific enquiry will somehow add up to a meaningful whole. And Nietzsche concludes this section of his third essay:

> It appears that today inquiry itself stands in need of justification (by which I do not mean to say that such justification can be found). In this connection let us glance at both the oldest and the most recent philosophers: to a man they lack all awareness that the will to truth itself needs to be justified. There is a gap here in every philosophy – how are we to explain it? By the fact that the ascetic ideal has no far governed all philosophy: that truth was premised as Being, as God, as supreme sanction; that truth was not allowed to be called in question. But once we withhold our faith from the God of the ascetic ideal a new problem poses itself, the problem of the value of truth. The will to truth must be scrutinised; our business now is tentatively to question the will to truth.

So, from the will to history to the will to truth. And Nietzsche is in no doubt about the psychological motivation for this: 'Any meaning is better than none.' Man does not mind suffering, hard work, deprivation, so long as he feels this is in the service of *meaning*. 'Let me repeat, now that I have reached the end, what I said at the beginning: man would sooner have the void for his purpose than be void of purpose.'

And now listen to another master of suspicion, not Marx or Freud but Kierkegaard. His tone is gentler, more ironical, but suspicion cuts quite as deeply here too and, as with Nietzsche, still speaks directly to our concerns. 'It is not improbable', he writes in the Introduction to his book *On Authority and Revelation*, written some twenty-five years before Nietzsche's essay on history:

that the lives of many men go on in such a way that they have indeed premises for living but reach no conclusions – quite like this stirring age which has set in movement many premises but also has reached no conclusion. Such a man's life goes on till death comes and puts an end to life, but without bringing with it an end in the sense of a conclusion. For it is one thing that a life is over, and a different thing that a life is finished by reaching its conclusion. In the degree that such a man has talents he can go ahead and become an author, as he understands it. But such an understanding is an illusion. For that matter . . . he may have extraordinary talents and remarkable learning, but an author he is not, in spite of the fact that he produces books . . . No, in spite of the fact that the man writes, he is not essentially an author; he will be capable of writing the first . . . and also the second part, but he cannot write the third part – the last part he cannot write. [This could be a commentary on Beckett's Trilogy, still a century away.] If he goes ahead naively (led astray by the reflection that every book must have a last part) and so writes the last part, he will make it thoroughly clear by writing the last part that he makes a written renunciation to all claim to be an author. For though it is indeed by writing that one justifies the claim to be an author, it is also, strangely enough, by writing that one virtually renounces this claim. If he had been thoroughly aware of the inappropriateness of the third part – well, one may say, *si tacuisset, philosophus mansisset.*

And Kierkegaard concludes with this pregnant aphorism: 'To find the conclusion, it is necessary first of all to observe that it is lacking, and then in turn to feel quite vividly the lack of it.'

Suspicion here, in Nietzsche and Kierkegaard, is not suspicion of this historian or that, this novelist or that, such as we might find it expressed by Dr Johnson or Dr Leavis; it is suspicion of the whole enterprise such as it is so solemnly, so passionately carried on in their (in our!) own time. By asking the questions: Why history? Why inquiry? Why three-decker novels? Nietzsche and Kierkegaard raise doubts which, once raised, will not go away.

Of course the practitioners of these disciplines might answer: why, I write in order to enlighten mankind; or, in order to manifest my genius; or, in order to earn my living. But, asks the master of suspicion, is this really the motive? And is it a sufficient motive? He asks this not in order to probe the individual pathology of the writer; rather, he wants to raise questions about communal pathology, to ask whether these are not ways, sanctioned by society, of hiding the truth from ourselves rather than revealing it.

Since the time of the first masters of suspicion their modern disciples, mainly French, have refined their insights and turned their attention to every aspect of life and culture in the West, from penal institutions to Blue Guides, from the workings of the family to the slogans of advertising, from Hollywood films to the history of science. This has led to some remarkable and illuminating works. At the same time they and their — mainly English and American — disciples have so completely accepted the premises and findings of the original masters of suspicion that what had been hard-won insights and ironical barbs have tended more and more to take on the character of a method and an orthodoxy. As a result the very nature of suspicion has been altered, and, I want to argue, its power blunted.

Once again, it is best to move from generalities to concrete examples. To make my point I want to look briefly at the career of the wittiest and most subtle of the modern French masters of suspicion, Roland Barthes.

In his early work, *Le Degré zéro de l'écriture*, Barthes set out to discover, Nietzschean fashion, the bad faith of the nineteenth-century novel. He showed how the use of the past tense and the third person works on us in such a way that we feel both safely insulated from the narrative and yet convinced of its truth: 'The finality common to both the Novel and narrated History', he writes, 'is to alienate facts: the *passé simple* is the very act of possession by society of its own past and its possibility.'

What Barthes dislikes about the nineteenth-century novel is that it pretends to be all of a piece, to exist 'out there', free of any personal choices by the author. But, as he remarks apropos of a novel of which he *does* approve, Michel Butor's *Mobile*, 'the discontinuous is the fundamental status of all communication; signs are only ever discrete'. A tree or a baby 'merely grows', as Wallace Stevens puts it in his delightful poem, 'Add This to Rhetoric', but a poem or a book is made up of sentences which are in turn made up of words which are in turn made up of letters, just as a painting is made up of brushstrokes and even *The Ring* is made up of individual notes. The central problem for the artist, says Barthes, is 'to know how to mobilise this fatal discontinuity, how to give it a breath, a time, a history'. Of course everything hinges on that word 'mobilise': what Barthes likes about Butor and dislikes about the classic novel is that the former is aware of the fact that this requires human choices, human skills, and makes sure that we are aware of it too, while in the latter the author conceals this fact from himself and from us.

The characteristic of the classic novel is the smoothness of its surface. Since it seems to exist 'out there', free of any maker, it offers no purchase for criticism. As a result commentators on novels have tended to speak in the very terms the novels themselves have presented them with – essentially, character and plot. When Barthes returned to the issue in his extended study of Balzac's novella, *Sarrasine*, he was determined to go against the grain of the narrative, to open it out for inspection, to return it to its discrete elements.

It is now generally agreed that the scheme he used in order to do so was hardly as rigorous and scientific as he tried to make out. But to dismiss *S/Z* for that reason is to fail to see the real target of Barthes's criticism. The old Barthes, the scourge of bourgeois modes of representation, who comes over in his early *Mythologies* as a much lighter and wittier version of Adorno, is still very much in evidence. Here he is on the last line of the novella: 'Et la marquise resta pensive.' (And the marquise remained pensive.) Barthes comments: 'Pensive, the marquise can think of many things which have happened, but of which we will never know anything: the infinite openness of pensiveness . . . withdraws that ultimate lexis from all classification.'

But since every element *in* the story is at the same time a part of the message *of* the story, Barthes is able to show that for Balzac as well as for the marquise this is in fact the perfect ending:

> Like the marquise, the classic text is pensive. Full of meaning
> . . . , it seems always to keep in reserve one last meaning, which
> it does not express, but whose place it keeps free and significant
> . . . Pensiveness (in faces, in texts) is the signifier of the inex-
> pressible, not of the unexpressed. For if the classic text has
> nothing more to say than it says, at least it wishes to 'have it
> understood' that it does not say everything . . . Just as the pen-
> siveness of a face signals that this head is full of language held
> back, so the (classic) text inscribes in its system of signs the sig-
> nature of plenitude: like the visage, the text becomes *expressive*
> . . . blessed with . . . interiority.

Barthes is still concerned to demythologise the novel, to show that its 'naturalness' is a pseudo-naturalness, its 'depth' and 'life' the product of (largely unconscious) rhetoric. And he still confesses that the attempt on the part of the novel to appear natural makes him sick, gives him nausea, suffocates him. But I detect a crucial change. In his early work the sarcasm at the expense of Mankiewicz's *Julius Caesar* or Barrault's *Oresteia* was polemical: he wanted to show up the meretriciousness of middle-brow art so as to clear the ground for the appreciation of genuine works of art, such as the novels of

Butor, Robbe-Grillet and Queneau. Now he no longer disguises the very real pleasure the work of unmasking gives him. In fact his own pleasure in the task becomes a central plank in his theoretical argument.

There are, he says, two kinds of reading which a work like Balzac's novella can give rise to. There is the ordinary, naive reading, which is pure consumption, and there is *his* kind of reading, which is in effect a *re*-reading, and which does not simply follow where the text leads but finds active pleasure in going *against* the text, breaking it up, unmasking it. 'Re-reading', he says, 'an operation contrary to the commercial and ideological habits of our society, which recommends "throwing away" the story once it has been consumed (devoured), so that one may then move on to another story, buy another book, and which is tolerated only in certain marginal categories of readers (children, the very old, teachers), re-reading is here proposed as the basic method, since only it saves the text from repetition (those who neglect to re-read are condemned to read the same story everywhere), multiplies it in its diversity and plurality . . . [so that] it is no longer consumption but game.'

Some very important moves are being made here, which will lead to much in Barthes's later work, notably his stress on pleasure. They are moves, too, which have a significance far beyond Barthes's own development. In effect, they herald the advent of what has come to be known as post-Modernism. Not that Barthes instigated the movement; rather, his remarkable nose for shifts in fashion enabled him, in no mere self-seeking manner, to change with the times.

His argument is perfectly logical: to read naively is to read as a consumer, accepting the product without questioning it; to read with suspicion is to counteract this, to retain our freedom. In parallel fashion, the writer will retain *his* freedom by recognising that all continuity, all interiority, is a false continuity, a pseudo-interiority. 'Today's writing', says Foucault in an essay which has much in common with Barthes's, 'has freed itself from the dimension of expression . . . Writing unfolds like a game . . . In writing, the point is not to manifest or exalt the act of writing, nor is it to pin a subject within language; it is, rather, a question of creating a space into which the writing subject constantly disappears.'

But though we seem to have got here quite logically we have arrived at the wrong place. The first part of the argument, the critique of consumption and interiority, I can go along with; but the second, the attitude it is suggested the enlightened reader and writer take up, with its stress on game as the answer to consumption, does not correspond to my experience either as a reader or as a writer. What, I ask myself, has gone wrong?

To begin with, both Barthes and Foucault operate with a simplistic historical model: there is 'the classic novel', and there is the modern (just as for Derrida there is 'Western metaphysics' and then his own kind of philosophy). But the classic novel is itself the product of specific and fairly recent historical forces. What of earlier forms of narrative? Are they, too, guilty of the same bad faith? May it not be that the reason why Kafka is attracted to the parable and the oral tale, why Joyce feels an affinity with Rabelais, Nabokov with Pushkin, Kundera with Diderot, is because these models are free of precisely the faults Barthes charges the classic novel with? And, if they are, how are *they* to be read?

Secondly, the view of the reader as either a consumer or as liberated is unconvincing. 'Those who neglect to re-read are forced to read the same story everywhere', Barthes says. In other words, those who read innocently, without suspicion, can never really respond to a work as something other than themselves. But is that true? Does it correspond to our experience? Do we not all know how a first reading can be the most illuminating one, making one suddenly aware of things one had – one now realises – always obscurely felt, but never been able to bring to consciousness? Certainly my own first reading of Proust and of Muriel Spark was such an experience, and no amount of subsequent re-reading has ever given me the same sense of a door suddenly being opened and yet also of a certain kind of coming home.

Thirdly, there is the problem of tone. There is something in itself suspicious about the ease of the solutions proposed by Barthes and Foucault, the triumphalism of their tone: re-reading 'saves the text from repetition': writing today 'has freed itself from the dimension of expression'. Remember Kierkegaard's aphorism: 'To find the conclusion, it is necessary first of all to observe that it is lacking, and then in turn to feel quite vividly the lack of it.' Barthes and Foucault certainly observe the lack, but do they feel vividly enough what this lack entails?

In the last of his pseudonymous works, the *Concluding Unscientific Postscript*, Kierkegaard seems to offer a striking portrait of the post-Modernist: 'Among so-called negative thinkers there are some who after having had a glimpse of the negative have relapsed into positiveness, and now go out into the world like town criers, to advertise, prescribe and offer for sale their beatific negative wisdom . . . These town criers of negativity are not much wiser than the positive thinkers, and it is inconsistent of the latter to be so wroth with them.' The genuine negative thinker, he goes on, 'constantly keeps the wound of the negative open, which in the bodily realm is sometimes the condition for a cure'.

Kierkegaard's 'genuine' negative thinker always recognises how easy it is for suspicion itself to harden into a new conviction, the conviction of the unquestioning value of suspicion. Kierkegaard never does this. In that regard his first major work, *Either / Or*, is exemplary. The young man who writes the first half sounds at times quite like late Barthes. In the little essay entitled 'The Rotation Method', for example, he deals with the problem of choice, which haunts all his thinking, in a highly original and witty way. 'All men are bores', the essay begins. 'Those who do not bore themselves usually bore others, while those who bore themselves entertain others. Those who do not bore themselves are generally people who, in one way or another, keep themselves extremely busy; these people are precisely on this account the most tiresome, the most utterly unendurable.' Such perpetually restless people, he goes on, imagine that they are doing something useful but they are in effect merely concealing their boredom from themselves. The young man who writes the essay, however, takes a different view of life: 'I assume that it is the end and aim of every man to enjoy himself', he says. Yet if life has no meaning and every course of action is as good or bad as any other, the mere unthinking pursuit of pleasure will soon pall. For this reason he has worked out a scheme designed to cause him the maximum enjoyment. It is based on the principle of crop rotation, which is at once arbitrary and rigorous. It is in effect a permutational principle like that which Schoenberg will develop as a compositional method in the following century. 'People usually think it easy to be arbitrary', he says, 'but it requires much study to succeed in being arbitrary so as not to lose oneself in it, but so as to derive satisfaction from it.' And he gives some examples of his procedure: 'You go to see the middle of a play, you read the third part of a book. By this means you ensure yourself a very different kind of enjoyment from that which the author has been so kind as to plan for you. You enjoy something entirely accidental; you consider the whole of existence from this standpoint; let its reality be stranded thereon.'

This little essay reminds me of that fine modern novel, Georges Perec's *La Vie mode d'emploi*. The central figure in that novel, a millionaire called Bartlebooth, determines early in life not simply to fritter away his time on earth but to do something with it. He hits upon a scheme: for ten years he will learn how to paint in watercolours; then for twenty years he and his manservant will tour the world, taking in a different port or seaside town every fortnight, where Bartlebooth will paint a watercolour of the seascape and have it despatched back to Paris, where it will be turned into a wooden jigsaw puzzle of seven hundred and fifty pieces, and put away in a box. Five hundred such boxes will await Bartlebooth on his return, and he will spend the next twenty years solving the puzzles, also at the rate of one a fortnight. As each is completed the original water-colour will be peeled away, taken to the spot where it was originally painted, and there a chemical solution will be applied to it which will dissolve it and leave only the original pristine sheet, which will be returned to him. Thus Bartlebooth will have lived from his twenty-fifth to his seventy-fifth year engaged in a pursuit that is wholly absorbing and totally useless. He will have enjoyed himself, harmed no-one, and by the end will have left absolutely no trace of his fifty years of concentrated activity. The scheme of a madman, perhaps, but also an image, lucidly conceived and unflinchingly carried out, of what we all do or do not do with our lives.

Kierkegaard's young man and Perec's Bartlebooth have much in common with Barthes and the Foucault of the essay 'What is an Author?' But the crucial difference lies in the fact that neither Bartlebooth nor the young man is simply the spokesman of the author. Kierkegaard's character is a young man in despair. He sees lucidly into the abyss that is facing him and refuses to be taken in by the slogans of the world: work hard, get married, live a useful life. He is answered in the second half of the book by an older man, a judge, who is himself married and, he says, at ease with the world. All your melancholy and despair, he says to the young man, stem from the fact that you won't commit yourself. Once you make a choice of a wife, a profession, all your problems will fall away. But how can I commit myself, we can imagine the young man answer-ing, when no one choice is any better or more meaningful than any other, when the world is divided into those who bore others and those who bore themselves? You say that, we can imagine the other replying, only because you have not made the choice.

Kierkegaard does not adjudicate between the two. It may be that the older man is in fact right, that he really does know what the young man is going through, that he has himself been through it and come out on the other side. But it may also be that the young man is right and the older man is simply conforming blindly and smugly to what the world expects of him. The problem will haunt Kafka as well: perhaps his father is right and he is simply being foolish and self-destructive in not complying with his wishes; yet he can't overcome his scruples, his suspicion of his father's attitudes, and make the commitments his father requires of him. Is he right in this? Is he wrong? Neither Kierkegaard nor Kafka knows the answers to these questions.

And Bartlebooth too, in Perec's wonderful novel, is no mere mouthpiece of the author. He dies, his project uncompleted, in mid-puzzle, foiled by the messiness of life, by its refusal to correspond to his plans. Perec's novel, itself written by means of the most complex permutational procedures ever used by a writer, Joyce included, both celebrates Bartlebooth and recognises his quixotic folly. Though it is an enormously funny book, it has none of the jauntiness, the triumphalism even, that pervades the texts of Barthes and Foucault. If the only pleasure is the pleasure of not being taken in, then, Kierkegaard and Perec suggest, it is a bitter pleasure indeed.

Kierkegaard's young man and Perec's Bartlebooth are, in a sense, both dandies. The dandy is a man in despair, a cynic who, lacking any trust in the world, tries in vain to substitute for that a sense of pleasure in his own performance. Barthes's notion of the pleasure to be derived from re-reading is the pleasure of the dandy: I am not going to be taken in, I am not going to become a consumer, I am going to treat all this as a game and enjoy my superiority and clear-sightedness in treating it as such.

In both Kierkegaard and Perec the focus is double: our sympathies go out to the dandy, but his struggle to make something of his life seems driven by an unacknowledged despair. Both of them, in other words, make us see that despair may be our necessary condition, but that this is hardly a cause for celebration. And in this they are not alone. For a great many writers, from the early Romantics on, suspicion is seen as a kind of blight. The cause of his dejection, Coleridge felt, was that now he could 'see, not feel, how beautiful' the natural world was. For Wordsworth the very onset of maturity and the thoughts that come with it mean that 'the things which I have seen I now can see no more'. Both Schiller and Kierkegaard, struggling to understand why their own work and that of their contemporaries seems so heavy, so lethargic, so weighted down with melancholy, are moved to contrast it with that of the ancient Greeks, who seem to them to have a lightness, a buoyancy, which they feel they can never recover. Eliot, on Margate sands, 'can connect nothing with nothing', and this hardly fills him with Barthian *jouissance*; while Kafka, in an early letter to Brod, can only confess: 'I haven't written a single line that I can accept, instead I have crossed out all I have written – there wasn't much – since my return from Paris. My whole body puts me on my guard against each word; each word, before even letting itself be put down, has to look round on every side; the phrases positively fall apart in my hands, I see what they are like inside and then I have to stop quickly.' Is this the death of the author that Barthes and Foucault so blithely celebrate?

The most extreme example of the sense of horror engendered by our living in the age of suspicion is perhaps the one Thomas Mann conjures up in his last major novel, *Doctor Faustus*. Adrian Leverkühn did not plan to become a composer; his corruscating clarity of mind, allied to his deep sense of the need for a firm centre to his life and his natural asceticism, impelled him at first towards theology. But gradually he realised that the only thing he really wanted to do was write music. The trouble is that he is too clear-headed not to see the meretricious and purely subjective nature of anything he might write. Once, he feels, composers were craftsmen; they worked within established traditions, turning out what their patrons required of them while feeling themselves at the same time to be working for the greater glory of God. Some of them, Josquin or Bach, did it supremely well; others did it efficiently enough. With Romanticism the ideas of tradition and craft disappeared; they became false, outmoded, and someone like Beethoven sensed that they could no longer support him. In their place he put his fiery imagination, his hope in the future, his abounding self-confidence. Instead of working for a patron he would work for himself. Now, in the aftermath of Beethoven, what have we got? Only our own little egos, our own little fantasies. And we cannot even believe that they are ours any longer. For we are somehow too late, producing everything at second hand. Or perhaps we only imagine that, but that imagining is destructive enough. We can, with enough hard work and enough sense of the marketplace, earn our living by our music, but what has happened to the high dreams of art as the most meaningful of human activities?

So the question is raised: is Leverkühn by nature too cold, too cerebral, too suspicious ever to allow himself to be taken over by the necessary inspiration? Or is inspiration itself a Romantic and bourgeois myth to which he is too discerning to succumb? What the devil offers this modern Faustus then is this: not wealth or glory or knowledge or happiness, but only the temporary release from the intolerable spirit of suspicion. It is a bargain he cannot refuse.

To the hard-headed post-Modernist all these examples will seem not only distasteful but positively misguided. They will reek to him of a worn-out metaphysics of presence and transcendence from which he feels he has, thankfully, escaped. The trouble with Eliot, Kafka and Mann, not to speak of Schiller and Kierkegaard, is that they still somehow believe in these fraudulent absolutes and so are, necessarily, broken on the back of contradictions that only exist in their own minds. Let us accept that all making is tainted and corrupt, that there is no meaning to life or art, he will argue, and let us rejoice in this rather than lamenting it, and amuse ourselves with it while we can, playfully unmasking false transcendence and bad metaphysics, whether in the making of artefacts or in the writing of criticism.

Such an attitude clearly satisfies the post-Modernist, but it fails to satisfy me. It may simply be a matter of temperament or circumstance, but I obscurely feel that Kierkegaard and Mann have a point which the post-Modernist is missing and that the solutions he offers are thin and unreal.

It is interesting to note that at least one author who holds a distinguished place in the pantheon of post-Modernism does not seem to share its confidence. Samuel Beckett is invoked time and time again by post-Modernists as the scourge of false transcendence, the spokesman for the death of the author, the man who will never take yes for an answer. But when Foucault quotes from *The Unnamable*, 'No matter who is speaking, someone says, no matter who is speaking', as evidence for the death of the author, he forgets that it is not Beckett saying this but one of his characters, and that the point about that character is that he is desperately seeking to discover *who* speaks, to recover himself as more than a string of words, to wrest an 'I' from 'someone says'.

You will remember Malone, lying on his bed, trying to pass the time as he lies dying. His plan is to tell himself four stories and then, with luck, die. But, even as he embarks on the first story, he finds that he cannot do it. He is incapable of playing such games. 'What tedium!' he notes. 'This is awful', he confesses. 'Can't do it', he laments. And the reason why he can't is that he is too serious, too grave:

Live and invent. I have tried . . . Invent. It is not the word. Neither is live. No matter. I have tried. While within me the wild beast of earnestness padded up and down, roaring, ravening, rending . . . That has been my disease. I was born grave as others syphilitic. And gravely I struggled to be grave no more, to live, to invent . . . But at each fresh attempt I lost my head, fled to my shadows as to sanctuary, to his lap who can neither live nor suffer the sight of others living. I say living without knowing what it is. I tried to live without knowing what I was trying.

If we are ever to lay to wild beast of earnestness to rest it will not be enough to assert that it does not really exist. Trust will only come by unmasking suspicion, not by closing our eyes to it. And here Kierkegaard and Nietzsche and Mann can help us because, by recognising that they too are implicated in what they are trying to understand, they, unlike their post-Modernist descendants, alert us to the fact that suspicion itself has a history. And after all, why should it alone be exempt? Perhaps, then, by tracing that history, by uncovering its genealogy, we may be able to understand what it is that it supplants and why, once it appears, it seems so irresistible.

To do this we must be prepared to substitute other pairs of terms for trust and suspicion, so as not to fall into the trap of thinking that it is merely a matter of defining words or concepts. Perhaps we should take a hint from Malone and talk of lightness and earnestness; or from Simone Weil and talk of gravity and grace; for even from Schiller and be prepared to fill out the implications of his terms *naive* and *sentimentalische* as applied to Homer and Shakespeare on the one hand and to his contemporaries on the other. In any case, the search for that elusive other which I have called trust and which perhaps only reveals itself in the moment that it succumbs to suspicion must start with the earliest works of poetry and narrative known to the West, with Homer and the Hebrew Bible.

2 Lightness and gravity

When the age loses the tragic it gains despair.

Søren Kierkegaard

Thomas Mann called Schiller's *On Naive and Sentimental Poetry* 'the greatest of all German essays', and one can see why he was drawn to it. Though it is usually taken as an attempt on Schiller's part to come to terms with the difference between his own art and that of his great friend and rival, Goethe, its aims are far broader: nothing less than to try and understand the difference between nature and culture, child and adult, ancient Greece and modern Europe.

We are the children of civilisation, he says, and we cannot simply turn our backs on that; rather, 'with free resignation, you must subject yourself to all the *ills* of civilization, respect them as the natural conditions of the only good; only its *evil* you must mourn, but not with vain tears alone'. It is nature, he goes on, which can console us for the ills of civilisation: 'If you march out toward her from your artificial environment she will stand before you in her great calm, in her naive beauty, in her childlike innocence and simplicity.'

Yet, he points out, this contrast of civilisation and nature is not one made by the ancient Greeks: 'One finds so little trace among them of the *sentimental* interest with which we moderns are attached to the scenes and characters of nature.' The ancient Greeks are precise and faithful in their descriptions of nature, but not more so than in their response to a tunic, or a shield or any domestic article: 'Nature seems to interest his understanding and craving for knowledge more than his moral feeling; he does not cling to her with fervor, with sentimentality, with sweet melancholy, as we moderns do.'

This is no vague idealisation of ancient Greece but a lucid and profound analysis of the difference between two civilisations. Ancient Greece is not a simple projection; Schiller is struggling with something real, though he is aware of the difficulty of his task precisely because he himself can only approach it from a 'sentimental' perspective. 'The poet of a naive and youthful world . . . is severe and modest like a virginal Diana in her forests . . . The dry truth with which he deals with the object seems not infrequently like insensitivity. The object possesses him entirely . . . Thus, for example, Homer among the ancients and Shakespeare among the moderns reveal themselves; two vastly different natures separated by the immeasurable distance of the years, but *one* in precisely this trait of character.' And he goes on to speak personally, saying that when he first read Shakespeare he was put off by his apparent coldness and insensitivity, jesting in the midst of the highest pathos, 'restraining himself where my sympathies rushed on, then cold-bloodedly tearing himself away where my heart would gladly have lingered'. Thus, he says, 'misled by acquaintance with more recent poets into looking first for the poet in his work, to find *his* heart, to reflect in unison with *him* on his subject-matter . . . it was intolerable to me that here there was no way to lay hold of the poet, and nowhere to confront him'. The same, he says, occurred with Homer, whom he got to know at a later period. And he goes on to give as an example the scene in Book VI of the *Iliad* where Glaucus and Diomedes come face to face in battle and, having recognised one another as guest-friends, exchange gifts. 'This touching depiction of the piety with which the rules of *hospitality* were observed even in battle', comments Schiller, 'can be compared with an account of the *knightly sense of nobility* in Ariosto.' Unlike Homer, the Italian poet cannot conceal his own wonderment and emotion, or the feeling of distance which separates him from his characters: it is really he and his feelings which are the subject of the poem.

What is so good about Schiller is his honesty in the face of his experience of literature. He describes his prejudices and how a reading of Shakespeare and Homer gradually overcame them, much as we will see Proust doing in the face of Giotto's paintings in a later chapter. And what he notes here is precisely what every reader of Homer is first struck by. We may at first feel that there is a kind of ruthlessness in describing a warrior falling off a chariot, a spear through his neck, as like a diver plunging into the sea; or a warrior, his face a bleeding mass, his neck broken, as like a poppy in a field beaten down by a spring shower. Such images in a modern novel *would* be designed to shock; the effect in Homer is quite different. He is merely seeing things, and asking us to see them, from some perspective other than that of the individuals engaged in the action. From this perspective the eruption on to the Trojan plain of a horde of armed men is simply one aspect of life on earth, like the flight of migrating birds or the sudden emergence of a swarm of bees. Human beings, for this poet, are like leaves on a tree, 'one generation springeth up and another passeth away' (vi. 146–8). Yet the effect is not at all like that of, say, Ecclesiastes, with its remorseless refrain that 'all is vanity'. Rather, it is strangely beneficial and heartwarming, a sense that we are not alone but part of a larger rhythm.

This aspect of Greek culture is what Kierkegaard is concerned to explore in an essay written fifty years after Schiller's. What, asks Kierkegaard, is the difference between ancient and modern tragedy? He begins by noting that Greek tragedy consists of lyrics and choruses as well as dialogue, whereas modern drama consists only of dialogue. Why? Well, if dialogue is the exchange between two individuals, then lyric and chorus represent precisely that which cannot be dealt with in psychological terms, 'the more', as he puts it, 'which will not be absorbed in action and situation'. And the reason why it is there in ancient Greek but not in modern drama is that in Greek culture 'even if the individual moved freely, he still rested in the substantial categories of state, family and destiny'. Modern man, on the other hand, stands alone and all his decisions are his alone. Thus tragedy as the Greeks knew it is alien to him, for by throwing 'his whole life upon his shoulders, as being the result of his own acts', he transforms tragedy into ethics. However, 'when the age loses the tragic, it gains despair', for now man, feeling fully responsible for what happens to him, becomes riven by feelings of guilt at not having acted otherwise than he has.

There is indeed a modern kind of tragedy, but because it is totally inward it cannot be the subject of drama. To demonstrate the difference Kierkegaard takes Sophocles' *Antigone* and contrasts it with a possible modern version. The classical heroine, he says, nurses a sorrow which is public and external to her. It will not go away, but the fact that it is public and external means that its burden is not all-engulfing. Sophocles' Antigone 'lives as carefree as any other young Grecian maiden', but not because of any thoughtlessness on her part or because she does not feel concerned about her family. On the contrary, her family is her destiny. 'If this is dark and cloudy, it is also unchangeable. This furnishes the keynote of the Greek soul, and this is sorrow, not pain.' Sorrow is both an inner and an outer thing, pain is only inner. In *Antigone* the tragedy concentrates itself around one specific point, the fact that the heroine has buried her brother in defiance of the king's prohibition. 'If this is seen as an isolated fact', says Kierkegaard,

> as a collision between sisterly affection and piety and an arbitrary human prohibition, then *Antigone* would cease to be a Greek tragedy, it would be an entirely modern tragic subject. That which in the Greek sense affords the tragic interest is that Oedipus's sorrowful destiny re-echoes in the brother's unhappy death, in the sister's collision with a simple human prohibition; it is, so to say, the after effects, the tragic destiny of Oedipus ramifying in every branch of his family. This is the totality which makes the sorrow of the spectator so infinitely deep. It is not an individual who goes down, it is a small world, it is the objective sorrow, which, released, now advances in its own terrible consistency, like a force of nature, and Antigone's unhappy fate, an echo of her father's, is an intensified sorrow.

Contrast the modern Antigone. Here we have to imagine an Oedipus who has killed his father and married his mother and begotten children upon her, but who has not been found out and punished for it. Oedipus is now dead. Antigone suspects the truth, but she is not sure of it. Anxiety and dread thus weigh on every moment of her life. She can tell no-one of her suspicions, for to do so would be to betray her father. She cannot even tell the man she loves and who is in love with her; yet how can she give herself to him while holding back so central a part of herself? 'My Antigone is no ordinary woman', says Kierkegaard, 'and consequently her dowry is unusual – it is her pain. She cannot belong to a man without this dowry . . . To conceal it from such an observer would be impossible, to wish to conceal it would be a betrayal of her love; but can she marry him with it? Dare she confide it to any human being, even to the beloved? . . . By whose hand then does she fall?' he asks. 'By the hand of the living or the dead? In a certain sense, the dead . . . ; in another sense, by the hand of the living, in so far as her unhappy love makes that memory kill her.'

This Antigone bears more than a passing resemblance to the young Kierkegaard, burdened by the knowledge of his father's guilty secret. But that should not take away, any more than in the case of Schiller, from the acuteness of his observation, from his fine sense of what is and what is not any longer possible in the realm of art. His youthful essay both deepens and broadens Schiller's analysis and opens the way to a renewed understanding of the relation between form and content in both Greek and modern art.

Forty years after Kierkegaard's essay Nietzsche was to take the discussion of the difference between the lightness of the Greeks and the gravity of the moderns one step further. This time it is not a static but a dynamic picture that he puts forward, not a conflict of essences – naive and sentimental, ancient and modern – but a historical struggle. 'The Greeks', he said more than once, 'were superficial out of profundity.' That state of affairs was destroyed, though, not by impersonal forces, but by man himself, or rather by a single man, Socrates / Plato. 'I recognised Socrates and Plato as symptoms of decay, as agents of the dissolution of Greece, as pseudo-Greek, as anti-Greek', he writes in the section of *The Twilight of the Idols* entitled 'The Problem of Socrates'. For Nietzsche Socrates / Plato destroyed Greek *insouciance* not through this or that specific attack on Homer and the tragedians, but because of the entire thrust of their philosophy, which was the product of envy and *ressentiment* and which touched a collective nerve. 'Ultimately my mistrust of Plato extends to the very bottom of him', he says. 'I find him deviated so far from all the fundamental instincts of the Hellenes, so morally infected, so much an antecedent Christian . . . In the great fatality of Christianity, Plato is that ambiguity and fascination called the "ideal" which made it possible for the nobler natures of antiquity to misunderstand themselves and to step on to the *bridge* which led to the "Cross".' His cure for all Platonism, he goes on, for its idealism, its hatred of the body, its mistrust of the world, its glorification of the spirit of dialectic, its belief in the ultimate oneness of reason and goodness, has been the realism of Thucydides, what he calls his 'unconditional will not to deceive' himself, 'and to see reason in *reality* – not in "reason", still less in "morality"'.

Nietzsche does not so much argue his case as fire as many rounds as he can in the general direction of his opponent in the hope of mortally wounding him. But again it would be wrong to dismiss his case for that reason. As with Schiller and Kierkegaard, this is no vague idealisation of ancient Greece but a powerful and reasoned examination of what it is that makes it so appealing and so different from us. That all three men were on to something supremely important is borne out by the fact that much of the best recent work on the Greeks has in a sense been nothing but a series of footnotes to them. I am thinking of the brilliant studies of Greek tragedy and ethics by John Jones, Bernard Williams and Martha Nussbaum, and of the equally illuminating work on Homer by Colin McLeod, Jasper Griffin and Oliver Taplin, and on oral cultures by Eric Havelock and Gregory Nagy. Is it possible, making use of their insights, to develop the issues raised by Schiller, Kierkegaard and Nietzsche and so come to a more informed understanding of the way suspicion and gravity took hold and of the lightness and trust which they replaced?

In Book III of the *Iliad* we find Helen on the walls of Troy, pointing out to the old men assembled there the Greek warriors they see in the plain below. Having identified Agamemnon, Odysseus and Ajax, she says: 'And now all the rest of the bright-eyed Achaeans do I see, whom I could well note, and tell their names; but two marshallers of the host can I not see, Castor, tamer of horses, and the goodly boxer Polydeuces, even mine own brethren, whom the same mother bare. Either they followed not with the host from lovely

Lacedaimon, or though they followed hither in their sea-faring ships, they have now no heart to enter into the battle of warriors for fear of the words of shame and the many revilings that are mine.' She spoke, says the narrative, 'but the life-giving earth already held them under, there in Lacedaimon, in their dear native land' (III. 234–44).

We are asked to enter imaginatively into two worlds which cannot, in the normal course of life, exist together: Helen's fond thoughts for her living brothers and the fact that they are dead, buried deep in the earth, and she will never see them again.

Such passages are often described as epic irony. But irony is the wrong word. What we have rather is a breath-taking reticence which is at the same time rich in implications. The earth holds Castor and Pollux and will never let them go; at the same time that earth is their 'dear native land', the land where each man hopes to die, and it is also life-giving, the very same earth in which seed is planted that will sprout and bring forth the corn out of which bread is made on which men feed. 'But to no man would great Telamonian Aias yield', we read in Book XIII, 'to any man that is mortal, and eateth of the grain of Demeter, and may be cloven with the bronze or crushed with great stones' (321–3). There it is again, the double vision: man eats of the fruit of the earth, yet how frail and vulnerable he is compared to the stone or bronze which can cut into him or crush him.

It is instructive to contrast Homer's poem with the Homeric *Hymn to Demeter*. The metre and diction are the same, but we are in a different world here, the world of myth and legend, precisely the world where death is no longer final and the double vision does not pertain. The *Hymn* tells how Persephone was abducted by the God of the underworld and then a compromise was reached and she was given back to her mother for two-thirds of the year on condition that she spend the other third with Pluto. Hermes is sent to fetch her and bring her to her mother: 'And when Demeter saw them, she rushed forth as does a Maenad down some thick-wooded mountain, while Persephone on the other side, when she saw her mother's sweet eyes, left the chariot and horses and leaped down to her, and, falling upon her neck, embraced her' (385–9). This is the world of late Euripides and late Shakespeare; it is not the world of Homer and Greek tragedy.

The *Iliad* itself seems to be aware of the central importance of death as finality to its purpose and of how the intrusion of the kind of reprieve found in the *Hymn to Demeter* would destroy its artistic integrity. In Book XVI the Trojan warrior Sarpedon, who happens to be the son of Zeus, is about to be killed by Patroclus. Zeus is plunged into grief and toys with the idea of saving him. Hera cannot believe her ears: 'Most dread son of Cronos, what a word hast thou said! A man that is mortal, doomed long since by fate, art thou minded to deliver again from dolorous death?' Do what you like, she goes on, but don't imagine the other Gods will approve. For if you save him now you must realise that in the future other gods will do likewise with *their* mortal offspring and then chaos will ensue (432). So Zeus lets Sarpedon go to his fate.

This is a poem which does not flinch from the fact that our dear ones die and we can do nothing about it. In the last six books we watch as Achilles struggles with the knowledge that his beloved Patroclus is dead, killed as he rushed into battle dressed in Achilles' armour. For the first time he has to confront a world which will not accede to his wishes, and he cannot bear it. His fury redoubles and he hurls himself into battle against the Trojans. But even when he has killed Hector, Patroclus' slayer, even when he has dragged the bodies of the Trojans round the grave of his friend, he is not appeased.

Achilles is sorrowful, in Kierkegaard's terms, and he is also in pain. He gives vent to his sorrow in cries of lamentation, and in his terrible slaughter of the Trojans. He even gives vent to it in the very public and stylised form of funeral games for his dead friend.

But it is still not enough. As the last book opens we still find him tossing and turning, unable to sleep, unable to assuage his sorrow. Yet in the course of that book he finds a kind of peace at last.

It comes in the form of Priam, who materialises suddenly inside his tent, having set out against the wishes of his wife with the crazy idea of begging for the body of his son from the very man who has killed her. His guide, as with Proserpina, has been Hermes, but no miraculous resurrection is about to occur here, only a miraculous change of heart. Before the startled Achilles can react Priam has clasped his hands and begged him to think of his own father, suffering from the absence of his son in his far-away home, and so to take pity on him. Suddenly a change occurs. In an extraordinary act of imaginative empathy Achilles – whose epithet has so often been *schetlios*, pitiless, usually coming at the start of the line for greater emphasis – suddenly grasps what Priam might be suffering. It is the only time in the poem, I think, when any of the warriors shows understanding of what his opponents may be going through. The poet does not try to psychologise or explain, he simply recounts what happens, but, as Schiller noted, his narrative is all the more powerful for that:

So spake [Priam], and in Achilles he roused the desire to weep for his father; and he took the old man by the hand and gently put him from him. So the twain bethought them of their dead, and wept; the one for man-slaying Hector wept sore, the while he grovelled at Achilles' feet, but Achilles wept for his own father, and now again for Patroclus; and the sound of their moaning went up through the house. But when goodly Achilles had had his fill of lamenting, and the longing therefor had departed from his heart and limbs, forthwith then he sprang from his seat, and raised the old man by his hand, pitying his hoary head and hoary beard; and he spake and addressed him with winged words.

(507–17)

Achilles weeps for his father and for Patroclus, while Priam weeps for his son Hector. It is this community of grief which seems at last to bring peace to Achilles: 'When he had had his fill of lamenting and the longing therefor had departed from his heart and limbs', says the poet, down-to-earth and factual as ever. At last Achilles has no need to lament any more. That need is a physical and psychological one, the two cannot be separated, and so the need departs from both his heart and his limbs. At that moment Achilles starts to live again. Lifting up the old man who has been kneeling in front of him he is able to offer words of comfort to him: 'Bear thou up and neither wail ceaselessly in thy heart; for naught wilt thou avail by grieving thy son, neither wilt thou bring him back to life.' Rather, he says, 'Let us twain . . . bethink us of meat; and thereafter shalt thou make lament over thy dear son, when thou hast borne him into Ilios' (549–51; 618–20).

Achilles is not 'reconciled to life'; that is the language of the counsellor, not of Homer. But the death of Patroclus, in this moment of shared grief, becomes something to be borne, to be accepted as part of the order of things rather than railed against in self-destructive fury. At this point both Achilles and Priam share the double vision of the poem: a sense of life in all its goodness, happiness, abundance; and death as finality, which must be accepted as part of that abundance. The poem, it is often said, confers *kleos*, fame, upon all the warriors it names. But beyond that the poem allows us to tolerate our losses by making us grasp the double vision: that our loss is never to be made good; and that life goes on, that our loss is one everybody suffers and has to learn to bear. That is why, though the 'world' of Homer has long since passed away, we can still make contact with what is central to it; ultimately his world of life and death is ours as well.

When death meets Patroclus or Hector, when Achilles accepts that it is better to die young, having done what had to be done, than to live out his life in an ignominious old age, we have entered the world of Greek tragedy, the world of Agamemnon and Oedipus and Ajax. For it is not just the sense of an inevitable doom that hangs over these people, it is that their response to their fate bathes them and the works of literature they inhabit with that feeling of lightness, joyousness even, which Kierkegaard and Nietzsche sensed and which John Jones has explored at length in his wonderful book, *On Aristotle and Greek Tragedy*. 'The Greeks', writes Jones, 'present us with a most brilliant awareness of personal identity which by and large they did not pursue beyond the grave; they just felt, and said, that death awaits life at the last. Their literature everywhere reflects this gesture of final self-surrender, so appealingly blithe and so strange.'

Coming back to the subject later in his book, he remarks: 'For the society which produced Sophocles, death is an experience which the life of the group comprehends . . . And for Sophocles himself, death is not so much the end of life's journey as it is all life's constant fringe.' This is beautifully put. And when he goes on to suggest that the blind Oedipus, feeling his way on the stage in *Oedipus at Colonus*, is the image of Sophoclean man, teleologically blind, yet moving 'with a shell-like containment of final ignorance and impotence', joyfully going to the death he knows awaits him, we are brought closer to an understanding of why the Romantics felt that the Greeks had got hold of something precious which we ourselves have lost.

In both Aeschylus and Sophocles, Jones argues, 'the moment when a man perceives the operation of the powers that are destroying him is one of solemn religio-tragic exaltation – not because the individual is "saved" thereby, but because Necessity and Fate and the ways of Zeus have been exposed for human consciousness in a flash of perfect clarity; a demonstration which is also a sufficient vindication'. Of course it need not be a male experience. Think of Cassandra in the *Agamemnon*. But what Jones has identified is the source of Oedipus' composure and of his healing realism, a realism akin to that of Achilles in his urging of Priam to eat now that he knows his son's body will be returned to him for public burial. 'My children', Oedipus says to his daughters just before he leaves them for ever, 'this day you lose your father; here and now there perishes all that is I, and you will not any longer bear the burden of tending me – a heavy burden, my children, as I know. And yet one word, quite alone, resolves all this pain. That word is love. Love was the gift you had from me as from no one else, and now you must live out your lives without me.' And Jones comments, very finely: 'He is not using the word solely to denote the fact of his love, he is looking at the word as at a half-domesticated life which remains still outward and alien at the moment of appropriation. For utterance *is* appropriation; the word *is* Oedipus's.'

Jones rightly insists that we damage Greek tragedy by trying to psychologise it, to 'enter the mind' of the hero. For it is not the hero but the whole tragic action, the *mythos*, as Aristotle called it, which is the focus of our attention. This is what gives Greek tragedy, like Homeric epic, its double focus. To try to enter the mind of the hero is, in Schiller's terms, to sentimentalise this art, to import both pathos and a false ethical judgement into an art which asks us rather to see human life and death as part of a larger rhythm.

There is nothing mystical in this, nothing 'religious' in our modern understanding of the term, but rather a profound realism. Shakespeare retains this essential quality when he has Edgar conclude *King Lear* with the words:

> The weight of this sad time we must obey,
> Speak what we feel, not what we ought to say,
> The oldest hath borne most; we that are young
> Shall never see so much, nor live so long.
>
> (V. iii. 324–7)

The central issue is not whether Lear is 'saved', but simply *that* the play has unfolded before us. In a moving essay the Holocaust scholar Lawrence Langer writes about a book of Holocaust paintings: 'But this is not an invitation to rhetorical speculation about "inner strength" and "spiritual determination" that might transform confrontation into a form of verbal coping. Haas's title, *Expecting the Worst*, to say nothing of the stark and gloomy draftsmanship, makes his intention unmistakable: Look and see, and, seeing, grieve.'

What this leaves out, of course, is that 'religio-tragic exaltation' of which Jones speaks, and which comes, in the *Iliad* and in Sophocles, from man's acceptance of what is to come, his trust in that which lies beyond his powers of comprehension, though not of experience.

To bring this out better let us contrast it with what Plato makes of death, for, as Nietzsche sensed, it is the influence of Plato and the tradition that stems from him, allied to a certain emphasis in Christianity, which makes the Greek view of life and death so hard for us to grasp. In the *Apology*, facing the sentence of death, Socrates actually compares himself to Achilles. When Achilles heard from his mother that if he killed Hector he too would shortly die, Socrates tells the court, 'he . . . made light of death and danger, and feared much more to live as a coward and not to avenge his friends' (28B–D). The way Socrates faces his death, his refusal to compromise, is indescribably moving. But it is not Achilles' way. Whether consciously or unconsciously, Socrates misreads Homer. In both the *Apology* and the *Phaedo* he stresses the fact that for the man who has truly thought out his priorities death holds no fears. When one adds to this the Platonic belief in the immortality of the soul one gets a picture of life in which the fear of death is a foolish and irrational thing, since death is in fact a condition we should welcome, the final shedding of that cumbersome body which is responsible for all our unhappiness. What we have in Homer, though, is something quite different. Achilles, it is true, accepts the fact of his early death, but he accepts it in full consciousness of what a calamity it is. 'Xanthus', he says to the immortal horse who has dared tell him his fate, 'why prophesy my death? There is no need. I know well myself that it is my fate to die here, away from my dear father and mother. But even so I shall not stop until I have driven the Trojans to their fill of war' (*Iliad*, XIX. 420–3). To die means to lose one's dear ones; it means to bring them sorrow; it means to cease to partake of the joys of life, joys so great that in the *Odyssey* the ghost of Achilles says that he would 'rather be the meanest slave on earth than lord over all the dead' (xi. 488–91).

For Plato, as Martha Nussbaum has so eloquently argued, the wise man is immune to the blows of fortune. Mistrusting the world and his body, he has total faith in his reason. His reason tells him what the world is like and that it is better to be released from it and partake of the joys of pure thought. For Homer and the tragedians, as for Thucydides, on the other hand, the world is only partially and momentarily intelligible, but we are not totally lost, for our traditions help us to live the good life. For Plato, however, tradition is what holds us back. We must escape its embrace and learn that we alone are responsible for our own fate. Armed with the light of reason we can rise above the pains and sorrows, the confusions and contingencies of the world, to perfect happiness in the contemplation of the Ideas.

For Plato all boundaries fall before the light of reason. But this, as both Nussbaum and Williams have pointed out, is not a self-evidently desirable state, it is only desirable for reason itself. Setting the radical Plato against the conservative Aristotle, Nussbaum writes: 'Plato suggested that there is available in the universe a pure transparent standpoint, from which the whole truth of value in the universe is evident. Aristotle (. . .) replies that this does not look to be the case. Lack of limit is itself a limit.'

It is when the traditions which underpinned Homer began to weaken, traditions which took for granted that man is embedded in a web of relations which support rather than hinder him, and that only the lived life, the life that accepts that it will be subject to the buffetings of fortune, can be called life at all – it is only then that the more voluntarist and purely ethical notions of Socrates and Plato start to seem commonsensical. Aristotle, though, still belongs to the old ways of looking at the world, and his suggestion that *looking* at the tragic action (and, looking, grieving) can help us live, rather than *understanding* what life *means*, is quite in keeping with the views we find expressed in Homer, Aeschylus and Sophocles. But it was precisely this attitude Plato felt was dangerous. Again and again we find in Plato, whether by chance or choice, a misconstruing of the nature of tradition. Thus in the early dialogue, the *Ion*, he argues that the rhapsode is merely repeating, without understanding, what Homer had first said, and thus is not fit to be listened to. But this is a travesty of what happens in oral tradition. As Eric Havelock and Gregory Nagy have shown, the singer of tales is the encyclopedic memory of the community. Like the nomadic carpet-weaver I referred to in the Introduction, he inherits a way of working and a repertory of motifs, and each of his songs is both totally traditional and slightly different from any other. It is only because of his failure or refusal to grasp how oral tradition works that Plato can score the points against it which he clearly feels constitute the last word on the matter.

Again, if, as Plato makes clear at the end of the *Republic* is the case with him, one holds that the display of excessive grief is both embarrassing to others and bad for oneself, then indeed both the *Iliad* and Greek tragedy will appear to be things which have to be banished for ever if society is ever to be healthy. Here Plato does not seem able to comprehend the important psychological role of public mourning and of the poets' transference of that from life to the realm of art, or to grasp what is in danger of getting lost once the individual is removed from what Kierkegaard called 'the substantial categories of state, family and destiny'. No wonder he felt that what Homer and the tragedians wrote was both shaming and shameful.

Reading Plato today one is forced to gasp in wonder at his inability to respond to Homer and Greek tragedy, or, as he would put it, at his quite justified suspicion of them and his determination not to be seduced by them. What he fails to see is the price that has to be paid for such an attitude. For denial of the dual vision, as I have described it, in the end entails a denial of the world we live in and, ultimately, of ourselves as embodied beings existing within that world. Yet such is the nature of suspicion that, once unleashed, it appears to produce a totally convincing and self-consistent world, not simply an alternative way of looking at things but the only way there can possibly be. This, as Nietzsche sensed, is the reason for Plato's enormous persuasive power, his hold on Western philosophy.

At the same time as Plato's version of life was taking hold suspicion began to triumph in another way. When Homer became not a living voice but a prized text, carefully stored in the great library at Alexandria, then the listener was replaced by the scholar and commentator, examining the text, collating manuscripts, trying to determine what was genuine and what spurious. We owe an incalculable debt of course to the early editors; were it not for them we might have lost Homer for good. But they too contributed to the demise of the very world they were intent on preserving. The questions they asked had not entered the minds of the audience that sat listening to the bard or the rhapsode singing of the anger of Achilles: questions about the unity of the text, the spuriousness or certain lines and episodes, origins and dating, and the historicity or otherwise of the subject matter. And these have remained the central questions of Homeric studies almost to our own day. For it is really only since the First and especially the Second World War that those prepared to listen, as Schiller and Keats had obviously listened, to the voice of Homer have joined the ranks of Homeric scholars and started to argue their case. It is only now, two hundred years after Schiller, that scholars, rather than poets and philosophical essayists, have started to encourage us to understand what it was that had got lost through the attitudes of mistrust and suspicion stemming on the one hand from Plato and on the other from the early editors and commentators. And it is not, I think, pure chance that this has coincided with the discovery, by writers and by the reading public, that there are other ways of writing narrative than those of the classic novel.

It is a curious and unfortunate fact that those who have been most acute in their understanding of the ancient Greeks have often tended to contrast them with what they will insist on calling 'the Judeo-Christian tradition'. Thus for Nietzsche Greek lightness is so different from the moralising ponderousness of the present because we are the heirs of 'the Judeo-Christian tradition'. And Kierkegaard, so acute on the ancient Greeks, seems to feel that when he is dealing with the Hebrew Bible he need make no effort of the historical imagination but can let the text speak directly to him, that he need not try to read for the *mythos*, the overall shape of the story, but only enter the minds and feelings of the protagonists. Of course such an attitude goes back to Luther and has always been a powerful part of the Protestant tradition which replaced the authority of the Pope and the Councils with the authority of Scripture. But that does not make it any less misguided, as misguided, indeed, as trying to read *Oedipus Rex* or *King Lear* solely in terms of the psychology of Oedipus or Lear.

One of the things I was trying to do in my own book on the Bible was to destroy the myth of a unified 'Judeo-Christian tradition' and to show that this is in fact a Christian construction, while the world of the Hebrew scriptures, and even of the Gospels, has more in common with that of Homer and the tragedians than with that of St Paul or St Augustine. I do not want to recapitulate what I said in that book, but it is important for my present argument to recall some of the conclusions I came to. As with Plato and Homer, there is an actual struggle between St Paul and the Hebrew scriptures, and, as with

Plato and Homer, this is partly conscious on the part of St Paul and partly the result of the fact that the two simply inhabit different thought-worlds and are thus bound to misunderstand each other.

There is also a curious symmetry between the scholarly response to Homer from the seventeenth to the late nineteenth century and the response to the Bible. Umberto Cassuto, the great Jewish Italian biblical scholar, once wrote a little book called *The Documentary Hypothesis*, in which he showed that at every stage the questions asked of the biblical text were the same as those asked at almost exactly the same time of the Homeric text: if human beings had written it, when and where had they done so? What kind of unity did it have? How many different layers or strands of tradition did it consist of? Was it possible to distinguish these strands? And so on. Reading this book has a strange effect, for one is made to realise that whereas these extremely learned men thought they were telling us something about Homer or the Bible, in fact they were telling us about the sensibility and cultural climate of Europe in the years 1650–1900. But, as with Homer, scholarly writing on the Bible has, in the past thirty or forty years, begun to ask different and, to my mind, more fruitful questions, such as: how do these narratives *work*? What is the role played by memory both within them and in their creation? How does their form reflect the meaning they convey? And so on.

When we stand back from Homer and the Bible and ask some general questions of both, the first thing that strikes us is that while the Hebrew scriptures have an attitude to death which is much closer to that of Homer, the Christian scriptures are evidently much closer to the *Hymn to Demeter* and to Plato. Thus, though in some of the later portions of the Hebrew Bible the notion of an afterlife is floated, in the main it accepts human death as final: 'I shall go to him, but he shall not return to me', as David says on learning of the death of his child. And, as with Homer, what is important is living the good life so as to die respecting oneself and respected by others.

Of course the heroic ethos of Homeric society means that such a death is likely to occur in battle, whereas the emphasis on the children of Israel as God's chosen people makes the best death that which takes place when one is 'old and full of years', surrounded by children and grandchildren. Nevertheless, there is more in common between the two than there is between both and the Christian notion that 'God hath both raised up the Lord, and will also raise up us by his own power', as St Paul puts it at 1 Corinthians 6:14.

Linked to the notion of an afterlife is the notion of revelation, the sense that history and human life are linear and that with the coming of Christ everything is revealed which had previously been hidden, while in each life as well a moment of illumination can be totally transformative: 'And he said unto them, Unto you it is given to know the mystery of the kingdom of God, but unto them that are without, all these things are done in parables' (Mark 4:11). The Hebrew scriptures, on the other hand, while being just as certain that God sees and understands everything, that 'The earth is the Lord's, and the fullness thereof; the world, and they that dwell therein' (Psalms 24:1), also make it quite clear that such understanding is not vouchsafed to men. And instead of faith, of a leap which will resolve all in a single moment of blinding insight, they stress the notion of trust, a confidence in God's ultimate beneficence and in the helping power of laws and traditions. Here the good man never gets to know the mystery of the kingdom of God; rather, he learns to walk in the way of the Lord.

This trust is made visible through a rhythm which pervades the universe and which is felt at the local level as parataxis ('and . . . and . . . and . . .'); in the poetry as parallelism ('The heavens declare the glory of God; and the firmanent showeth his handiwork'); and at the narrative level as variation. By contrast the Christian emphasis on a primal Fall and a consequent redemption and revelation affects everything, from the way the Christian Bible is constructed (one great arch stretching from Creation to Last Judgement) to the attitude to individual characters.

We saw with Homer, in my example of Helen on the walls to Troy, that the way the poem is told is part and parcel of what it is saying. The same is true of the Bible. Take the use of the particle *wa*. This can mean 'and' and 'but' and 'therefore', and so on; its force lies precisely in its fuzziness. This is by and large respected by the translators of the King James Bible, but modern translations, infected by that fatal need to clarify, against which Williams and Nussbaum warned, consistently seek to distinguish 'and' and 'but' and 'therefore'. Even the King James translators sometimes fall into the trap. Thus at the end of 2 Samuel 6, for example, we are told how David danced before the ark as it was brought in triumph to Jerusalem, and how his wife Michal rebuked him. The episode ends, in the King James version: 'Therefore Michal the daughter of Saul had no child till the day of her death.' But the Hebrew does not say this. It says: '*Wa* to Michal, the daughter of Saul, there was not to her a child till the day of her death.' And this makes an enormous difference. If God has made Michal barren *because* she rebuked David we will naturally think quite differently of God than we would if there was no direct relation asserted between her action and her barrenness. This is quibbling, someone will say. But is it? Leaving the issue open leaves the world mysterious rather than explainable in terms of action and reward or punishment. The Hebrew Bible's use of *wa* is its way of 'knowing when to stop' as Wittgenstein would say, its wisdom in not pressing for clarity beyond a certain point: Michal did this and then a certain thing happened to her. Maybe there's a connection, maybe not. What is certain is that the world will not yield itself fully to human enquiry. But this is not a matter for despair. It would only be that if we felt that it *should* so yield itself. As things are, walking in God's way and accepting our limitations are enough.

This is true of the Greeks as well. Tragedy arises when men press for full knowledge or believe that they are in total control. We can

see this with both Achilles and Oedipus. It takes the death of Patroclus and the revelations about his birth to bring Achilles and
Oedipus against the hard rock of the Other, of a world which is not
as we would have wished it to be. In the Hebrew Bible the pattern
is even more strongly emphasised. Nearly every major character
begins his life as the hero of his own fairy-tale; then comes a
point at which the world and his desires come into conflict and his
eyes are opened both about his own errors and the nature of life.
We see this in the case of Adam, of Jacob, of Moses, of Samson, of
Saul and of David. We even see it in the case of Jesus. In the garden
at Gethsemane and on the cross Jesus comes to see and accept
that life is other than he had imagined it: 'Abba, Father, all things
are possible unto thee; take away this cup from me; nevertheless
not what I will, but what thou wilt' (Mark 14: 36). How that
squares with the Resurrection is of course the central problem for
Christian theology.

To have your eyes opened does not mean to be 'redeemed' or
'saved'. That language belongs to Christianity. What Aristotle says
about Priam, though, could well apply to David: 'For many rever-
sals and all sorts of luck come about in the course of a life', he
remarks in the *Nichomachean Ethics*, 'and it is possible for the
person who was most especially going well to encounter great
calamities in old age, as in the stories told about Priam in the Trojan
war' (1100a5–9). When David saw Bathsheba bathing he was
tempted and fell. Before that his life had unfolded like a dream.
Now he summons her, sleeps with her, tries to conceal his role in
her pregnancy and even has her husband killed in the process. When
he realises that God has found him out, though, he immediately
repents and begs for mercy. God forgives him, but the price he has
to pay is a stiff one. His first son by Bathsheba dies, his other sons
begin to feud, and his favourite, Absalom, ousts him from the throne
and then is himself killed in battle with David's forces, to David's
inconsolable grief. Yet David dies in his bed, telling his son

Solomon: 'I go the way of all the earth', and then, the narrator tells us, 'David slept with his fathers and was buried in the city of David' (1 Kings 2: 2, 10). Like Odysseus, David is no paragon of virtue but, rather, cunning, cautious, decisive when the need arises, and, above all, lucky – that key attribute which, it is said, Napoleon always looked for in his generals.

Napoleon would not have recommended St Paul for promotion, though he was apparently rather good at harassing Christians before his conversion. For St Paul, like Kierkegaard's modern Antigone, cannot seem to free himself from self-torment: 'For the good that I would I do not: but the evil which I would not, that I do ... O wretched man that I am! who shall deliver me from the body of this death?' (Romans 7:19–24). We are in a different world here from that of David or Odysseus. Yet the struggle within oneself of warring factions is something that later literature has made us so familiar with that it is hard to realise that it is not the only way of conceiving of the self. Indeed, one could say that what distinguishes the heroes and heroines of Homer, Greek tragedy and Hebrew scripture is precisely that they have no 'view of the self'. This does not mean that they do not have a sense of themselves; only an obsessed theoretician would want to claim that. Rather, it is that they do not have the time or space to ask who or what they are, and not only do they manage quite well like that, they seem to manage considerably better than those, like St Paul, who do ask such questions.

Rejecting tribal descent in favour of spiritual kinship, rejecting the rituals of the Jews or turning them into an allegory of the spirit, St Paul casts himself on the mercy of a God who cannot be known by any outward manifestation. With this step he opens up a whole new world of inwardness. It is a world he explores with passion and anxiety, and which will always have room for fresh explorers, not only his direct descendants, Augustine, Pascal and Rousseau, but most of the great novelists of the nineteenth century. His mode of self-questioning is still what fuels the energies of the modern biographer. Yet the cost of opening up this new world was high. Like the heroes and heroines of Homer and Greek tragedy, the men and women of the Hebrew Bible are essentially light in spirit, for they trust the traditions into which they are born even when they are led to subvert them and walk their own way. With St Paul, as with Plato, this quality of trust has gone. Perpetual vigilance is now required, perpetual self-questioning and self-examination. Suspicion reigns: suspicion of the world, of others and, above all, of oneself. No wonder the question they both ask is: 'Who shall deliver me from the body of this death?'

A tale of a heel and a hip

It is a curious fact about the Bible, not sufficiently noted, that this book, which is the source of so much of our morality and theology, should also be the repository of so many stories which seem almost deliberately designed to question both morality and theology. Of course there are plenty of places in the Bible where moral judgements are easy to make: in the episode of the Golden Calf Aaron and the Israelites are clearly at fault; Moses is clearly a good man and Ahab clearly a bad one. But what of Jonah? And Saul and David? Can we say that Saul is bad and David good? Obviously not. Is Saul then simply unlucky and David lucky? That is not quite right either.

It is not that these stories seem indifferent to morality or theology but rather that they seem to be carefully designed to confuse the moralist and the theologian, to say to him: take us seriously if you dare and see what happens!

This is particularly true of the story of Jacob, which takes up the entire second half of the Book of Genesis, and which is marked by deception, trickery and betrayal from start to finish; which begins with a grabbed heel, climaxes with a twisted hip and concludes with crossed hands. If we are to take it seriously we have to understand how grabbing, dislocation and deception are part of what the Bible is *about*.

Let us begin at the beginning, with the birth of Jacob. Rebecca, Isaac's wife, conceives twins and the Lord says to her:

Two nations are in thy womb, and two manner of people shall be separated from thy bowels; and the one people shall be stronger than the other people; and the elder shall serve the younger.

(Genesis 25: 23)

That, at least, is how the translators of the Authorized Version render the Hebrew, and most modern translations follow them. The Hebrew, however, concludes: *verav ya'avod tza'ir* – which could equally well mean 'and the elder shall enslave the younger'. Given the pattern of Genesis, where the younger son invariably overcomes the elder, the usual translation is probably the correct one, but it is important to notice that the Hebrew produces an ambiguity which has to be worked at in order to determine which of two meanings is the correct one, and thus suggests that any meaning is provisional and dependent on how the rest of the story is read.

The first twin emerges, ruddy and hairy all over, and is called Esau, from the verb *'asah*, 'he made', suggesting perhaps that he is completely formed. 'After that', we are told, 'came his brother out, and his hand took hold on Esau's heel; and his name was called Jacob' (25: 26). His name seems to derive from the fact that his hand is grasping Esau's heel or *'aqueb*. Jacob is a grabber from the start and thus, in our modern sense, a heel, one who does things others would consider unsporting in order to gain an unfair advantage. We are also, I think, meant to recall God's punishment of the serpent at Genesis 3:15: 'it shall bruise thy head, and thou shalt bruise his heel'.

So far so clear. But in the very next sentence we are told that the boys grew, and that while Esau was 'a cunning hunter, a man of the field', Jacob was 'a plain man, dwelling in tents' (25: 27). This would seem to contradict what we have just learned about the twins, for now it is Esau who is cunning and Jacob is – well what? What does 'a plain man' mean?

We can dispose of Esau fairly quickly. The Hebrew says that he was 'a man who knew how to hunt', who was 'canny' at hunting. So the word 'cunning' is an Elizabethanism and should not detain us. But the problem of Jacob is not disposed of so easily. Jacob, we are told, is an *ish tam*, a man who is *tam*. What does *tam* mean? It is not a word usually applied to individuals, though it is applied to Noah and to Job. Noah, we are told, was an *ish tzadik tamim hayah bedorotav*, 'a just man and perfect in his generations' (6: 9) as the Authorized Version puts it. As for Job, in the first verse of the first chapter of the book devoted to him we are told that he was 'perfect and upright, and one that feared God, and eschewed evil' – *vahayah ha'ish hahoo tam vayashar v'ireh elohim vesar mera'a* (Job 1:1). The word in fact would seem to have connotations of integrity, uprightness and innocence. Its root meaning is *complete*, and the verb means 'was ended, was completed, was finished'. As an adjective it encompasses, in ways we can, I think, understand, 'complete, perfect; innocent, artless; naive; without blemish'. Thus in Psalm 26:1: 'Judge me, O Lord; for I have walked in mine integrity [*betummi halakhti*]: I have trusted also in the Lord; therefore I shall not slide.' In Genesis 20: 5 Abimelech defends himself against the accusation that he has 'taken' Sarah in full knowledge that she was Abraham's wife by saying: 'Said he not unto me, She is my sister? and she, even she herself said, He is my brother: in the integrity of my heart [*betam levavi*] and innocency of my hands have I done this.' And God absolves him, saying: 'Yea, I know that thou didst this in the integrity of thy heart [*betam levavkha*]; for I also withheld thee from sinning against me' (20: 6).

So which is Jacob? Is he a heel or a pure-hearted man? Those commentators who have noted the contradiction have resolved this by the simple expedient of saying that we are here faced with an irony. Even Robert Alter, one of the most subtle and most sensitive readers of biblical stories, takes this line in his recent fine translation of Genesis: 'There may well be a complicating irony in the use of this epithet [*tam*] for Jacob, since his behavior is very far from simple or innocent in the scene that is about to unfold.' But this is too easy a way out. It absolves us from having to make the imaginative effort to reconcile the two views of Jacob. I think, however, that such an effort can yield rich rewards, that if we can come to understand how the two epithets complement rather than contradict each other we will be able to read not only the story of Jacob as it was meant to be read, but much of the Bible and of other ancient literatures besides.

We have lost the sense of how it is possible to be a heel *and* a man of integrity partly because of Christianity, especially the Pauline emphasis in Christianity, and partly because of Kant – though what Kant did, of course was to encapsulate and articulate the inarticulate assumptions of his time. Much recent work in moral philosophy, particularly the work of Bernard Williams and Martha Nussbaum, has been devoted to trying to free us from the grip of this particular view of morality, and has done so by going back to the Greeks, not just to Aristotle, but, more importantly, to Homer and the tragedians and Thucydides. The Bible would have been just as helpful to their enterprise.

Think first of Odysseus. He is, we are told, 'many-wiled', *polumêtis*, or, as the first line of the *Odyssey* has it, *polutropon*, a man of many devices, but he is also *polutlas*, 'much-enduring' and *dios Odysseus*, 'godly Odysseus'. Again, as in the case of Jacob, how, we ask, can he be both? Certainly he tells lies, sometimes for no good reason except that that is how he is; certainly he is devious; yet there is a basic innocence and humanity about him when compared, say, to the suitors: he leaves the nymph Calypso who offers him immortality if he will stay with her, in order to return to his ageing wife, whom he loves, and though he is often willing to sacrifice his men to satisfy his curiosity about the dangers he meets with on his wanderings, all those who know him, including his old dog, both trust and love him. John Winkler, who has brought out brilliantly how Odysseus' cunning and constancy are echoed by that of Penelope, makes the further point, with the help of modern studies of Greek village life, that lying and deception have never had the stigma attached to them in the Mediterranean that they have in the Protestant north, and he reminds us of the pride fathers in Greek villages take in the lies their sons tell: a good liar will know how to fight his corner and keep the patrimony alive and increase it.

The willingness to deceive, not only for defensive and aggressive purposes but simply as a habit of life – to keep in practice, as it were, should be taken together with the style of speaking and the comportment described in the previous chapter: cautious, guarded, and sensitive to the unspoken. That quality is summed up in the notion of a 'reined-in mind'. When Odysseus shares with Telemakhos his plans to remove the armor from the hall and to test the various members of his household, he says forcefully, 'If you are truly my son and of my blood, let no one hear that Odysseus is inside', and Telemakhos replies, 'Father, you will soon know what kind of spirit I have – slackminded never!' (16.300–1, 309–10). 'Slackmindedness' (*khaliphrosunê*) is a trait of children who have not yet learned to control their public personalities with constant vigilance by erecting a wall of discretion

(*pais . . . nêpios êde khaliphrôn*, 19.530; 4.371). The opposite of the
man with a reined-in mind is the babbler who guilelessly reveals
to others information that may be used against himself or his
friends. Athena praises Odysseus for being 'close-minded' (*ankhi-
noös*) and 'mentally restrained' (*ekhephrôn*, 13.332), that is, he
always has his wits about him, reveals nothing to anyone without
cause, and suspects in others a deviousness that might be equal
to his own . . . *Ekhephrôn*, of course, is a frequent epithet for
Penelope . . .

What Winkler says here will help us understand the contrast the
Bible sets up between the twins Esau and Jacob. But before turning
to them let us examine a few more examples of our theme. Think
of Job. He is, we are told, *tam veyashar*, perfect and upright. And
the sign of his *tam*-ness would seem to be his willingness to argue
with God. Why does he do this when the comforters would not
dream of it? The feeling that comes through the Book of Job is that
Job is more serious about life than they are; he is not content simply
to repeat what he has been told, he tries to think things through for
himself. Like Abraham, who also argued with God, over the fate of
Sodom and Gomorrah, Job's trust in God and the created world is
so deep that he feels that what is happening to him is an affront to
his sense of the meaning of the universe to which he is unwilling
to submit in silence. But he is also prepared to be surprised, to revise
his views. Like Odysseus, he has a kind of primal innocence which
is ultimately rewarded.

Think now of Saul and David. Saul does nothing terribly wrong,
but he lacks self-confidence, so is driven to blame others for his own
mistakes. He is, we feel, someone who will always be unlucky,
though whether that is because he lacks self-confidence or whether
his bad luck is due to lack of self-confidence we cannot of course
tell. David, by contrast, is both lucky and self-confident. He seems
to sense from the start that God is with him; but that doesn't mean

he can just sit back and wait for good fortune to happen to him. On the contrary, the fact that God is with him means that he must make every effort to ensure his own success. And though he commits sins and crimes much more terrible than any committed by Saul, he accepts his guilt as soon as he is found out – and God forgives him, though he has to pay a heavy penalty as his children turn against each other and then against him.

In all these cases – Odysseus, Job, David – innocence and cunning go together, and a deep trust in God (or the gods, in the case of Odysseus) with a canny sense of suspicion of strangers and even of friends. Shakespeare – amazingly – understood this kind of morality and how it conflicts with Christian, and especially Protestant morality. The most famous speech in *The Merchant of Venice* is of course the one that universalises man: 'Hath not a Jew eyes? Hath not a Jew hands, organs, dimensions, senses, affections, passions? – fed with the same food, hurt with the same weapons, subject to the same diseases, healed by the same means, warmed and cooled by the same winter and summer as a Christian is? If you prick us, do we not bleed? If you tickle us do we not laugh? . . .' (III. i. 51–7) This is fine rhetoric, and it achieves its effect. In our post-Enlightenment times it seems to be the only kind of moral sentiment that makes sense.

But there is another side to Shylock. One which asserts his belonging to the tribe of Jacob and his *difference from* rather than identity with the Christians with whom he has to deal. This emerges most fully in I. iii, his first confrontation with Antonio. The topic is, of course, interest:

SHYLOCK: Well then, your bond. And let me see – but hear you,
Methoughts you said you neither lend nor borrow
Upon advantage.

ANTONIO: I do never use it.

SHYLOCK: When Jacob grazed his uncle Laban's sheep –

This Jacob from our holy Abram was,

As his wise mother wrought in his behalf,

The third possessor; ay, he was the third –

ANTONIO: And what of him? Did he take interest?

SHYLOCK: No, not take interest – not as you would say

Directly int'rest. Mark what Jacob did:

When Laban and himself were compromised

That all the eanlings which were streaked and pied

Should fall as Jacob's hire, the ewes being rank

In end of autumn turnèd to the rams;

And when the work of generation was

Between these woolly breeders in the act,

The skillful shepherd peeled me certain wands,

And in the doing of the deed of kind

He stuck them up before the fulsome ewes,

Who then conceiving, did in eaning time

Fall parti-colored lambs, and those were Jacob's.

This was a way to thrive, and he was blest;

And thrift is blessing if men steal it not.

ANTONIO: This was a venture, sir, that Jacob served for,

A thing not in his power to bring to pass,

But swayed and fashioned by the hand of heaven.

Was this inserted to make interest good?

Or is your gold and silver ewes and rams?

SHYLOCK: I cannot tell; I make it breed as fast.

But note me, signior –

ANTONIO: Mark you this, Bassanio,

The devil can cite Scripture for his purpose.

An evil soul producing holy witness

Is like a villain with a smiling cheek,

A goodly apple rotten at the heart.

O what a goodly outside falsehood hath!

(I. iii. 64–98)

No anthropologist could have presented us with a more powerful picture of the clash of two cultures. For Shylock, as for most Jews, believing and unbelieving, even today, the Hebrew Bible is not the repository of moral sentiments but of tales of abiding interest and relevance, tales which have the feel of stories about one's immediate family more than about far-off or mythical times. Trying to talk to Antonio Shylock does what comes naturally to him, he explains himself by means of the re-telling of a story in Scripture. Antonio, it becomes clear in the course of their exchange, is not familiar with either the mode or the story. Shylock has no sooner started, and named Jacob, Laban and Abraham, than he interrupts him sneeringly: 'And what of him?' And when Shylock, unperturbed, proceeds to re-tell a highly complex episode, which takes half a chapter in Genesis (30: 28–43), in fifteen dense lines, he responds by expressing his sense that something is somehow being put over him, and falls back on two inter-related clichés: that the devil quotes Scripture for his own purposes, and that the smiling exterior hides the villain within.

The attitude of the two men to biblical narratives marks their differences; but so does their attitude to what is actually *in* this narrative. For Shylock Rebecca is Jacob's 'wise mother', who 'wrought' on behalf of her son, and in a sense taught him how, to be blessed, one must be resourceful, or perhaps that resourcefulness is a result of blessedness. For Antonio, in so far as he can understand what Shylock is going on about, 'This was a venture, sir, that Jacob served for, / A thing not in his power to bring to pass, / But swayed and fashioned by the hand of heaven.' Resourcefulness, in Antonio's culture, is merely another word for (Oriental) cunning and deceitfulness, and since Jacob is a patriarch, father of Judah from whom eventually Jesus himself will descend, he cannot be tainted with even a hint of deceitfulness; on the contrary, all that he did he did at God's bidding, and even, we could say, he did not do it at all but had it done for him by God. It is easy to see that such a view of human nature would fit naturally with the notion that there is an inside and an outside to men, and that some men are of the Devil's brood and some of God's.

It is quite extraordinary that Shakespeare, who, so far as we know, was never exposed to Jewish tradition, should have been able so to step aside from the prejudices of his age (and ours?) as to see – not that Jews are human beings like everyone else, but the much more difficult thing – that the world-picture of the Jew is, though completely different from that of the Christian, every bit as coherent and persuasive, for those inside it, as is the Christian.

Jacob, then, is both a heel and *tam*. Once we grasp that there is no contradiction between the two terms all the major episodes of his life fall into place.

The first, of course, we have already looked at. At birth Esau comes out first, but Jacob follows quickly, gripping his brother's heel. Three verses later we are already plunged into the second episode, where Esau is persuaded by Jacob to sell his birthright for the famous mess of potage, 'this red red stuff' (*ha'adom ha'adom hazeh*), as the Hebrew has it, whence his name, Edom. As Robert Alter points out, 'the famished brother cannot even come up with the ordinary word for "stew" (*nazid*) and instead points to the bubbling pot impatiently as (literally) "this red red"'. Esau is not just physical and sensual, he is, in John Winkler's terms, 'slack-minded', 'a trait of children who have not yet learned to control their public personalities with constant vigilance by erecting a wall of discretion'. The biblical narrative is quite clear about this: 'thus Esau despised his birthright' (*vayivez esau et habkhorah*) (25: 34).

The next major episode is briefly alluded to by Shylock: Esau, having exchanged his birthright for the red stew, is now blatantly tricked out of the parental blessing by the wiles of his mother Rebecca. The blind and aged Isaac is led to believe that Jacob, covered all over with the skins of kids and goats and offering the food he asked for, is his hairy elder son Esau. Though he is puzzled by the fact that the voice seems to be that of his younger son, he cannot deny the evidence of his hands: 'The voice is Jacob's voice, but the hands are the hands of Esau' (27: 22). Nevertheless, to make quite sure, he asks him: 'Art thou my very son Esau?' and Jacob replies, 'I am' (*vayomer ani*). Whereupon he blesses him: 'See, the smell of my son is as the smell of a field which the Lord hath blessed: Therefore God give thee of the dew of heaven, and the fatness of the earth, and plenty of corn and wine: Let people serve thee, and nations bow down to thee: be lord over thy brethren, and let thy mother's sons bow down to thee: cursed be every one that curseth thee, and blessed be he that blesseth thee.' (27–9)

Our modern sensibilities are outraged at this. How can someone who, on being asked if he is someone else, answers 'yes', who perpetuates an elaborate deceit on his father and brother, be allowed to get away with it? But in the Hebrew Bible, as in pre-Socratic Greek culture, honesty counts for little in the face of such sacramental acts as blessing and cursing. Of course, as Alter points out in his note to verse 23, 'And he discerned him not', 'This crucial verb of recognition will return to haunt Jacob when he is deceived by his sons and then will play through the story of Judah and Tamar and of Joseph and his brothers', but that is the way of the Bible: not — or only rarely — overt moral judgements, but not indifference to morality either. Once Jacob has been given the blessing it cannot be taken away. Isaac may be furious and Esau may set up a great cry of lamentation, but what is done cannot be undone: 'Thy brother came with subtilty [*bemirmah*], and hath taken away thy blessing' (35). All the wretched Esau can say is: 'Is not he rightly named Jacob? for he hath supplanted me these two times: he took away my birthright: and, behold, now he hath taken away my blessing.' As Alter notes: 'At birth, Jacob's name, *Yaʿaqob*, was etymologized as "heel-grabber" (playing on *ʿaqueb*, "heel"). Now Esau adds another layer of etymology by making the name into a verb from *ʿaquob*, "crooked", with the obvious sense of devious or deceitful dealing.'

Jacob escapes from the wrath of his brother and heads for Padan Aram, urged by both his father and mother to go there and find a wife for himself from the daughters of his mother's brother Laban. (Esau marries into the family of Ishmael, Abraham's son by the handmaid Hagar.) On the way he stops at Bethel for the night, takes stones from the ground and puts them under his head as pillows, and dreams of a ladder stretching from earth to heaven, with the angels or messengers of God running up and down it, and the Lord standing above it. The Lord tells him he is the God of his father Isaac and his grandfather Abraham and promises him and his seed the land 'whereon thou liest', and then goes on to confirm Isaac's blessing: 'in thee and in thy seed shall all the families of the earth be blessed. And, behold, I am with thee, and will keep thee in all places whither thou goest, and will bring thee again into this land; for I will not leave thee, until I have done that which I have spoken to thee of.' (28:14–15) Whatever tribulations Jacob will have to endure, he now knows that the Lord is with him. This is how it is. We are never told whether Jacob deserves this or not. One could argue that he is hungrier for the blessing than his brother and therefore deserves it; or that he obtained it by deceit and so does not deserve it. The Bible does not even consider the issue, as *Oedipus Rex* does not pause to consider whether Oedipus deserved his fate or not: this is how it was, look and see and, seeing, grieve. Tragedy is not the mode of the Bible, but the refusal to separate destiny and character is common to both ancient cultures. What is made clear in the story of Jacob, and by the next episode in particular, is that having the blessing does not mean that you can just sit back and wait for good fortune to smile on you, as Antonio seemed to imagine.

For at the house of his uncle Laban Jacob meets his equal in cunning. Having worked for the beautiful younger daughter Rachel for seven years, Jacob, the younger son who tricked his elder brother out of his birthright, is tricked by Laban into first marrying his elder daughter, the much plainer Leah, and has to work another seven years for Rachel. After that it is his turn to get the better of his father-in-law, in the way described by Shylock. And as Jacob flees back to the house of his parents with his two wives, his children and his flocks, it is the turn of Rachel, the younger daughter, to trick her father, stealing his household gods and successfully concealing them when he comes after Jacob and searches her tent. Thus in the course of this episode Laban tricks Jacob, Jacob tricks Laban, and Rachel tricks her father. However, as Israeli Peace Now activists are fond of saying, you don't have to love your neighbour to make peace with him, and it all ends with a treaty between Jacob and Laban, followed by sacrifice and a communal meal, 'and early in the morning Laban rose up, and kissed his sons and his daughters, and blessed them: and Laban departed, and returned unto his place' (31: 55; 32:1 in the Hebrew).

But what of Esau? Will peace be possible with him? It seems he is on his way, with his men, to meet Jacob, and Jacob does not know what to expect. Ever cautious, he divides up his company, sends presents ahead to Esau, and brings his family over the ford of the Jabbok river. He himself stays alone that night on the other side: 'And Jacob was left alone; and there wrestled a man with him until the breaking of the day' (32: 24/25). Commentators have been much concerned about who exactly this 'man' was: was it God, one of his 'angels', a man sent by him, or what? But the story doesn't say and it doesn't matter. Here, at the start, he is a man (*ish*), and at the end of the episode Jacob says: 'I have seen God face to face' (*ra'iti elohim panim el panim*) (30/31), whereupon he calls the place Peniel or face of El. What is important is that from the start of his life Jacob has been involved in trials of strength and cunning: with Esau, with Isaac, with Laban. Now at last he meets someone who is not merely a match in cunning, as Laban was, but a match *tout court*, someone who gives him a sense of the *limits* of his cunning and strength.

Jacob, we are told, is left alone on one side of the river: *vayivater ya'akov levado*. Not even Abraham at the moment of the sacrifice of Isaac was so alone – and this chapter has many parallels with Genesis 22. There we were told: 'the two of them went together' – *vayelkhu shnehem yahdav* (22: 6). Here there is no mother to guide and protect him, no son to be concerned for: he is quite alone and night has fallen. A man wrestles with him and neither comes out the winner. The man twists Jacob's hip (probably; the Authorized Version gives 'thigh'), but Jacob won't let him go unless he blesses him. Whereupon the man first asks him his name, not so much because he does not know it as to ritualise the occasion, for when Jacob tells him, he says: 'Thy name shall be called no more Jacob, but Israel: for as a prince hast thou power with God and with men, and hast prevailed' (32: 28/29). His name will no longer be 'heel' or 'crooked', but 'the one who strives with God'. Rashi, the medieval Jewish commentator, brings out the implications of this: 'It will no longer be said that the blessings come to you through deviousness but instead through lordliness and openness.' Nevertheless, Jacob's name is not changed for good, as is Abram's; *Jacob* and *Israel* become synonyms, a practice, as Alter notes, 'reflected in the parallelism of biblical poetry, where "Jacob" is always used in the first half of the line and "Israel", the poetic variation, in the second half'. But not quite synonyms either, for, as the Israeli novelist Meir Shalev has pointed out, there is a tendency in what remains of Jacob's story to identify the *person* with Jacob and the *public figure* with Israel, though this division is not strictly adhered to.

What then is the meaning of this episode? In my book on the Bible I pointed out how frequent was the pattern in the Hebrew scriptures – and even in the New Testament – of a move from fairy-tale to reality in individual lives. From Adam to Jesus, passing by Jacob, Moses and David, we find a life beginning like a happy dream and ending with the protagonist coming smack up against a reality which is other than his wishes and desires. Here, at the river Jabbok,

Jacob comes up against his reality. Until then it has always been a matter of getting the better of an opponent, sometimes by instinct, as when in the womb he clutches his brother's heel, sometimes with the help of others, as when his mother shows him how to trick his aged father, sometimes after an initial setback, as with Laban. Now he is not only face to face with an opponent who will never yield to him, they are actually locked together, body to body. In one sense Jacob wins again: his desire to wrestle with God, like Job's, is rewarded; his cunning is, as it were, cast in a new light, and he is re-named and blessed. Before, he had won both birthright and blessing by trickery; now he earns it by his simple willingness to fight, his refusal to let go. The encounter with reality is thus not tragic, as it is in the case of Oedipus; it is not even such as to inspire dread and awe, as is the case with David after the episode with Bathsheba and Uriah or Jesus after Gethsemane. And this is more in keeping with the tenor of the Hebrew Bible: you come up against a reality you have not chosen and do not necessarily like, and you accept it and live on, renewed by the encounter. Nevertheless, reality extorts a price: Jacob will walk with a limp for ever after. In an extraordinary shift of perspective, whose only parallel I can think of is the opening of the final chapter of William Golding's *The Inheritors*, we move from within the orbit of Jacob's body and consciousness to a point outside and above him: 'And as he passed over Penuel the sun rose upon him, and he halted upon his thigh' (31/32; perhaps better as Alter has it: 'he was limping on his hip').

Jacob had, until this moment, been a grabber. Now, in the wrestling with the 'man', he accepts that life cannot be grabbed. The 'man' brings home to him the limits of his world, as it were, and the reality of the world of others. But, as with David after the episode of Bathsheba, the discovery also marks the end of his years of growth and development. After this there is only the long decline into old age and death. And, as with David, this is marked by trouble given him by his children.

After the encounter with Esau, which goes much better than he had feared, the children take centre stage. First there is the episode of Dinah and her brothers, in which the brothers trick Schechem and Hamor and then slaughter them and their men. Then comes the saga of Joseph. At the end of chapter 37 Jacob is tricked by his sons as he had tricked his father, when, bringing him Joseph's multi-coloured cloak, stained with blood, they persuade him that his favourite is dead. Later he is made to part from the other loved son of his beloved Rachel, Benjamin, and though all turns out well, and neither Joseph nor Benjamin dies in his lifetime, the shock of learning that Joseph is alive is almost too much for the old man to bear: 'And Jacob's heart fainted, for he believed them not' (45: 26). He revives, though, and is persuaded that Joseph is indeed alive and living in Egypt: 'And Israel said, It is enough; Joseph my son is yet alive: I will go and see him before I die' (28).

So he goes down to Egypt and meets Pharaoh, who asks him his age. His reply involves a startling confession: 'The days of the years of my pilgrimage [*megurai*, my sojournings] are an hundred and thirty years: few and evil have the days of the years of my life been, and have not attained unto the days of the years of the life of my fathers in the days of their pilgrimage [*megureyhem*, their sojournings]' (47:9). As Alter points out:

> Jacob's somber summary of his own life echoes with a kind of complex solemnity against all that we have seen him undergo. He has, after all, achieved everything he aspired to achieve: the birthright, the blessing, marriage with his beloved Rachel, progeny, and wealth. But ... although he gets everything he wanted, it is not in the way he would have wanted, and the consequence is far more pain than contentment. From his 'clashing' (25: 20) with his twin in the womb, everything has been a struggle. He displaces Esau, but only at the price of fear and lingering guilt and long exile. He gets Rachel, but only by having Leah

imposed on him, with all the domestic strife that entails, and he loses Rachel early in childbirth. He is given a new name by his divine adversary, but comes away with a permanent wound. He gets the full solar-year number of twelve sons, but there is enmity among them (for which he bears some responsibility), and he spends twenty-two years continually grieving over his favorite son, who he believes is dead. This is, in sum, a story with a happy ending that withholds any simple feeling of happiness at the end.

But there is one final twist before death arrives. Joseph brings his two sons, Manasseh, the elder, and Ephraim, the younger, for the old man to bless. He carefully places the older on the side of his father's right hand and the younger on the side of his left, but the perverse old man crosses his hands and puts his right hand on the head of the younger and his left on that of the older. Though, like his own father's, his eyes are dim with age, there is no confusion here, since when Joseph remonstrates with him: 'Not so, my father: for this is the firstborn; put thy right hand upon his head', Jacob refuses, saying: 'I know it, my son, I know it: he also shall become a people, and he also shall be great: but truly his younger brother shall be greater than he, and his seed shall become a multitude of nations.' (48:18–19) So a central theme of Genesis is repeated for one last time: the elder shall serve the younger for no other reason than that that is how it has to be.

There is a final, formal set of blessings and curses on the twelve sons and then, like David, Jacob dies in his bed, allowed his last words: 'I am to be gathered unto my people: bury me with my fathers in the cave that is in the field of Ephron the Hittite' (49: 29). To Joseph, when he had brought his two sons to be blessed, Jacob had spoken of his beloved Rachel, the first time he had mentioned her since her death, and showing that she is still present to him. Now he asks to be buried with his fathers and with Leah in the cave of Machpelah, as though in death he has himself become simply a public figure and it no longer matters what his feelings might have been in his lifetime. As we listen to his words we watch him passing from a living, sentient being, tricked and tricking, loving and resenting, to a figure who will simply remain in the memory: Abraham, Isaac, Jacob. And with that final letting go he can embrace his death: 'And when Jacob had made an end of commanding his sons, he gathered up his feet into the bed, and yielded up the ghost, and was gathered unto his people' (49: 33).

Jacob's life story, as it is told in Genesis, illustrates no moral or theological argument. What we are presented with, rather, is a complicated, contradictory life, full of pain and suffering and joy. It is the story of a man who is at once *tam* and *ʿaquob*, a man for whom life is never easy, who gains much and loses much, but of whom it can never be said that he didn't strive. More than that of Abraham the obedient one or Joseph the dreamer, it is the archetypally Jewish life.

3   Dante: trusting the mother tongue

That man should speak is nature's doing; but whether thus
or thus . . .

Dante

'What meaning have yesterday's conclusions today? They have the
same meaning as yesterday, are true, except that the blood is oozing
away in the chinks between the great stones of the law.'

Thus Kafka, in his diary for 19 January 1922. Writing pins down.
It holds. But by the same token it freezes the flux, the continual
movement of existence, and so distorts it. There seems to be no possibility of reconciliation between the two; the best we can do is be
aware of the conflict. Kafka, because that is what he is like, sees this
tragically: the law is what is written; it is made up of great stones;
they are there for ever; at the same time the blood, our blood, oozes
away in the chinks between the stones.

Such considerations, naturally, did not trouble Homer or the
writers of the biblical narratives. But they did trouble Dante.
Indeed, the paradox goes right to the heart of his lifelong struggle

to make a poetry that would endure and yet that would speak for the whole man, for the blood flowing in his veins and his sense of time passing and his need to do something with his life, and his sense too of eternal laws governing both the universe and individual lives.

For Dante, given the time and place in which he wrote, this meant coming to terms with two different but, as we will see, interrelated questions: what meaning the Incarnation had for him personally, and how to write an authoritative work in the vernacular.

The first thing to understand is that in the culture of the Middle Ages Latin was not simply the universal language of the Church, it was, even for those who chose to write in the vernacular, the natural language of the universe. As Jacques le Goff puts it: 'All who do not speak Latin are barbarians, do not really speak, have no language, merely shriek like animals.' Latin, in fact, is frequently a term synonymous with language itself, as when Dante writes of his ancestor Cacciaguida: 'Ma per chiare parole e con preciso / latin rispuose quello amor paterno' ('But in clear words and with precise discourse [*latin*] that paternal love replied') (*Paradiso* XVII. 34–5). In the first troubadour, William IX of Aquitaine, as in Chrétien de Troyes, the very birds sing 'en leur latin' – in their own tongue.

But Latin was not only the universal language of Christendom, it was also the language of classical Rome, and, for a poet with epic ambitions, the language of Virgil, *the* poet of imperial Rome. But of course Latin for Virgil was his vernacular; to write in Latin in thirteenth-century Italy would therefore be in a sense a betrayal of Virgil. On the other hand how could a modern poet, conscious of the many different vernaculars in Europe alone, trust himself to his mother tongue, knowing that it was only one among many, would not be understood beyond its borders, and was subject to change and decay? What good would it do then to write in Tuscan? How could one write something that would be authoritative and permanent, that would do for Tuscany what Virgil had done for Rome, in so unstable a medium?

Fifty years after Dante the question was dead (only to be revived, in different guise, in the Renaissance). In a letter to Boccaccio Petrarch shows his disapproval of the vernacular and, by implication, of Dante's adherence to it, though he concedes that Dante was 'ille nostri eloquii dux vulgaris', the leader of us all in vernacular eloquence (*Seniles*, V. ii). Boccaccio himself, in his *Trattatello in laude di Dante*, his Little Treatise in Praise of Dante, defends Dante in a manner that gives the game away. Dante, he says, actually started the *Commedia* in Latin, but abandoned the project when he realised that his audience was not up to the task of deciphering it. Dante, he goes on, realised then that it would have been useless to put the good hard bread of Latin into the mouths of those who still suckled at the breast. For both authors the vernacular is a kind of baby-talk, while only the use of Latin is the sign of the mature author. And when Petrarch came to write *his* epic, *Africa*, he of course wrote it in Latin.

The irony is that Dante's whole life was spent trying to understand the continuity between the baby at its mother's breast and the mature, authoritative author. But the door he pushed open was firmly shut by the humanists who followed him: thus are options foreclosed for centuries and sometimes for ever in the history of human culture.

Dante's first poems were love lyrics, mainly sonnets, in the sweet new style, the *dolce stil nuovo*, of his older contemporaries, Guido Guinizelli of Bologna and Guido Cavalcanti of Florence. Yet his first mature work, the *Vita Nuova*, like Virgil's *Eclogues*, is already a warning of ambitions far in excess of his contemporaries'. By placing the lyrics within a prose frame Dante is already asserting his desire to speak the truth in the form of an extended fiction: not this or that poem in praise of his lady, but a story about what she meant both to him as a private individual *and* to the world at large.

The *Vita Nuova* was written when Dante was in his late twenties or early thirties. In 1300 he was thirty-five, in the middle of his life according to the biblical time span, a time, as he says in the *Convivio*, when a man is at the height of his powers. Two years later, though, an event took place which, along with Beatrice's death, would be the most important one in Dante's life: he was exiled, for political reasons, from his beloved Florence, 'cast forth,' as he puts it, 'through well-nigh all the regions whereto this tongue extends, a wanderer, almost a beggar . . . Verily, have I been a ship without sail and without helm, drifted upon divers ports and straits and shores by the dry wind that grievous poverty exhales' (*Conv.* I. iii).

We know the link between exile and linguistic innovation in the case of such modern writers as Joyce, Beckett and Nabokov. In Dante's case it is important to understand that it was not simply the loss of his beloved Florence and the break-up of the *stilnovisti* circle which affected him. More heart-breaking was another factor, the end of his career in politics and what that meant to someone who, like him, fervently believed in the Aristotelian notion that man is a political animal, only fully himself when engaged in the affairs of the *polis*. And yet, in mitigation of that, was the fact that Latin, the language of Christendom and of universal learning, was, after all, available to the man without a *polis* as it was not to his modern counterparts. We have only to think of Erasmus, two centuries later. Exiled, he became a wandering European, exchanging letters with the good and the great, fêted wherever he went, a universal and no longer merely a Dutch intellectual.

Indeed, Dante's next few works are either written in Latin or deal with themes usually treated in Latin, and they are an attempt to prove to himself that he could do without either *polis* or mother tongue, that such things are clung to by the child and the adolescent but that the adult must go his way supported by his Christian faith and his faith in Reason.

Yet it is clear that these admirable sentiments hardly convince their author. Not only do elements in the books directly contradict their ostensible argument, but the fact that none of these works was ever finished, that they were picked up with enthusiasm but then dribbled away into silence – and this from the pen of a man with perhaps the most powerful sense of form in the entire history of world literature – suggests that these were years of torment and confusion. Rather like Proust almost exactly six centuries later, Dante, in the years 1303–8, gives the impression of someone searching desperately and in vain for a form and a subject that will appease him and fulfil his burning ambition and overflowing talent. As with Proust, it would be a foolish reader who tried to read the work in terms of the life, but it would also be a foolish reader who did not wish to stand back and contemplate the extraordinary shape of such a life, visible to us now with hindsight but, for him, a life to be lived in all its darkness and confusion.

The *Convivio* turns its back resolutely on death – Beatrice's death and the death that is exile – and tries to find solace in Reason. Dante revisits his old odes and, by allegorising them, tries to prove that they deal not with love for a living woman but with the mind's search for Reason and Truth. He tells us in the second treatise that he was able to turn from real women to philosophy with the help of the works of Boethius and Cicero, who taught him how the intellect familiar with philosophy 'remains free and full of certainty'. 'And so', he ends the second treatise, 'I declare and affirm that the lady of whom I was enamoured after my first love was the most fair and noble daughter of the Emperor of the universe, to whom Pythagoras gave the name of Philosophy' (II. xvi).

Yet the fact that Dante abandoned the work after allegorising only three of a projected fourteen odes suggests that, like Proust with his book on Sainte-Beuve, he felt at one and the same time that if he was forced to go forward he would have to think matters through rather than relying on his feelings, *and* that, in the end, thinking did not turn out to be the answer. And we know that, like Proust, he reverted in his last great work to the mode of his youth, to poetry and fiction, to real and not allegorical ladies, and to all the uncertainties such an enterprise entails.

The first treatise of the *Convivio* should have warned us that this might happen. It is a justification of his writing the work in the vernacular. Latin, he explains, is nobler than the vernacular because of its immunity to corruption. The vernacular is changeable even within one man's lifetime. For this reason Latin cannot be used as a means of commenting on vernacular verse. Latin is lord, and so cannot be servant to the vernacular, as commentary is servant to the text on which it comments. But, as Dante proceeds, we find that we are witnessing the birth of something quite new out of this tactful acknowledgement of Latin's superiority. For when he has finished his reasoned defence of his choice of the vernacular he moves in to the attack. He has, he says, been motivated by 'the natural love of my own tongue' (I. x), which he learned at his nurse's breast. Had it not been for the vernacular, he goes on, he himself would not be alive, since it is the vernacular that brought his parents together and allowed them to speak to each other. It is, he says, a house which he enters with pleasure, a table on which a banquet is laid, a new life, a new sun, the bread he dispenses to his readers. As he proceeds he grows more and more extravagant in his praise of the mother tongue, and moves from seeing himself first as son and then as father and finally as priest, while his banquet takes on strongly eucharistic overtones.

Where the *Convivio* is written in Italian, yet acknowledges the superiority of Latin, the *De vulgari eloquentia* is written in Latin and yet comes out in favour of the vernacular. The book was probably begun at roughly the same time as the *Convivio* and abandoned shortly afterwards, again less than half finished. It is, as many scholars have pointed out, in effect the first European essay in comparative linguistics. Now the vernacular is openly called nobler – *nobilior* – and not just emotionally closer than Latin. Latin is now seen as dead. On the one hand there is the spontaneous tongue and on the other there is *grammatica* – the living blood of men, as it were, and the dead stones of the law.

But if the vulgar tongue is indeed nobler than Latin, what *is* the vulgar tongue? Provençal? Bolognese? Tuscan? Chapter xvi of Part I suggests an answer: just as white is the measure of all colours though not itself a colour, so 'the supreme standards of those activities which are generically Italian are not peculiar to any one town in Italy, but are common to all; and among these can now be discerned that vernacular language which we were hunting for above, whose fragrance is in every town, but whose lair is in none'. Thus, he concludes, 'we declare the illustrious, cardinal, courtly and curial vernacular language in Italy to be that which belongs to all the towns in Italy but does not appear to belong to any one of them, and by which all the municipal dialects of the Italians are measured, weighed and compared' (I. xvi).

In Part II he sets about determining what this ideal vernacular would consist of. The worthiest subjects of poetry, he says, are war, love and the acquisition of virtue; the most serious subject is tragedy; the worthiest form is the canzone; the best words are those which are neither childish (like *mamma* and *babbo*), nor soft and feminine (like *dolciada* and *piacevole*), nor rural (like *greggia* and *cetra*). Then, as he is discussing what is the best kind of stanza, the book peters out. And it is easy to see why. Dante has rejected the authority of *grammatica*, of Latin and the forms of the classic authors, but he has simply put other authorities in their place. What he comes to see, I suspect, is that we cannot start by leaning for sustenance and authorisation on *any*thing: not on a poetic form which is predetermined; not on a poetic style; not on a poetic vocabulary. The *Commedia*, when it comes to be written, will have a wholly original form, a wholly original method of dividing up its units, and a wholly inclusive attitude to vocabulary. Indeed, as we will see, it will employ a vernacular that stretches all the way from *mamma* and *babbo*, via the feminine and the rural, to the most exalted forms of language, and *that will forcefully assert* a continuity between all these.

It is as though Dante, in a gesture unparalleled in earlier art, had recognised that for his work to be genuinely authoritative he would have so to work on the mother tongue that the artefact he made would acquire its own authority. This gesture of trust – in work, in time, in language – is inseparable from his growing sense that his efforts to shore up his feelings of loss by turning from the living, dying Beatrice to the immortal Lady Philosophy, and from history and fiction to allegory, had led him to a dead end. Only by trusting to memory and imagination, only by confronting imaginatively the pain of the loss of both Beatrice and his civic role, could he find a way to escape from the confusions of exile, could his ship cease to be buffeted by the winds of change and he reach the port he so desired. It would be no geographical port and there was no certainty that he would arrive, but then he had just been forced, after five years of fruitless work, to grasp the fact that to imagine there is such a certainty is to ensure that you never arrive. It was time to go forward into the unknown, and to do so by revisiting the past. His tools would be the poetry he knew he could write better than any of his contemporaries, and the mother tongue he loved.

In the *Convivio* Dante had dated his exile, the moment of disaster, to the middle of his life. The poem he starts to write around 1308 begins:

> Nel mezzo del cammin di nostra vita
> mi ritrovai per una selva oscura,
> che la diritta via era smarrita.
>
> (*Inferno*, I. 1–3)

In the middle of the journey of *our* life *I* found myself again, or perhaps just 'I found myself', or, indeed, 'I came to' – the Italian *mi ritrovai*, like the French *je me suis retrouvé*, is a perfectly ordinary expression which is nevertheless remarkable for the way it spans the physical and the spiritual, the commonplace and the unique. It is extraordinary too, when we think of it, as a way of beginning an epic of overwhelming ambition and encyclopedic scope – like Proust's 'Longtemps, je me suis couché [that reflexive again!] de bonne heure', but even simpler, closer to the basic premise of the adventure story: suddenly, something happened ... Dante is no longer informing the reader of this or that truth of which he is the custodian; rather, he is both recounting what happened to him and describing what *is* happening as he starts to write. Before, there was nothing, a dark wood; now there is this: all that is to follow.

But we have not exhausted the implications of that opening gambit. By writing in the first person, but accepting that before writing starts there is only darkness, he actually makes it possible, in the course of the journey, to recover his lost self, to bind up the disparate parts of himself, so that by the end of his journey the straightening of his will becomes one with the recovery of his past.

The self that Dante finds or finds again hardly exists as yet. 'I' is merely a marker. It will only be at the very end of the poem, and even then, as we will see, hardly there, that it will have achieved a certain fullness. We have a long way to go before that happens, and so does Dante – both the wayfarer within the poem and the poet making the poem. But the wayfarer will help the poet and the poet the wayfarer, so that it often becomes impossible to tell which is which.

Dante does not know where he is going, but he has found the two essential elements that will help him on his journey: an 'I' that is nevertheless only an example of a communal 'we', and the *terza rima* stanza.

As John Freccero has pointed out, the essential thing about the *terza rima* is that it is always on the move: aba bcb cdc ded e . . . But, as another fine Dante scholar, Teodolinda Barolini, has also noted, the beauty of the *terza rima* is that it goes backward as well as forward, proceeding, like the pilgrim himself, in a kind of spiral. Each line of the tercet, Dante decides, will consist of eleven sylla-bles, which is as natural a container in Italian as the pentameter is in English, but which has the advantage of giving him 33 syllables for each tercet, a kind of doubling of the Trinity and an echoing of the 33 cantos which make up each canticle. Thus from the smallest to the largest element Dante makes the choices; he is indeed what the Middle Ages called the poet, a *maker*. Every line of the poem, as we say it to ourselves, makes us subliminally aware of something made, of a controlling impulse, even though the natu-ralness of the language and the conscious realism of Dante's mode simultaneously draws attention away from that and towards the world he is describing.

Dante, alone, struggling out of the dark wood and, seeing the light shining at the top of a great mountain, starts to rush up its steep side — only to be driven back almost at once by three wild beasts which bar his way. As Freccero has again noted, what is being enacted here, at the very start of the poem, is a little drama about the rejection of the philosophical and the embracing of the fictional. For the nature of Lady Philosophy, as she appeared in the *Convivio*, is such that, once the mind has turned towards her, she can lead it directly to its goal. The mind, grasping the truth, takes no time to reach its goal, nor does it have to cover any terrain to arrive there. But Dante's experience with his philosophical writings of the previous decade showed him that a journey which could be made in the blink of an eyelid was not one which could bring him any permanent satisfaction. The little drama with the three beasts is designed to show that human beings are not made up of mind alone. Dante at first imagines that they are, and, seeing the sun at the top of the mountain, tries to rush straight up to it. But he is driven back. Because he has a body, because he is human, he will have to go down before he can climb up, down into himself and into the depths to face the manifold temptations of the world and of language. At the same time, of course, this primal failure, this discovery that we are embodied, not made up of mind alone, opens up a space for fiction, for the story–poem that is to follow.

The Christian tradition Dante inherited had an explanation for this, as for most things, and it was, as we might expect, a theological and not a psychological or aesthetic explanation. In Canto VII of *Paradiso* Beatrice explains to Dante the dynamics of salvation history: 'Your nature, when it sinned totally in its seed', she says, 'was removed from these dignities, even as from Paradise; nor could it recover them, if you consider carefully, by any way except the passing of one of these fords: either that God alone, solely by His clemency, had pardoned; or that man should of himself have given satisfaction for his folly' (*Par.* VII. 85–92). However, man could never of himself make satisfaction, since he is incapable of descending as far in humility as he had intended to ascend through pride. Therefore it was necessary for God to step in, and, taking on the flesh of man, to make that profound descent. Only God could make himself so heavy, as it were, to sink right down into the depths of Hell. And, because God has gone down to the very bottom of Hell in our flesh, we too can now follow, and so we too can now rise up (86–120).

The great medieval English equivalent to Dante's *Commedia*, *Piers Plowman*, makes the same point in its opening Passus, in a characteristically homely and rural manner:

For Truth telleth that love is triacle [treacle] of heaven: May
no sin be on him seen that that spice useth,
And all his works he wrought with love as him list,
And lered [taught] it Moises for the levest thing and most
like to heaven,

And also the plant of peace, most precious of vertues;
For heaven itself might nat holden it, so was it heavy of
himself,
Till it had of the earth eaten his fill.
And when it had of this fold [earth] flesh and blood taken,
Was never leaf upon lind [linden tree] lighter thereafter,
And portatif and persaunt as the point of a needle,
That might noon armour it lette [stop] ne none high walls.

(Piers Plowman, B text, I. 148–58)

In the previous chapter I argued that there is a lightness, an innocence, in Homer and the narratives of the Hebrew Bible, which is
lost forever when those grave men, Plato and St Paul, start to ask
their suspicious questions. Dante's poem, like Langland's, suggests
that God gave us the means to make ourselves so heavy in order that
we might become light again. In artistic terms this means that it is
only by facing the full consequences of suspicion and gravity that
gravity can be overcome. Kleist, as we will see in a later chapter, was
to make a somewhat similar suggestion, shorn, this time, of all
Christian connotations.

It took another, Dante and Langland suggest, to help us find ourselves. And Dante's poem, as that first canto of the *Inferno* proceeds,
begins its slow work of reparation by demonstrating the crucial
importance of community if the self is to fulfil itself. Alone, Dante
might well have tried to run up the mountain again as soon as he
had got his breath and courage back from his encounter with the
three beasts. Instead, Dante, 'ruining down into the depth', as the
poet graphically puts it, finds himself suddenly in the presence of
another. 'When I saw him in that vast desert', he writes, 'I cried to
him, "Have pity on me whatever you are, shade or living man!"'
' "*Miserere* di me", gridai a lui, / "qual che tu sii, od ombra od omo
certo!" ' (*Inf.* I. 65–6)

Miserere – have pity on me. Why does Dante use a Latin word, a word from the liturgy, moreover, for his very first word of direct speech in the poem? Italian, after all, has a perfectly good phrase for 'to have pity on' – 'aver pietà di' – as well as for 'to help' – 'aiutare'. Why not choose one of those? I think Dante is signalling here his recognition that his earlier distinction between *grammatica* and *vulgare* was a mistaken one. All speech is both one and the other: it is the one because it issues from the same throat as once uttered inarticulate childish cries; and it is the other because *all* speech is an acceptance of the fact that we are not alone, that we form part of a community. In other words, the plainest vernacular, no less than Latin, is *grammatica*. It is only our sentimental and Romantic age that thinks Hemingway's language is more 'real' than that of Henry James, that *Trainspotting* is closer to the stuff of life than *The Ballad of Peckham Rye*. The truth is, that all four are equally far from reality, that all are equally made up of words. To touch reality in art it is always necessary to go by the roundabout way; try going straight for it and the three beasts will inevitably push you back.

Dante often helps us by placing a parallel passage in a corresponding later canto. The parallels between *Inferno* I and *Purgatorio* I have often been noted: the deserted shore, the sea left behind, the mountain, the setting forth with a guide. What has not so often been seen is the way that *miserere* in *Inferno* I is answered by a phrase in *Paradiso* I. There, at the very start of the last canticle, Dante places an invocation which sets the tone for all that is to follow: 'The passing beyond humanity', he writes, 'may not be set forth in words: therefore let the example suffice any for whom grace reserves that experience' (*Par.* I. 70–2). Thus the English. But it conceals much that is there in the original. I don't say the Italian, because, of the seven words Dante uses, only four are clearly Italian: 'Trasumanar significar *per verba* / non si poria.' Dante first of all invents a word, 'trasumanar', 'to transhumanise oneself', for precisely that which cannot be set forth in words, the going beyond the human; then he presents us with a Latin phrase – *per verba* – instead of the expected 'con le parole', partly because 'con' means with' while 'per' means 'through', which answers his needs better; but also as though to balance his daring invention of a new word by reminding us and himself that language is always *grammatica*, that once you are in the world of words you are in the world of the stones of the law. Yet of course what the poem also demonstrates for us is that Kafka's harsh and radical division between law and individual is only one way – perhaps a peculiarly post-Romantic and modern way – of talking about the relationship of language to self and world.

The encounter with Virgil, which sets the tone – of wonder, of courtesy – for so many of the later encounters in the poem, provides a wonderful response to the Romantic Bloomian notion of the anxiety of influence. Learning who this figure is who has risen up before him, Dante ceases to think about his own terror as wonder and delight flood through him: 'Are you, then, that Virgil, that fount which pours forth so broad a stream of speech? . . . O glory and light of other poets, may the long study and the great love that have made me search your volume avail me! You are my master and my author. You alone are he from whom I took the fair style that has done me honour.' In the past his poetry had brought honour to Dante; now he prays only that the gift of Virgil's poetry may help him in his hour of need: 'vagliami'l lungo studi e'l grande amore / che m'ha fatto cercar lo tuo volume' (*Inf.* I. 79–84).

Beatrice, Virgil tells him, summoned him to this spot to help Dante: 'Assist him [*l'aiuta*]', she had said to him, 'so that it may console me' (*Inf.* II. 69). And she in turn was sent on this mission by Lucia who was herself sent by none other than the Virgin Mary. The question of why Dante 'came to' in the dark wood is left open: was it Dante's essential goodness, or grace from heaven? Philosophy would need to resolve this; fiction does not, wisely sensing that to probe too deeply is to invite the wrong kinds of answers. What is before the poem is the dark wood; what follows is the mother tongue and the *terza rima*. That is enough.

The *Inferno* is the canticle of temptation and of those who have yielded to it. Central to it is the perversion of language. Scholars have alerted us to the ways in which Francesca, Ulysses, and indeed every character Dante and Virgil meet in Hell distorts language consciously or unconsciously for his or her own ends. I want to pursue the theme of the need to use the mother tongue and the dangers that involves by looking briefly at the most extreme of these cases, that which is set before us in Canto XXXI.

Here Dante and Virgil, in the very depths of Hell, come across a giant with a horn round his neck. He speaks a language neither they nor we can understand: 'Raphèl mai ècche zabì almì', he howls, and Virgil answers him: 'Stupid soul, keep to your horn and vent yourself when rage or other passion takes you.' Turning to Dante, he explains: 'He is his own accuser; this is Nimrod, through whose ill thought one language only is not used in the world.' Nimrod was thought to have been the chief builder of the Tower of Babel. Now he, who had wanted to by-pass speech and build a tower that would allow him to reach the heavens, is robbed of speech. Dante makes the point that the love of self, which is what has brought all these sinners to Hell, is inextricably bound up with their attitude to language. The baby cries when it wants food; learning to talk involves a sacrifice, it involves time and effort and the giving up of the power to scream and shout. But learning to talk gives the baby a new mastery of the world and allows it to become a part of human society. Nimrod, unwilling to give up immediate gratification, unwilling to humble himself in order to rise, has been reduced to the level of a beast. 'Let us leave him alone', Virgil says, turning away, 'and not speak in vain, for every language is to him as his is to others, which is known to none' (*Inf.* XXXI. 67–81).

Once again, though, our full understanding of this episode will have to wait till we come across Nimrod again in a different context. When Dante meets Adam in Paradise Adam explains that 'the tongue which I spoke was all extinct before the people of Nimrod attempted their unaccomplishable work; for never was any product of reason durable for ever, because of human liking, which alters, following the heavens. That man should speak is nature's doing; but whether thus or thus, nature then leaves you to follow your own pleasure' (*Par.* XXVI. 124–32).

In the *De vulgari eloquentia* Dante had repeated the currently held belief that Hebrew was the first language. Here, in line with the new radicalism of the *Commedia*, he presents us with a different explanation. Hebrew is no better than Tuscan, only different, just as Giotto is no better than Cimabue, only more famous at the present time. History cannot provide authority, and neither can any one language, not even Hebrew. Nimrod imagined that he could build a tower that would reach up to God and challenge him, but he was wrong; a sort of Rimbaud before his time, his desire to speak only the language of his immediate feelings has led to his inability to say anything at all. What *Dante* then has to do in his poem is to fashion meaning, to develop authority, in the course of writing, by speaking of what is meaningful to him and trusting his medium: the language he has grown up with and the *terza rima*.

'Before I descended to the anguish of Hell', Adam tells Dante, 'the Supreme Good from whom comes the joy that swathes me was named *I* on earth; and later He was called *El*, and that must needs be, for the usage of mortals is as a leaf on a branch, which goes away and another comes' (*Par.* XXVI. 133–8). Giuseppe Mazzotto has some pertinent remarks on this passage.

The mutations of the names of God – first *I* and later *El* – show that the relationship between words and their referents is not sustained by a necessary etymological bond as one finds in Cratylism

... In *Paradiso* XXVI the names of God are empty leftovers, ephemeral designations for that which cannot but remain inaccessible. In effect, Adam's recitation makes the 'proper' of the proper name vanish, and he thereby annihilates the myth of an Edenic language in which there is a necessary, natural, and stable relation between words and things. It is from the perception of the shattered unity between *res* and *signa* that Dante gets the impulse to establish a poetic order capable of gathering within itself the scattered fragments of language.

One way in which he does that is, like Proust, to widen his scope and speak of just such things; to speak, that is, about how his journey is both a journey to God and a journey to the poem. Another is, as I have suggested, to leave everything provisional, waiting to be corrected or altered by something else. Thus we cannot fully understand the nature of Dante's journey until we have encountered Ulysses' antithetical journey; we cannot properly understand Francesca until we have encountered Beatrice and La Pia; we cannot even understand the dark wood of the opening till we enter the Edenic wood at the top of Mt Purgatory.

But it is not simply a later figure or episode which alters our understanding of an earlier one. The poem is constantly working at re-defining its key concepts through a variety of different means, allowing us gradually to enlarge our comprehension as we move forward, so that the process, though in one sense powerfully linear, is also more like the gradual covering of a field or the gradual excavation of a buried treasure.

One such key concept is that of the childish babble and of its place in our adult lives. We have already seen that in the *De vulgari eloquentia* Dante argued that the serious poem should eschew words like *mamma* and *babbo*. Dante seems to be still of the same opinion when, in the invocation at the start of *Inferno* XXXII, he writes: 'It is not without fear that I bring myself to speak; for to describe the bottom of the whole universe is not an enterprise to be taken up in sport, nor for a tongue that cries mamma and dadda' ('... né da lingua che chiami mamma o babbo') (7–9). But of course in saying this he shows that he is prepared to use precisely such words in his poem. Moreover, when we reach the equivalent place in *Paradiso*, we find this: 'Now will my speech fall more short, even in respect of that which I remember, than that of an infant who still bathes his tongue at the breast' ('che d'un fante / che bagni ancor la lingua a la mammella') (*Par.* XXXIII. 106–8).

It is not as if these are isolated instances of the use of this topos. Among the many other things it has been doing, the poem has been quietly working away at deepening our understanding of just what is involved here. In the episode of Nimrod we saw the giant reverting to mere babble, babble and Babel coming together here to hint at the fact that the essential language of Hell, of those locked in the prison of their own egos, is precisely that: babble. In *Purgatorio* XIX Dante has a dream of 'a woman, stammering, with eyes asquint, and crooked on her feet' ('una femmina balba, / ne li occhi guercia, e sovra i piè distorta') (7–8). As he looks at her she is transformed into a seductive siren, singing beautifully, 'her speech ... / unloosed'. She it is, she sings, who drew Ulysses with her song, 'and whosoever abides with me rarely departs, so wholly do I satisfy him (22–4). Fortunately Virgil is at hand to save Dante from her clutches and return her to her true and vile appearance. But the episode is designed to remind us not only of the contrast between Dante and Ulysses but also of two distinct attitudes to life and art which are nevertheless almost impossible to distinguish in practice. After all, we recall, Dante first addressed Virgil as 'that fount which pours forth so rich a stream of speech', and now here we read of the siren who sings so seductively, 'with her speech unloosed'. What is the difference between these two streams, these rivers of language that transform words into a kind of natural force? When Dante and Virgil had first arrived at the base of Mt Purgatory they had encountered Dante's old friend, the musician Casella, who, upon being asked by Dante to 'comfort my soul somewhat' by singing a song of love, complied and began to sing one of Dante's own odes, one of the very poems he had vainly tried to turn into philosophical allegory in the *Convivio*, 'Love that discourses in my mind'. He began so sweetly, Dante says, 'that the sweetness still within me sounds'. Dante and Virgil and the other souls who have gathered round to listen are entranced, but Cato comes rushing up to them, crying: 'What is this, you laggard spirits? What negligence, what stay is this? Haste to the mountain to strip off the slough that lets not God be manifest to you' (*Purg.* II. 112–23).

Song takes over the body, soothes the mind and limbs, like balm poured over it. Virgil's own 'broad stream of speech' made Dante into the poet he is. Yet being taken over by the song of another, like the nostalgic hearkening to the singing of one's old songs, leads to destruction. Plato and St Paul would no doubt try to find an essential difference between the two; Dante is content to raise the point that things in themselves are not good or bad, it is only a question of what we do with them. It is easy enough to see how Paolo and Francesca both use and are used by the love story of Lancelot and Guinevere to free themselves of any responsibility for their actions; and it is easy enough, once Virgil has revealed her for what she is, to see the Siren as wholly evil. But the ambiguities of the seductive nature of art, which tormented Plato and which runs like a dark thread through the entire Middle Ages, are not so easily resolved.

Yet the poem demonstrates that there is a key difference between the active play of mind, which rejoices in its god-given abilities, and the dangerous seductions of passivity and nostalgia. In Canto XVI of *Purgatorio*, at the very centre, therefore, of the entire poem, Dante presents us with a model, as it were, of the whole. He tells the little story about the childish soul, a story so simple and enchanting that Eliot translated it almost word for word and made

it into the opening of one of his most charming poems, 'Animula':
'From His hands who fondly loves it before it exists', Marco Lom-
bardo tells Dante, 'comes forth after the fashion of a child that
sports, now weeping, now laughing, the simple little soul, which
knows nothing, save that, proceeding from a glad Maker, it turns
eagerly to what delights it. First it tastes the savour of a trifling
good: there it is beguiled and runs after it, if guide or curb bend not
its love' (*Purg.* XVI. 85–93). Nature in itself is neither good nor bad;
it has the energy of the child and it all depends on how that energy
is directed. Thus Dante provides a Christian answer to both Plato
and Virgil, for both of whom nature is dangerously wicked and
needs to be kept in check or transcended. In Dante – blending St
Augustine and Aristotle – it is a matter rather of the right and
wrong uses of desire. It is not that the child in us must be suppressed,
its desires rooted out, its babblings transformed into *grammatica*;
rather, all this must be channelled in the right direction, and the
surest way to do that is to make it recognise what happens when the
wrong direction is taken. Teaching, whether of the child by the
adult or of the reader by the poet, will not consist in laying down
the law, in prescribing this or that course of action, but rather in the
exploration of what is involved in different kinds of choice.

There is a second aspect to the passage which is less easy to
analyse and which is bound up with the first. The Creator 'fondly
loves' the little soul even before it exists; He is a 'glad Maker', and
his gladness in the existence of the little soul is reflected in the soul's
'turning eagerly' to 'what delights it'. Dante is clearly drawing here
on his own sense of the playful pleasure of making art, of knitting
even Nimrod and the Siren into his eleven-syllable line and his *terza
rima*. Such making is joyful of itself and Dante is convinced that it
reflects the joy of the primal Maker and that this is the essential
quality of the universe, if only we would recognise it. Paolo and
Francesca, the poem implies, could never have written Canto V of
the *Inferno*, nor could the Dante who listened entranced to Casella

in the scene in which that encounter is described. By unleashing Dante's own flow of speech Virgil, the archetypal poet of tears and melancholy, taught Dante how to rejoice, and this, the poem will teach *us*, is not only the most precious of gifts, but the key to the universe.

All teachers, though, must eventually be left behind, their teachings internalised by each of their pupils. When Beatrice finally appears to Dante at the top of Mt Purgatory, it is not as a gentle mother that she speaks to Dante but as a stern father. Indeed, it is Virgil who is sought by Dante as a comforting mother at this point, but Virgil has gone for ever: 'As soon as on my sight the lofty virtue smote that had already pierced me before I was out of my boyhood, I turned to the left with the confidence of a little child that runs to his mother when he is frightened or in distress, to say to Virgil: "Not a drop of blood is left in me that does not tremble: I know the tokens of the ancient flame." But Virgil had left us bereft of himself . . .' (*Purg.* XXX. 40–51). Instead, there is Beatrice, echoing the siren in the double naming of hearself – 'Ben son, ben son Beatrice' – and telling Dante not to weep for the loss of his guide and mentor because there are more important things to weep for, such as his own past errors. And she proceeds to remind him of how he forgot her at her death, so much so that in order to turn him back to the right path it was necessary to show him 'the lost people'. Dante listens to all this with a growing sense of shame: 'As children stand ashamed and dumb, with eyes on the ground, listening conscience-stricken and repentant, so stood I. And she said, "Since you are grieved through hearing, lift up your beard and you will receive more grief through seeing"' (*Purg.* XXXI. 64–9). Dante's answer to this makes clear what is at stake here: the notion of adult responsibility. 'With less resistance is the sturdy oak uprooted, whether by wind of ours or by that which blows from Iarbas' land, than at her command I raised my chin; and when by the beard she asked for my face, well I knew the venom of the argument' (70–5). Iarbas' land is Africa, but, as so often, Dante uses periphrasis to make a complex intertextual point. Iarbas was Dido's African wooer in the *Aeneid*, and in *Aeneid* IV. 446 Aeneas stands like a great oak, refusing to be moved by Dido's please. As Peter Hawkins puts it in a fine article, drawing a contrast between the unmoved Aeneas and Dante here, 'In Purgatorio . . . the storm represents a kind of liberation. Virgil's stoic hero becomes a Christian pilgrim meant to be uprooted, to yield before a feminine wind that overcomes him precisely in order that it – that she – may raise him up. A Virgilian "no" becomes a Dantesque "yes".'

The little child must be allowed to babble, then taught to speak. The adult must never forget his childish roots, but must never seek refuge in a reversion to childishness either. These themes, present as an underground current right through the *Commedia*, re-surface powerfully in the final canto, where their ultimate significance becomes clear.

Canto XXXIII of *Paradiso* is usually seen as the grand climax to Dante's journey, the triumphant vision of the end. But again, as at the end of Proust's novel, it is not closure that is being worked for but a final openness, not a vision that is being presented to the reader but the understanding of how, once the work has been read, he himself may start to live; how, indeed, the reading of the poem has itself led us to the point where, like Dante at the top of Mt Purgatory, we can dispense with our motherly guide and, 'free, upright and whole', be ready to act in accord with the prompting of our will.

The canto begins with St Bernard's prayer to the Virgin, to which we listen without the intermediary of the narrator. Then Dante picks up his story once again: 'Bernard was signing to me with a smile to look upward, but I was already of myself such as he wished; for my sight, becoming pure, was entering more and more through the beam of the lofty Light which in Itself is true' (*Par.* XXXIII. 49–54). But then comes an interruption, a screen thrown between ourselves and the vision. 'Thenceforward', writes Dante, 'my vision was greater than speech can show, which fails at such a sight, and at such excess memory fails. As is he who dreaming sees, and after the dream the passion remains imprinted and the rest returns not to the mind; such am I, for my vision almost wholly fades away, yet does the sweetness that was born of it still drop within my heart. Thus is snow unsealed by the sun; thus in the wind, on the light leaves, the Sibyl's oracle was lost' (55–66).

Dante denies us the sight we too have come to long for, and gives us instead something we have by now got to know well: his own inability as pilgrim and poet. But it is not simply an account of failure: he gives us images of how wondrousness affects human lives, of the sweetness left imprinted on the heart by a joyous dream, of snow gradually melted by the sun, and, at this supreme moment in the poem, of the Sibyl, whose prophecies, Virgil tells us, are always being scattered by the wind. And no sooner has he done this than he switches direction once again, this time to prayer: 'O Light Supreme that art so far uplifted above mortal conceiving, relend to my mind a little of what Thou didst appear, and give my tongue such power that it may leave only a single spark of Thy glory for the folk to come . . .' (67–72). And God – or perhaps the exigencies of the poem itself – seems to respond to his prayer. As he looks into the heart of light the pessimism of *Aeneid* VI is replaced by a kind of triumph: 'In its depth I saw ingathered, bound by love in one volume' – as, of course, Dante's own poem is now gathered as it approaches its end – 'that which is dispersed in leaves throughout the universe' (85–7). And he knows that this is so 'because, in telling this, I feel my joy increase'. Pilgrim and poet are gradually becoming one, and the reader too is being drawn into the orbit of both. The joy that floods him as he now tells it is proof of what he says; and for us, by now, our total trust in that first-person narrator, a trust which has grown in the course of the journey precisely because the pilgrim was, like us, so often confused, and the poet, like us, so often at a loss for words — our total trust in him allows us too to feel that joy.

But we are not yet done with images of negation and failure. 'A single moment makes for me greater oblivion than five and twenty centuries have wrought upon the enterprise that made Neptune wonder at the shadow of the Argo', Dante writes, and the dense web of words, the complex mingling of the senses created by the image, leaves us in a state of baffled openness. It is at this point that Dante utters the lines I have already quoted: 'Now will my speech fall more short, even in respect to that which I remember, than that of an infant who still bathes his tongue at the breast' (94–6; 106–8). And so he looks and looks and sees at last the image of the Trinity within the pure circle. 'But', he confesses for one last time, 'my own wings were not sufficient for that, save that my mind was smitten by a flash wherein its wish came to it. Here power failed the lofty fantasy; but already my desire and my will were revolved, like a wheel that is evenly moved, by the Love which moves the sun and the other stars' (139–45).

These, the last lines of the poem, leave us with an image not of rest and ending but of plenitude and joyous activity. Even the syntax keeps us wheeling, for we think at first that the subject of the sentence is 'my desire', only to find that it is in fact 'love', as those key words, played with and worked on throughout the length of the poem, *amore* and *muovere*, to love and to move, appear for one last time:

> ma già volgeva il mio disio e'l *velle*,
> sì come rota ch'igualmente è mossa,
> l'amor che move il sole e l'altre stelle.

Douglas Biow puts the second point I wish to make about these last lines extremely well: 'What fails [the poet] is never his awareness of the truth or the causes of the things he saw, but his memory and his language. Yet even in the last moment of the poem, when he strains to describe the ineffable and yearningly strives to recall the vision of God . . . his failing memory and language may still be understood as assurance that he, in fact, was there.' And he concludes his fine essay with a remark that goes to the heart of my subject: 'To lose faith in the wonder of the poem, to assert that it is all put there by Dante, is to move toward the highly parodic Ariostean world of Astolfo's marvelous but instructive flight.'

Ariosto is of course the darling of the post-Modernists, the favourite poet of Calvino and Celati. They cannot find it in themselves to enter the Dantean world, and perhaps they are right in so far as their own work is concerned. But Dante's poem exists for us, can still be read by us. To withhold assent from it is to deny ourselves what it has to give us: the greatest example of relaxed control in the literature of the West. And this, I have been arguing, stems from Dante's sense of trust in the world and in the vernacular, a trust which, unlike Homer's and that of the authors of the Hebrew Bible, has had to be fought for and earned; and from his demonstration that the acknowledgement of failure, of our human limits, is precisely that which can lead us forward and help us out of the spiral of egoism and self-pity into which the refusal of such acknowledgement, the clinging to the self we know, will lead us. Dante's poem is about making the will right through voluntary submission which will bring about the possibility of real self-expression. That is the story it tells. But it is also the story it enacts in its work on language, for the poet, in the course of his poem, reveals himself to be not a master or a slave but a maker, not the triumphant controller of his language or the humble follower of authority, but one who finds his freedom in what to others would be impossible constraint.

Kafka's extraordinary and powerful image of the blood oozing between the stones of the law impresses us as profound truth;

Dante's career and poetry asks us to imagine differently. It asks us to recognise that there is a continuity between the child and the man, between even the most exalted language and the infant's cry of *mamma* and *babbo*. Language, as Adam tells Dante in paradise, is inherently changeable. We must find it in ourselves to live with that changeability, to renounce ready-made certainty for a living language that can be worked on and which will then in turn work on us.

We must not forget our roots, forget the earth on which we stand. Our roots, though, do not lie in this or that spot on earth, in this language or that; they lie in our common, vulnerable humanity.

4 Shakespeare: trust and suspicion at play

ALBANY: Well, you may fear too far.

GONERIL: Safer than trust too far.

(*King Lear*)

A performance is about to take place:

> Why, then the champions are prepared, and stay
> For nothing but his majesty's approach.
> > (*Richard II*, I. iii. 5–6)

Trumpets sound, and the king enters with his nobles. After a few preliminary rituals a herald calls out:

> Harry of Hereford, Lancaster, and Derby
> Stands here for God, his sovereign, and himself,
> On pain to be found false and recreant,
> To prove the Duke of Norfolk, Thomas Mowbray,

A traitor to his God, his king, and him,
And dares him to set forward to the fight.

(I. iii. 104–9)

A second herald responds:

Here standeth Thomas Mowbray, Duke of Norfolk,
On pain to be found false and recreant,
Both to defend himself and to approve
Henry of Hereford, Lancaster, and Derby
To God, his sovereign, and to him disloyal,
Courageously and with a free desire
Attending but the signal to begin.

(110–16)

A marshall calls out: 'Sound, trumpets, and set forward combatants.'
But then something unexpected happens: 'Stay!' cries the marshall,
'The king hath thrown his warder down' (117–18).

Richard II's action at this moment destroys the spectacle we were
about to witness and precipitates instead the play Shakespeare has
in store for us. But it does more. I want to suggest that it opens the
way for the flowering of Shakespeare's mature art.

To understand why this should be the case we have to go back to
the first scene of *Richard II*. This play, when it has been looked
at historically, has too often been seen as being 'really' about
Elizabethan politics – indeed, the Queen herself is famously supposed to have taken it like that. But there is never a single explanation as to why the work of a great writer is as it is. Without wanting
to deny its relevance to Elizabethan politics, I would like to suggest
that here, at the chronological start of the entire sequence of Shakespeare's two great linked tetralogies concerning English history, the
playwright is presenting us with a world which is just about to be
lost, a world in which we can trust because inner and outer are inti-

mately related and God still speaks directly to us, as he did to Abraham and Moses, and as Achilles' mother did to him.

The first scene is going to bring that world to life, just as the third, from which I began by quoting, is going to show its disappearance for ever. Two nobles square up to each other, each adamant that he is telling the truth, each accusing the other of slander and lies. They, in keeping with the times, are not interested in arbitration: they are determined to prove the truth of their claims *with* their bodies, *on* the body of their opponent. Bolingbroke says:

> for what I speak
> My body shall make good upon this earth
> Or my divine soul answer it in heaven.
> Thou art a traitor and a miscreant . . .
>
> (I. i. 36–9)

Mowbray answers:

> 'Tis not the trial of a woman's war,
> The bitter clamor of two eager tongues,
> Can arbitrate this cause betwixt us twain;
> The blood is hot that must be cooled for this.
>
> (48–51)

This is not just a quarrel between two angry men. When Bolingbroke says: 'Besides I say, and will in battle prove', and Mowbray rejoins: 'Then, dear my liege, mine honour let me try', they are appealing to the right to trial by combat, a variant of the ritual of the ordeal.

The ordeal has had a bad press since it passed out of fashion. The idea that you could decide if a woman was a witch by throwing her into a pool and seeing if she floated, or that a man was guilty of stealing cattle if he was found not to be able to hold a hot iron in his hand for a certain period of time – this strikes us as barbaric and superstitious. But, as Peter Brown points out in one of his many remarkable forays into the *mentalité* of the early Middle Ages, 'Ordeals had depended on an easy passage between the sacred and the profane.' They were, he explains, 'an instrument of consensus and . . . a theatrical device by which to contain disruptive conflict', by which to bring to an end those family feuds which might otherwise have rumbled on for generations.

The ordeal was a public spectacle. It demonstrated to a non-literate society through the forms of ceremony how things really stood, and it did so in a highly dramatic way, so as to imprint it on the memory of the community. 'The hand that has held the hot iron', writes Brown, 'the hand that has been plunged into boiling water, are solemnly sealed and reopened again before witnesses three days later. If the wound heals "normally", then the case is adjudged decided: God has spoken in the most elemental way, by an assertion of the integrity of a man's rights symbolized by the sur-viving integrity of his physical body in contact with extreme heat.' If one of the two combatants is killed then God has spoken in a way no-one can gainsay: that man was guilty and the victor innocent. Thus in the *Chanson de Roland*, 'when the traitor Ganelon is defeated in trial by battle, he is killed and the thirty kinsmen who mobilized behind him are hanged. That, for the writer of the poem at least, was the last of it.' But, as Brown points out, it is important to understand that 'it is not a judgement *by* God; it is a remitting of a case *ad iudicium Dei*, "*to* the judgement of God"'. Thus, 'by being brought to the judgement of God, the case already stepped outside the pressures of human interest, and so its resolution can be devoid of much of the odium of human responsibility'.

However, Brown argues, by the end of the twelfth century the concept of the ordeal was withering in the face of multiple pressures – the centralisation of power, the new concern with law, the shift from community to hierarchy. *Richard II* is set of course in the late fourteenth, not the twelfth century. Nevertheless, it seems

to me clear that Shakespeare, with his remarkable ability to con-
dense and concentrate in one powerful dramatic incident the
ethos of a whole culture, has captured in a single scene the essence
of a vanishing world. Once we are alerted to it we can see that
the whole play, in the way it is written as well as in its subject
matter, is meant to make us aware of a culture in the process of
disintegration. One has only to contrast its garden scene, so
starkly emblematic and 'medieval', with the great orchard scene
of *2 Henry IV*, aptly compared by Tony Nuttall to a scene in
Chekhov, to see what I mean.

The last representative of that older world is of course John of
Gaunt, aptly called 'time-honored Lancaster' in the very first line
of the play. And it is in keeping with this that it is John of Gaunt
on his deathbed who delivers the famous speech about the perfection and integrity of feudal England, 'This royal throne of kings,
this sceptred isle', a speech which, like Ulysses' parallel speech on
order in *Troilus and Cressida*, is no more representative of
Shakespeare's own views than any other passage in his works. Of
course even that speech is not quite Gaunt's last, and we leave him
punning desperately on his own name, seemingly infected by the
new spirit which is already seeping into the play and which will
culminate in Richard's own desperate play with words as he tries to
make sense of what is happening to him.

Why exactly does Richard halt the trial by combat? We are never
told. It could be because he has a guilty conscience, knows that
Mowbray is implicated in his uncle Gloucester's murder, and at his
own orders – something strongly hinted at in the play. It could be
because of his civilised refinement, which modern historians have
certainly discerned in him, and which would make him see trial by
combat as a barbaric survival, not fit for the modern age. The simple
fact is, though, that by his intervention he reveals his own fatal lack
of trust in the process that tradition has ordained. And what Brown
says about the decline of the ordeal has an important bearing not

just on the way this play develops, but on our understanding of Shakespeare's relation to tradition.

Brown sees the decline of the ordeal as directly related to the shift from consensus to authority which occurs in the course of the twelfth century. This, he suggests, was bound up with a shift in the relations between inner and outer, subjectivity and objectivity; for the supernatural, 'which had tended to be treated as the main source of the objectified values of the group, came to be regarded as the preserve . . . of intensely personal feeling'. It led too to the growth of rationality, 'for appeal to reason in clerical controversy invariably implied . . . that men could be expected to obey rapid and trenchant decisions – the outcome of syllogisms, the production of an authoritative written text'. Simultaneously, the majesty of the sacraments was heightened. 'The same Lateran Council of 1215 that forbade clerical participation in the ordeal sanctioned the doctrine of transubstantiation. The two decrees sum up a shift in mentality. Laymen were no longer allowed to expect that the untold majesty of God might any day shine out for their benefit in a law suit: but if they went to church, the transmutation of bread and wine into Christ's body was certain to happen.'

This polarisation between authority on the one hand and subjective truth on the other, when once consensus breaks down, is immediately apparent in Shakespeare's play. No sooner has Richard thrown his warder down and stopped the fight than he starts to exercise extraordinary arbitrary authority. First he exiles Mowbray for life and Bolingbroke for ten years; then, taking pity on Gaunt, he changes his mind and commutes the sentence on Bolingbroke to six years. The latter rightly comments:

> How long a time lies in one little word!
> Four lagging winters, and four wanton springs
> End in a word, such is the breath of kings.
>
> (I. iii. 213)

Gaunt, for his part, bitterly remarks that six years or ten makes little difference since he will be dead anyway by the time his son returns; and when Richard tut-tuts this, saying, 'Why, uncle, thou hast many years to live', he is quick to respond:

> But not a minute, king, that thou canst give.
> Shorten my days thou canst with sullen sorrow
> And pluck nights from me, but not lend a morrow.
> Thou canst help time to furrow me with age,
> But stop no wrinkle in his pilgrimage.
>
> (226–30)

There are limits to the powers of even a tyrant; not even a Tamburlaine can conquer time.

These two speeches suggest that Richard is now at odds with the workings of nature, which makes his assertion that he is God's vicar on earth all the more shrill and unconvincing. As the play progresses it splits, as a reading of Brown could have told us it would, into the objective and the subjective, and it grows clearer and clearer that power is the only arbiter and yet Richard grows more and more insistent that God will help His anointed:

> Is not the king's name twenty thousand names?
> Arm, arm, my name! A puny subject strikes
> At thy great glory.
>
> (III. ii. 85–7)

But the king's name is actually worth nothing at all; in a world shorn of consensus and the acceptance of tradition a name is a word like any other. But this fact is more than Richard can bear; for it is not only his personal world that is crumbling before his eyes, but his whole sense of the ultimate meaning of the universe – though, as I have suggested, it is probably the case that he protests so much because deep down he had never had Gaunt's confidence in such a meaning. All he has left then is his sense of himself as victim. 'I thought you had been willing to resign', says Bolingbroke. 'My crown I am', answers Richard,

> but still my griefs are mine.
> You may my glories and my state depose,
> But not my griefs. Still am I king of those.
> (IV. i. 191–3)

He can at moments comfort himself with the thought that during the long winter nights old men will 'tell the lamentable tale of me', and he can try to evade the truth by acting out the role of the broken king, and even of Christ, rejected and betrayed, but we know it is only a matter of time before the words of which he has now become the master – since he is master of nothing else – will be stifled in his throat by Bolingbroke's command. Even in death, though, Richard clings to his extreme version of the old order:

> Exton, thy fierce hand
> Hath with the king's blood stained the king's own land.
> Mount, mount, my soul! thy seat is up on high;
> Whilst my gross flesh sinks downward, here to die.
> (V. v. 109–12)

It has often been pointed out that what we see in this play is the transformation of Richard from king to actor. This is true but trite. What needs to be understood is that by portraying this transformation on the stage Shakespeare discovered how the death of the old order cleared a space for a secular drama. Richard discovers that his words are mere words, incapable of pushing back armies or ensuring his survival. But then all actors on stage are condemned to utter mere words and their victories over their enemies are always 'for play' and never 'for real'. In *Richard II* Shakespeare both mourns this condition and discovers in it one of his abiding themes. Where Marlowe had embraced the new powers given him by the Elizabethan stage by placing on that stage men whose power over both their fellows and the audience depended on their rhetoric, men with whom we feel Marlowe the playwright identifies, Shakespeare, more realistic, more responsible, made his plays out of the recognition of the ambiguous nature of *play*. Marlowe, like Verdi, exults in the ability of the protagonist, through his voice, his speech, his song, to transcend reality, to give body to our desires, and we love him for it and pay to be thus transported. Shakespeare, like Mozart, never forgets the limits of that power as well as its dangerous ambiguity. We pay to witness this ambiguity at play.

Was Schiller wrong then to see Shakespeare as essentially a naive artist, like Homer? Our modern tendency is to be deeply suspicious of the image of Shakespeare as the untutored child of nature, even when that image goes back almost to Shakespeare's own time. For it goes back of course to Ben Jonson's encomium printed at the head of the First Folio, with its lines about Shakespeare's 'small Latin and less Greek', and its view that 'Nature herself was proud of his designs, / And joyed to wear the dressing of his lines!' It goes back to Dryden's 1668 remark that Shakespeare 'needed not the spectacles of books to read Nature; he looked inwards, and found her there'. And it becomes a commonplace in the eighteenth century. It may be, as Emrys Jones has suggested, that the English needed to have as their national poet someone more like a force of nature than a great intellect, that Shakespeare was, as it were, a gift to English anti-intellectualism. But Jones, drawing on Baldwin and other scholars of Renaissance rhetoric, brings out brilliantly in the first chapter of his *The Origins of Shakespeare* how it is possible to reconcile this view of Shakespeare with that of a young man deeply immersed in school rhetoric of the kind which had been the daily fare of the grammar schools since Erasmus's friend Colet had founded St Paul's in the early sixteenth century.

Jones does not say this, but all we have to do is to substitute the word *craft* for the word *nature* for everything to fall into place. For Shakespeare, as the scholarship of the past fifty years has made clear, was firmly embedded in a craft tradition of the kind I described in my Introduction: an artist whose mind was stocked with examples both linguistic and existential from the tradition, and who thought of himself as a maker, not a thinker, a craftsman whose primary allegiance was to the production of a play on time and for a particular occasion. In this he was like Bach, Mozart or Haydn, and unlike Beethoven and Schoenberg. Wittgenstein, like Schoenberg a product of *fin-de-siècle* Vienna and with roots in German Romanticism, could not conceive of a great artist, which is what the world told him Shakespeare was, as anything other than a version of Beethoven, and so was deeply puzzled by him. ' "Beethoven's great heart" – nobody could speak of "Shakespeare's great heart" ', he writes. 'I do not think Shakespeare would have been able to reflect on "the lot of the poet". Nor could he regard himself as a prophet or as a teacher of mankind. People stare at him in wonderment, almost as at a spectacular natural phenomenon.' This is curious, because, as we shall see, Wittgenstein's own philosophical work can in fact help us grasp the nature of what it means to be involved in a craft tradition. But it is often the case that pioneers are the most conventional of people when they turn from what is their passion to comment on the world at large.

However, Wittgenstein's comments in *Culture and Value* help us, negatively, to see what people might have meant throughout the ages when they spoke of Shakespeare's *naturalness*: a sense that there is no need for him to exert his will, that he is quite happy to disappear into the tradition and re-mould it from within. As Emrys Jones puts it, talking of the death of Falstaff described in *Henry V* and its similarity to the death of Socrates as described by Plato in the *Phaedo*: 'What is Shakespearean about such a passage is the freedom and casualness and audacity with which the classical text is put to work in a new vernacular context and then used in such a way as to stimulate the mind into entertaining a number of different possibilities.'

I think that what is so remarkable about Shakespeare, as about Mozart, and what gives their work its special tone, is that at the same time as they were exploring, as no-one had explored before them, the breakdown of trust and the corrosive effects of suspicion, they nevertheless trusted completely in the craft tradition in which they were working. That is why they are so different both from Milton and Beethoven who came after them, and from Homer and Bach who came before.

If it was in *Richard II* that Shakespeare finally faced up to the fact that he was writing in a world in which trust had given way to suspicion, it was perhaps only in *A Midsummer Night's Dream* that he finally grasped what belonging to a craft tradition entailed. The play is so difficult to talk about precisely because its perfection feels neither frozen nor imposed but is inherent in a gathering rhythm which unleashes potential without disintegrating in the process.

One obvious reason for this lies in the way it is constructed. It does away with the linear plot of romance and tragedy and with the tight plotting of farce. Instead of plot, subplot and complication leading to crisis and dénouement, it presents us with four distinct plots, variations on one another, and treats the complications that arise from each and from the way they impinge on one another so lightly that all is resolved by the end of Act IV.

But it is not only the plot of *A Midsummer Night's Dream* which seems to be of the flimsiest; the four lovers can hardly be said to have characters. But then this is, in a sense, what the play is about: the fluidity of character. Do the lovers know what they want, except that it should not be what others want for them? as W. D. Snodgrass nicely puts it. Does the play even teach them what they want, or is that too serious a way of reading it? Curiously, we in no way resent the pairing off at the end of Lysander and Hermia, Demetrius and Helena, in the way we resent the pairing off of the Duke and Isabella, Angelo and Mariana in *Measure for Measure*. The reason, I think, is that in this play all the choices we make in life are presented as both arbitrary and inevitable. The play does not fail to deliver 'deep' characters; rather, it asks us to imagine a world where character is always 'light'.

'Translation', in effect, is the key. Helena wishes to be 'translated' into Hermia, who is pursued by both men. In the woods she gets her wish and finds she doesn't like it. Everyone is 'translated' in the forest and the moonlight. This does not mean that they are turned into beasts, like Odysseus' crew by Circe, nor does it involve a 'transhumanising' such as Dante talked of at the start of *Paradiso*. Simply the sense that our characters sit very lightly upon us, that to be 'true' to ourselves does not mean making sure that there are firm boundaries around ourselves but rather that we realise our potential.

That of course flies in the face of the troubadour romantic ethos which underlies *Romeo and Juliet* and still underlies our view of character. To be true in this tradition is to be single and absolute; what *A Midsummer Night's Dream* teaches us, on the other hand, is that we are full of contradictory desires and that the more we try to live up to a false ideal of truth to ourselves the more foolish we become. That is why the play has to end with a burlesque of *Romeo and Juliet*.

It is the mechanicals who make the play what it is, and it is appropriate that the last act should belong to them. It is they who provide the ballast, the 'bottom', which allows the play to sail away into the skies. How do they do that? Or rather, how does Shakespeare do it through them?

It is easy to grow solemn over them, and over Bottom in

particular. Bottom wants all the roles – Lover, Lady, Lion, Moon. As Snodgrass wittily says: 'He wants to play the tyrant; if there is to be no tyrant the next best thing is to be the director.' But even Snodgrass can't resist deepening Bottom: he is, he remarks, like a baby who has trouble keeping straight the parts of the body and their proper roles: 'I see a voice; now will I to the chink / To spy an I can hear my Thisby's face.' He seems determined to annihilate all distinctions, dissolving the meanings of words and the barriers between species: 'There is not a more fearful wild fowl than your lion living.' But is he for that reason really the symbol of anality that Snodgrass wishes to make him? That is once again to substitute a meaning for the absurd, wise, living and changing creature Shakespeare gives us, to substitute an idea for the play Shakespeare has presented to us.

Patricia Parker, in an equally interesting exploration of the play, rightly stresses the role of Snug the Joiner, the way the play reveals the *joints* in both psychology and rhetoric, and she brings out skilfully how it plays with the humanist contrast between 'rude mechanicals' and courtiers and gentlemen. After quoting Thomas Wilson's *Rule of Reason*, a humanist rhetorical treatise, she says: 'All this description of the necessity of "order" – by the author of a text on the "rule" of "Reason" – has to do with a shaping of "matter" . . . , the forming of the formless or "rude".' Yet, she rightly says, what we have in *A Midsummer Night's Dream* is the depiction of how 'rude mechanicals' misjoin both language and bodily parts, 'where Bottom's body is monstrously joined to the head of an ass, and where lovers disjoined in the interlude in the woods outside Athens finally wander, grope, and stumble in the dark, unable to find their way.' This is excellent, but Parker can't help bringing in Marx on class wars and Benjamin on mechanical reproduction – none of which is exactly irrelevant, but reference to which seems to destroy the lightness of the play, to substitute a final 'meaning' for the playful exploration of possibilities.

I think the effect of the mechanicals, their inability to join anything properly, is to force *us* into becoming part of a craft tradition.
It is we who are made to do the work of joining properly, even as
we see how absurd and condescending are the comments of the
assembled courtiers when the play is finally performed. Even
Theseus, wise and humane as he is, and fully justified in his plea to
others to be generous, evinces a confidence in his own ability to
emend where emendation is needed which we, who have experienced the rest of the play as Theseus has not, will find it difficult
to accept. Theseus is the perfect humanist, wise and just and
confident in the powers of reason and imagination – yet where
Hippolyta, who is merely bored by the play, can see in the story of
the lovers 'something of great constancy; / But howsoever, strange
and admirable', he can only say dogmatically: 'I never may believe
/ These antic fables nor these fairy toys' (V. i. 26–7; 2–3).

Each of the characters and each of the commentators is looking
for a bottom to this play, a base or core. Yet if the play has a bottom
it is the moment when Bottom wakes up from his dream and says:

> I have had a most rare vision. I have had a dream, past the wit
> of man to say what dream it was. Man is but an ass if he go about
> to expound this dream. Methought I was – there is no man can
> tell what. Methought I was and methought I had – But man is
> but a patched fool if he will offer to say what methought I had.
> The eye of man hath not heard, the ear of man hath not seen,
> man's hand is not able to taste, his tongue to conceive, nor his
> heart to report what my dream was. I will get Peter Quince to
> write a ballet [ballad] of this dream. It shall be called 'Bottom's
> Dream', because it hath no bottom.
>
> (IV. i. 203–14)

It is not enough to say that Bottom is misquoting St Paul here. He
is, rather, putting everything St Paul stands for into question. 'Eye

hath not seen, nor ear heard', wrote St Paul, 'neither have entered into the heart of man, the things which God hath prepared for them that love him. But God hath revealed them unto us by his Spirit: for the Spirit searcheth all things, yea, the deep things of God.' (1 Corinthians 2: 9–10) St Paul knows the answers. They have been revealed to him on the road to Damascus. If only men could be brought to see the truth as he has seen it they would be saved. Bottom in his wisdom discovers that the dream is bottomless and that man is but an ass if he go about to expound it. And Shakespeare in *his* wisdom shows us that men are changeable and inconstant, and yet that out of the web of interlocking lives something of great constancy can emerge.

To respond to this play is to discover how crushing and restrictive are both law and subjectivity, and even understanding itself. Yet it is not an anarchic play; no less than in Greek tragedy, its trust of the world is never confused with a construal of the world, but rather with a sense of constancy as the wellspring of the world. That is why it is so pleasurable and releasing to watch and so difficult to talk about.

A Midsummer Night's Dream is Shakespeare's coming of age as master of his craft, as joiner *extraordinaire*. But Shakespeare, like Mozart, could never rest on his laurels. He had to subject his craft to greater and greater tests. In *Twelfth Night* we see such testing taking place, and how the craft tradition in Shakespeare's hands can still deal apparently effortlessly with such tests. Here the power of ego to blind one to the world takes on a dangerous edge, for there is no Theseus to control the realm of mortals and no Oberon to control that of the supernatural. Orsino, Olivia, Sir Toby and Malvolio all have it in their power to do harm to others, wittingly or unwittingly, in the pursuit of their desires. All that Viola has on her side is her trust that time will untangle all the knots and somehow set things to rights.

Two Ovidian images polarise the play: that of Actaeon torn to

pieces by his own dogs and that of Arion riding the dolphin. Both
appear at the very start of the play. First, Orsino:

> O, when my eyes did see Olivia first,
> Methought she purged the air of pestilence.
> That instant was I turned into a hart,
> And my desires, like fell and cruel hounds,
> E'er since pursue me.
>
> (I. i. 20–4)

Then, the Captain to Viola:

> True, madam; and, to comfort you with chance,
> Assure yourself, after our ship did split,
> When you, and those poor number saved with you,
> Hung on our driving boat, I saw your brother,
> Most provident in peril, bind himself
> (Courage and hope both teaching him the practice)
> To a strong mast that lived upon the sea;
> Where, like Arion on the dolphin's back,
> I saw him hold acquaintance with the waves
> So long as I could see.
>
> (I. ii. 8–17)

Orsino, Olivia, Sir Toby and Malvolio are all pursued by their hounds
and all will in some way or other be torn by them. They have never
experienced what it means to be subject to the waves of chance, and
so imagine the world will yield them what they want. Viola and her
brother, schooled by misfortune, discover in misfortune both courage
and hope, which teach them the practice of riding on the waves of
the world, *holding acquaintance* with them, a wonderful phrase
which socialises our dealings with the world without in any way
diminishing the frightening aspect of what is involved.

Only Malvolio will have to endure anything as frightening. It would no doubt have been possible for Shakespeare to show us how Malvolio's true, trusting nature was brought out into the light of day by what he had had to endure in the darkness of prison and impending madness. But he chooses not to do that. Malvolio, in the end, turns his back on the world of reconciliation into which Olivia beckons him: 'I'll be revenged on the whole pack of you' (I. i. 367).

Yet though there is strain, the world of Shakespeare's comedy seems able to expand and accommodate it as perhaps it cannot quite accommodate Shylock. When the characters have all departed the Clown is left alone to sing a song that acknowledges that even within comedy Malvolios will always exist as much as Violas, that 'the rain it raineth every day', that the world began a long time ago and all we can say is that now the play is done.

I said earlier that Wittgenstein's remarks about Shakespeare are curiously at odds with the thrust of his later philosophy, which, had he but realised it, would have found in Shakespeare's drama luminous examples of what he was struggling to articulate. When Wittgenstein is discussing how we know we are using language correctly – i.e. trustworthily – he says that we want to formulate the rules, but we can't do this and we have to trust simply in 'what we do'. There is, he says, 'a way of grasping a rule which is *not* an *interpretation*'. Here language is functioning normally, is not 'on holiday'. In the two comedies I have been looking at Shakespeare presents us with dramatic examples of what happens when language goes on holiday and what happens when – as in the case of Viola and Sebastian – it functions as a practice to be learned by contact with the buffetings of the world. Malvolio, like Iago after him, needs to interpret in order to control; as a result he *mis*interprets and makes a fool of himself. The Clown, like Viola, earns our confidence because he accepts that 'the rain it raineth every day' and no man can stop it.

Buoyed by his complete confidence in his craft, Shakespeare was able to take a closer and closer look at the nature of suspicion.

Hamlet, like *A Midsummer Night's Dream*, is a celebration of exuberance, of that *copia* which every Renaissance artist delighted to display. Hamlet himself is the archetypal Renaissance courtier: soldier, scholar, horseman, fencer, wit – he would not have been out of place in *Love's Labour's Lost*, and could, in a different play, have been the Fool. His remarks to Polonius and to Rosencrantz and Guildenstern are very like those of the Fool in *Twelfth Night* or *King Lear*. Unfortunately, while the Fool is 'licensed', has his precise role in the community, even if it is to question that community, Hamlet, far from being the voice of tradition and of the ultimate sanity of the community is, in Schiller's terms, a sentimentalist in a naive world, a figure who stands outside precisely because he does not know what role he has.

The naive world in which Hamlet finds himself is the world of Old Hamlet and Old Fortinbras, the world to which the jester Yorick belonged, as Sterne sensed. It is a world in which revenge is a simple matter: once you know that someone has been responsible for killing one of your kinsmen you have the duty to avenge his death as quickly as possible. That is what the ghost of Old Hamlet enjoins Hamlet to do. But he can't. Not, like Richard II, because he no longer has the means, but because the simple world inhabited by his father is no longer his world. And the reason for this is quite simple: had Claudius merely killed Old Hamlet there would be no problem; had he killed him and seduced his wife there would still be no problem. The problem arises because Gertrude seems to have married him willingly.

The naive world of the older generation seems to be inhabited by members of Hamlet's generation: Laertes, Fortinbras, Horatio. Each still feels he has a role to play and plays it to the hilt. To Hamlet, though, it seems that they are *overplaying*. Like bad actors they 'saw the air' too much with their hands and forget that 'in the very torrent, tempest, and (as I may say) whirlwind of your passion, you must acquire and beget a temperance that may give it smoothness' (III. ii. 4–8). Hamlet, like Kierkegaard, has too strong a sense of tradition not to see that those who pretend or imagine that they are still part of it have failed to see how things have changed, and that as a result everything about them is false. And, like Kierkegaard, he knows that he too is not exempted, despite his greater awareness of what is at stake. When the time comes the only way he himself can act is to leap after Laertes into Ophelia's grave and start to rant quite as violently as any Marlovian hero - though even here he catches himself in the act and concludes: 'Nay, an thou'lt mouth, / I'll rant as well as thou' (V.i.270–1).

This is why Hamlet so appealed to the Romantics. His play-acting, his prevarication, was something Coleridge and Kierkegaard understood only too well, for they too understood with varying degrees of clarity that in a world bereft of tradition only the fools and the knaves go on as though nothing had happened, but that being neither a fool nor a knave is of little comfort. For they lack Bottom's ability to accept that there is no bottom and that this is something to wonder at and celebrate.

Hamlet, unlike Richard II, is well aware that he is acting, playing; unlike Bottom, he cannot be saved by that knowledge. The play's hold on the Western imagination stems from this double perspective. It is close to Greek drama and to *A Midsummer Night's Dream* in its sense of confidence in the craft tradition and in its ability to use effortlessly all the elements it needs from that tradition; yet its hero is at the centre of a Kierkegaardian modern tragedy in which the really important things can never be said, in which the excesses of language and incident only hide the terrible silence suffocating the hero.

By contrast *Othello* is almost a copy-book demonstration of what happens when trust and suspicion come into contact. Othello, like David in the Hebrew Bible, like Odysseus, is a foreigner to introspection; he is what he does and what he can relate. His way of speaking is not to argue but to tell a story – to the senators of

Venice as much as to his future wife. And this holds right through to the end:

> I pray you, in your letters,
> When you shall these unlucky deeds relate,
> Speak of me as I am.
>
> (V. ii. 340–2)

He does not want them to sum him up – mighty warrior or black ram – but to *relate a deed*. And this deed he then proceeds to enact before them. That Othello and not Iago has the last word, in keeping with the promise of the title, is borne out by the play's concluding line: 'This heavy act with heavy heart *relate*.'

To Iago of course this mode of being and telling is nothing more than an attempt to dignify human affairs with 'bombast circumstance'. For him ' 'Tis in ourselves that we are thus or thus. Our bodies are our gardens, to the which our wills are gardeners' (I. iii. 319–21). For him we are alone in a hostile world, but if we can recognise this and not be fooled by men's rhetoric we can remain masters of our destinies. Thus he urges Roderigo to cheer up and put money in his purse, for 'If sanctimony and a frail vow betwixt an erring barbarian and a supersubtle Venetian be not too hard for my wits and all the tribe of hell, thou shalt enjoy her' (352–4).

Othello, like the oral story-teller he is, tells a tale; Iago, like a novelist, sums up the characters of others in two words: 'erring barbarian', 'supersubtle Venetian'. The play, it has often been said, charts the way in which Iago's language gradually infects that of Othello and how, when that happens, Othello is doomed. That is true; but it also charts the way in which the language of a culture of suspicion infects the language of a culture of trust.

Iago sows the seeds of suspicion in Othello's mind by asking him to *interpret*, to get to the bottom of things. The ancient tragedian and the oral story-teller answer the question: what happened? The novelist and the modern playwright answer the question: what *really* happened? A small difference, it might be thought, but, in effect, a monumental one.

Take the scene (III. iii) where Iago and Othello are shown watching Cassio and Desdemona. As Cassio leaves Iago remarks in one of his pretended asides: 'Ha! I like not that.' Othello, as he is meant to, rises to the bait: 'What does thou say?' 'Nothing, my lord.' But to say 'nothing' is of course quite different from not saying anything, for 'nothing' already conjures up a 'something'. Othello asks if it wasn't Cassio they saw leaving, and Iago has already won: 'Cassio, my lord? No, sure I cannot think it, / That he would steal away so guilty-like, / Seeing your coming' (III. iii. 35–40). We ourselves have seen Cassio leaving and seen that there was nothing guilty about it. Or was there? How did he in fact look? Wittgenstein would say, he didn't look 'like' anything, he simply went away. But Wittgenstein isn't around to counsel Othello, and the fact of the matter is that once an action is taken out of its place in the continuum language goes on holiday and it becomes open to suspicion.

Iago guides Othello into seeking a 'bottom', into precisely that area which Bottom the Weaver understood is best left alone. He does just the same with Roderigo in an earlier scene (II. i). First he calmly tells him that Desdemona is lusting for Cassio, having tired of the Moor. 'I cannot believe that in her', says the bewildered Roderigo. 'She's full of most blessed condition.' 'Blessed fig's end!' retorts Iago. 'The wine she drinks is made of grapes ... Blessed pudding! Didst thou not see her paddle with the palm of his hand? Didst not mark that?' 'Yes, that I did; but that was but courtesy.' 'Lechery, by this hand!' snarls Iago. 'An index and obscure prologue to the history of lust and foul thoughts' (II. i. 245–53).

Courtesy is too weak a concept to stand up for long against the idea of lechery. Or rather, it is weak because it is not a concept at all but a part of the fabric of life. As such, it is taken for granted until the moment comes when, being questioned, it crumbles. Not because it is inherently false, but because it cannot withstand the corrosive effects of suspicion. What we saw in the case of Homer and Plato, of the Hebrew scriptures and St Paul, is being played out here once more, though neither of the protagonists is of course conscious of their exemplary status.

When we look at Shakespeare's career as a whole we see that it was imperative for him to subject that older culture, from which he himself derived the confidence to make his plays, to greater and greater testing. Iago is a destroyer; he is also a better man of the theatre than either Bottom or Hamlet. The play he plans he carries out to perfection. After *Hamlet* and *Othello* it is as if both the notion of *copia* and of dramatic plot have to be openly shredded before our eyes. This is what happens in *King Lear*. Hamlet had said that he had that within which passes show, but he said it with the confidence in language of the born showman. All Cordelia can say is: 'What shall Cordelia speak? Love, and be silent' (I. i. 62). And when asked to speak in public and tell her love she can only say: 'Nothing, my lord' (87), Iago's very words, but, this time, meant. However, 'nothing' is not a word Lear will accept or a playwright can tolerate. 'Nothing?' 'Nothing.' 'Nothing will come of nothing. Speak again.'

This is the great play of negation, steadily undoing what the earlier plays had done, rather as the Book of Job undoes Genesis. Those five 'nothings' will be matched by the five great 'nevers' of the climax. But before we reach that point much will still have to be undone.

First of all, language. The playwright must have felt as uneasy as we do with what follows. Cordelia, ordered by Lear to speak, does so with:

> Unhappy that I am, I cannot heave
> My heart into my mouth. I love your Majesty
> According to my bond, no more nor less.
>
> (I. i. 91–3)

Later readers have taken Cordelia's words too much for granted. After all, she says what they want to hear, that the heart has its reasons which reason cannot speak. What is not so often remarked upon is that, no less than Iago with Othello, Lear has here forced her to speak *his* language, albeit reluctantly. Lear is determined to strip away all falsehood from the self: he will get rid of the trappings of office and the conventions of courtesy so as to be left with only the pure language of the heart. Later, on the heath, he will be driven even further along this road and almost joyfully attempt to strip man of all his trappings till he reaches rock bottom: the poor bare forked animal. What the play demonstrates in almost clinical fashion is that such an enterprise is doomed from the start: there is no essence of man or of humanity; we are our trappings, our modes of speech. Once, of course, this was seen as self-evident: a person was the role they played within the community in which they grew up and functioned; what has changed is that this is now seen, by a Iago, a Lear, as merely hiding the essential self.

Cordelia's refusal to play Lear's game does still, to some extent, play it, in its too sharp — and rhetorically undistinguished — division between heart and mouth, inner and outer. A moment later he forces her into another kind of contradiction when, in answer to his: 'So young, and so untender?' she responds: 'So young, my lord, and true.' (106–7) For 'trueness' is not something one says about oneself; it is best left to other people to say. In the normal course of things only those planning treachery or the creatures of an incompetent playwright protest their trueness. Finally she breaks and the words come flooding out: she is lacking, she says, 'that glib and oily art' which 'speaks not what it purposes'; then, turning to her sisters:

> I know you what you are;
> And, like a sister, am most loath to call
> Your faults as they are named. Love well our father.
> To your professèd bosoms I commit him;

But yet, alas, stood I within his grace,
I would prefer him to a better place.
So farewell to you both.

(269–75)

We feel, surely, that there is some justice in Regan's answer: 'Prescribe not us our duty.'

Cordelia's words leave us uneasy because they make her appear smug and priggish. That Lear has forced her into this posture is part of the strange discomfort generated by the scene. That discomfort will only be left behind when we have seen and heard the sisters in action, when we have noted Goneril's acid reply to Albany's 'Well, you may fear too far' – 'Safer than trust too far' (I. iv. 319). And when we have seen how the ethos of suspicion and naked egotism eats up those who would live by it.

The sisters' words then, are ground up in small pieces and thrust back in their faces – but not before Cordelia and Lear have lost their lives. Before that happens, though, we will have been shown how foolish it was of Lear to imagine he could do without the trappings of authority and the conventions of courtesy, how vain it is to think one can get down to the poor bare forked animal as though to an essence of the human.

At the same time both language and plot are themselves ground into small pieces by this terrible machine. Where *A Midsummer Night's Dream* threw plot and character into the air to reveal that both are as insubstantial as moonbeams and that our potential for change is an index of our humanity, the storm scene in *Lear* breaks down both character and language to reveal the chaos that comes to those who think they are in control. Shakespeare here dips into what Jones calls the native tradition and comes up only with shards: 'O, do, de, do, de, do, de. Bless thee from whirlwinds, star-blasting, and taking. Do poor Tom some charity, whom the foul fiend vexes.

There could I have him now – and there – and there again – and there –' (III. iv. 57–60). When Hamlet plays the madman we know that he is at least partly in control; when Edgar plays the madman it only adds to our sense of dislocation, for here language itself has broken down. And yet Shakespeare, unlike Webster, say, retains his poise even here, for what we are witnessing, after all, is not madness but the acting of madness. And, Shakespeare being Shakespeare, even out of this maelstrom of broken language and shattering thunder come strange words of human solidarity: 'Prithee, nuncle, be contented; 'tis a naughty night to swim in.' There is no contentment, though, for Lear: 'There's hell, there's darkness, there is the sulphurous pit; burning, scalding, stench, consumption. Fie, fie, fie! pah, pah!' (IV. vi. 127–9).

But it is not just language that must be destroyed in an attempt to free it of its falsity. The well-made play must go the same way. I am thinking here of the apparently quite innocent scene of summing up and sorting out that occurs after the violence: Edgar has defeated his brother and Cordelia's forces have triumphed. Edgar now speaks to the assembled company: 'List, a brief tale.' Then he proceeds to recount how he assumed 'a madman's rags' (V. iii. 182–222), how he met his blind father, and so on. This is the sort of thing plays end with. Unfortunately in this play that is not the end. Moreover, such speeches usually take place in the dead time when the action is over. Not here. The audience knows as Edgar does not that time is still ticking away and that the time we spend listening to the story is the time it is taking for Edmund's instructions to have Cordelia killed to be carried out. In life, this play tells us, there is no dead time; it is only in plays that we have the luxury of a summing up.

Edgar is interrupted by the news that Goneril has killed herself after poisoning her sister. Edmund confesses, the two bodies are brought out, and then – only then – does Edmund seem to recall the orders he had earlier given: 'Quickly send – Be brief in it – to th'castle, for my writ / Is on the life of Lear and on Cordelia' (V. iii. 245–7). But it is too late. Lear enters with Cordelia dead in his arms.

As Lear himself dies on stage before us, his old heart cracking at last, we are finally ready for the real last words, words which, I suggested in an earlier chapter, draw the play into the orbit of Greek tragedy, words which seek neither to sum up nor to aportion blame, and which ask us neither to empathise nor to moralise, but to 'look and see and, seeing, grieve'.

The radical questioning of language and the forms of theatre that is *King Lear* seems to have made it possible for Shakespeare, in his last plays, to jettison all that the craft tradition had taught him and yet to go on writing drama. Those last plays do indeed return to a tradition, but, like *The Magic Flute*, to an older tradition than that of the plot-driven dramas that had come before, to what Richard II had gestured towards when he had talked of how, during the long winter nights, old men would recount his story. At the climax of *The Winter's Tale* the audience is specifically enjoined to let go its suspicion, to trust what we see before us, so that in return we may be vouchsafed a glimpse of grace in action. After the seriousness, the suspicion, of the first half of the play, Shakespeare reverses the trend I have been suggesting was irreversible, and makes lightness triumph over gravity, trust over suspicion. Not every viewer or reader thinks it works, and that is as it should be, for what trust rests on is the goodwill of another: 'But release me from my bands / With the help of your good hands', Prospero begs the audience. 'As you from crimes would pardoned be, / Let your indulgence set me free' (Epilogue 9–10; 19–20). And that 'let' reminds us that even at the time when he was most obsessed with the workings of suspicion Shakespeare had found it possible to strike that strange note of trust; not in a play, it is true, but in that mysterious little poem, 'The

Phoenix and the Turtle', whose theme is the giving up of the self in trust of another. As the twin pillars of selfhood, the twin bastions, it has often been said, of the coming age of Enlightenment, Reason and Property, are confounded by the love of the two birds, Reason itself cries out: 'Love hath reason, reason none, / If what parts can so remain.' And he composes this threnody, which is as near as Shakespeare ever came to telling us what lay at the heart of his mysterious trust:

> Beauty, truth and rarity,
> Grace in all simplicity,
> Here enclosed in cinders lie . . .
>
> Truth may seem, but cannot be;
> Beauty brag, but 'tis not she;
> Truth and Beauty buried be.
>
> To this urn let those repair
> That are either true or fair;
> For these dead birds sigh a prayer.

Red blood white snow

We could be looking at one of those luminously clear yet mysterious Renaissance paintings entitled 'Portrait of a Jealous Man'. As often with such pictures, it would take us some time to read it. At first we would be dazzled by the clear gaze and noble tilt of the head: 'Sicilia cannot show himself overkind to Bohemia', Camillo says in the first scene of *The Winter's Tale*. 'They were trained together in their childhoods; and there rooted betwixt them then such an affection which cannot choose but branch now. Since their more mature dignities and royal necessities made separation of their society, their encounters, though not personal, have been royally attorneyed with interchange of gifts, letters, loving embassies; that they have seemed to be together, though absent; shook hands, as over a vast; and embraced, as it were, from the ends of opposed winds. The heavens continue their loves!' (I. i. 21–31) 'I think', the other courtier replies, in choric antistrophe, 'there is not in the world either malice or matter to alter it' (32–3). And he goes on to cap this by introducing another theme, that of the King's son, 'your young prince Mamillius': 'It is a gentleman of the greatest promise that ever came into my note' (34–5). Camillo responds by embroidering on this new theme: 'It is a gallant child – one that indeed physics the subject, makes old hearts fresh. They that went on crutches ere he was born desire yet their life to see him a man.' (37–40) Though he is no Christ child, making the lame walk and the blind see, nevertheless, he gives hope even to those seemingly without it, quickening in the old and decrepit the desire to stay alive long enough to see him grow and flourish.

This note of joy in life itself is maintained when we meet the principals of *The Winter's Tale* in the next scene. Polixenes, the visiting King of Bohemia, explains to Hermione, the wife of his host, Leontes, the King of Sicily, that

> We were, fair queen,
> Two lads that thought there was no more behind
> But such a day to-morrow as to-day,
> And to be boy eternal.
>
> (I. ii. 62–5)

When she asks who was 'the verier wag o'th'two?' he replies that there was nothing to choose between them:

> We were as twinned lambs that did frisk i'th'sun,
> And bleat the one at th'other. What we changed
> Was innocence for innocence: we knew not
> The doctrine of ill-doing, nor dreamed
> That any did.
>
> (67–71)

Hermione, as is the way with Shakespeare's women, seeks to punc-
ture this idealised image of Edenic bliss: 'By this we gather / You
have tripped since.' But Polixenes will not be deflected into banter.
Of course, he says, temptations have come my way since then, and
in those days I had not met my wife nor Leontes you. Are we then
the snakes who destroyed your Eden? she quips. And when Leontes
approaches and asks her if she has managed to persuade his friend
to stay in Sicily for a while the theme of the role of women in an
innocent world shifts effortlessly to their own situation. You have
never spoken to better purpose, her husband tells her. Never? she
asks. Well, you did, once, he says. When was that? she asks:

> My last good deed was to entreat his stay.
> What was my first? It has an elder sister,
> Or I mistake you. O, would her name were Grace!
> But once before I spoke to the purpose. When?
> Nay, let me have 't; I long.

> (97–101)

Leontes does not answer directly, but in the way of these late
Shakespeare plays, develops the theme almost as though he were
giving her a chance to cap his images, which she proceeds to do:

LEONTES: Why, that was when
            Three crabbèd months had soured themselves to death
            Ere I could make thee open thy white hand
            And clap thyself my love. Then didst thou utter
            'I am yours for ever.'
HERMIONE: 'Tis Grace indeed.
            Why, lo you now, I have spoke to th' purpose twice;
            The one for ever earned a royal husband,
            Th' other for some while a friend.

> (101–8)

And she gives that hand to the friend as she speaks. Whereupon
Leontes' jealousy erupts:

> Too hot, too hot!
> To mingle friendship far is mingling bloods.
> I have *tremor cordis* on me: my heart dances,
> But not for joy, not joy. This entertainment
> May a free face put on, derive a liberty
> From heartiness, from bounty, fertile bosom,
> And well become the agent. – 'T may, I grant.
> But to be paddling palms and pinching fingers,
> As now they are, and making practiced smiles
> As in a looking-glass . . . – O, that is entertainment
> My bosom likes not, nor my brows.
>
> (108–19)

What has happened to trigger this off? And have we and the
courtiers been misreading the signs so far?

We have, I think. Or rather, as is the way with these things, we
have been storing them up and allowing the tone to dictate our
response to them; now that the tone has changed we can see that
we had felt all along that something was amiss. In fact, two themes
have been jostling each other in these opening exchanges, themes
which looked as though they were reinforcing each other but which,
in retrospect, we can see were really in competition.

One is the theme of time and change and growth, the theme of
hope, and it is there in the opening line of the play: 'If you shall
chance, Camillo, to visit Bohemia . . .' We would say today: 'If you
should happen to visit', but the sense is the same: the mood, as the
grammarians say, is optative: some time in the future this may
happen . . . The theme is pursued in Camillo's speech about the
youthful loves of the two kings, but he chooses to link past to future
in a natural image which to a large extent precludes chance: 'There

rooted betwixt them then such an affection, which cannot choose but branch now.' Human affections are likened to a tree which, once rooted, has no option but to grow and put forth branches. This is not quite accurate, of course, for a tree may wither if its source of water is cut off and may die if struck by lightning, but, unless such natural calamities occur, growth there will be. Camillo, however, ends his speech with a covert acknowledgement that human beings are not plants: 'The heavens continue their loves!' In other words, it is as well to give them our good wishes, to invoke heaven in the knowledge that, where human beings are concerned, it is not simply natural calamities which can lead to a change in their relations – we would not think to utter such an invocation to a tree – but some subtle change in the individuals themselves, whose sources are too complex ever to be fully explainable.

The two themes persist into the opening exchanges of the second scene. Polixenes' first words summon up the theme of time and change:

> Nine changes of the wat'ry star hath been
> The shepherd's note since we have left our throne
> Without a burthen.
>
> (I. ii. 1–3)

Stanley Cavell, for one, has noted this, but instead of focusing on the literal meaning he has, in keeping with his Freudian orientation, rushed to link it with Hermione's pregnancy and Leontes' repression of the thought that he is perhaps not the father of the child. 'Nine' is certainly not fortuitous (though it is typical of Cavell that he notes triumphantly that there are nine lines to Polixenes' speech, as though that vindicates his reading; but Shakespeare does not work in this way, though Dante does, and the number of lines is a distraction, a false imposition of meaning, and therefore a hindrance to response rather than a help). Shakespeare does of course want to make it possible for us to imagine that the child may be Polixenes'; but what is central to the speech is the introduction of the notion of change, mutability, linked to the emblem of mutability, the moon. Leontes urges Polixenes to stay, whereupon he replies that 'I am questioned by my fears of what may chance / Or breed upon our absence' (11–12). That again is merely the normal Elizabethan way of putting it, but nevertheless it does remind us that things may happen 'by chance' in human affairs as they do not where trees are concerned, and that the master of the house had better be around to make sure he is controlling that chance.

It is with this as background that, as Hermione tries to persuade Polixenes to stay, he comes up with the extraordinary account of his childhood friendship with her husband, when 'What we changed / Was innocence for innocence: we knew not the doctrine of ill-doing'. We do not need Freudian explanations of the love of the two boys. What we need to see is that, by Polixenes' account, they lived in a timeless world of innocence, precisely the state which theologians have ascribed to Eden before the Fall. Hermione, as we have seen, is quick to point out that, if the analogy is pushed too far, she and Polixenes' wife will be cast into the roles of the serpent and, of course, of Eve, who is so easily elided with him. That is the context for her exchange with Leontes which leads to his outburst. She starts by saying that the 'elder sister' of her successful persuasion of Polixenes to stay was her acceptance of Leontes as her husband. With a kind of natural respect for the powers that govern men's lives and perhaps a natural desire to propitiate them, she interjects a brief prayer: 'O, would her name were Grace!' Leontes enters into the spirit of her speech and responds with something that seems to be merely choric and yet which, with the following speech in mind, we can see to be already functioning within a different world from hers. What he says, in essence, is that it took him three whole months of wooing to persuade her to give him her hand in token of betrothal and say: 'I am yours for ever.' What he actually says, though, is:

> Why, that was when
> Three crabbèd months had soured themselves to death
> Ere I could make thee open thy white hand
> And clap thyself my love. Then didst thou utter
> 'I am yours for ever'.

$$(101-5)$$

The months were crabbed and sour because Hermione would not yield to him; nevertheless, when taken in conjunction with what Polixenes has just said and with what is to come, we are left with the feeling that Leontes is a man ill at ease with the passing of time and the changes it brings: he wants to live in an eternal Edenic present and is likely to respond badly to having to wait for what he wants. The image of the hand, which is his alone, leads of course to his seeing – and our seeing with him, in retrospect – that same white hand now clasped by Polixenes, and to seeing those two hands, neither of which belongs to him, 'paddling palms and pinching fingers' – no wonder it sets his heart dancing, 'But not for joy, not joy'.

For those who wish to avoid chance, the vagaries of time and of human beings (though not of plants), to fix time and to ensure that what they possess now will remain theirs for ever, the possibility that the world does not function so as to make that certain is an intolerable affront. Leontes does not move from trust to suspicion; he was always suspicious, hence always uneasy with the passing of time, for trust is precisely the acceptance of time and whatever changes it may bring. This, it seems to me, is the significance of Hermione's appearing before us as someone subject to the moon, to change, appearing before us, that is, as obviously pregnant. Cavell's fantasies about Leontes' fear of being a father, of his dread of being responsible for the change that is taking place in her and in his world, even more than his dread of someone else's being responsible for it, are again at once both acute and misdirected. What Leontes fears, we come to realise, is not fatherhood but change, of which fatherhood is an instance. And he fears it because he cannot be in control of it.

Of course he is already a father. And both what we have already been told about Mamillius and what we now see of him and of Leontes' relations with him bring the conflict between the two themes out into the open. Mamillius, we recall, was said by Archidamus in scene i to be 'A gentleman of the greatest promise that ever came into my note', to which Camillo replies that he is indeed a wonder, that he 'makes old hearts fresh' and awakens the desire to live on even in those who have reached the ends of their lives. He is, in other words, the embodiment of all that Leontes fears. So it is not surprising that he reacts to his suspicions about his wife's relations with his best friend by trying to co-opt Mamillius as an ally, or perhaps to measure the distance he himself has travelled from those Edenic days to the present: 'Art thou my boy?' he asks him, and when the child replies, 'Ay, my good lord', he mutters an oath and goes on:

LEONTES: Why, that's my bawcock. What, hast smutched
    thy nose?
  They say it is a copy out of mine. Come, captain,
  We must be neat – not neat but cleanly, captain,
  And yet the steer, the heifer, and the calf
  Are all called neat. – Still virginalling
  Upon his palm? – How now, you wanton calf?
  Art thou my calf?
MAMILLIUS: Yes, if you will, my lord.
LEONTES: Thou want'st a rough pash and the shoots
    that I have,
  To be full like me; yet they say we are
  Almost as like as eggs . . .

            (121–30)

Mamillius lacks the horns Leontes feels sprouting on his forehead, yet people say he is the spitting image of his father. And then, after an aside on the falseness of women, he looks into his son's face and sees himself as he was a quarter of a century before. Once again the Edenic image of innocent childhood floods the surface of the play, but now we understand it as only an aspect of Leontes' present jealousy and the polar opposite of the genuine innocence of the little boy, who is growing unawares into the man all admire. The next lines confirm this: 'Go play, boy, play. Thy mother plays, and I / Play too, but so disgraced a part, whose issue / Will hiss me to my grave.' (187–9)

Hermione's Grace, that elder sister who guided her to her marriage, has become the disgrace of the cuckold, whose fall from grace will not end with his death but be a blight on his memory for ever. When Camillo responds naturally to a query about Polixenes he feels that the whole world is conspiring against him: 'They're here with me already, whisp'ring, rounding / "Sicilia is a so-forth." 'Tis far gone, / When I shall gust it last.' (217–19) And when Camillo fails to pick up his hints he rounds on him: 'I have trusted thee, Camillo, . . . But we have been / Deceived in thy integrity, deceived / In that which seems so.' (235–41) When Camillo vehemently denies this, he cuts him short: 'Ha'not you seen, Camillo – / But that's past doubt, you have, or your eye-glass / Is thicker than a cuckold's horn . . .' (266–8). Camillo is appalled: 'Good my lord, be cured / Of this diseased opinion, and betimes, / For 'tis most dangerous' (295–7). But Leontes is ready to back his suspicions against the world. Shakespeare, however, makes sure we side with the world. Hamlet had his suspicions and he was justified: the ghost of his father ratified them for him and for us. But there is nothing to back Leontes' suspicions, and everything we learn, from Camillo, from Polixenes, from the verbal texture of the play, makes it clear to us that Leontes' suspicions are completely groundless. When Camillo, whom Leontes has tried to persuade to kill his old friend, tells Polixenes what is happening, Polixenes protests his innocence, but Camillo has had enough insight into Leontes' state to enable him to say:

> Swear his thought over
> By each particular star in heaven and
> By all their influences, you may as well
> Forbid the sea for to obey the moon
> As or by oath remove or counsel shake
> The fabric of his folly, whose foundation
> Is piled upon his faith, and will continue
> The standing of his body.
>
> (422–9)

Like the sceptic – to that extent Cavell is right – Leontes has total faith in his suspicion; it is his new God, the very ground of his being. Once it has established itself it grows as naturally as a tree. But it is not that suspicion, or jealousy, or scepticism has taken the place of trust. What Act I shows us is that what it has replaced was not trust at all but a pathological refusal to envisage growth and change, and therefore a profound mistrust of the world. Genuine trust, the play will show us, is precisely that which can live with change and uncertainty. 'How should this grow?' asks the bewildered Polixenes, meaning: what is to come of this? 'I know not', answers Camillo, in a response which those critics who would peer behind the opening of the play to the origins of Leontes' jealousy would do well to bear in mind, 'but I am sure 'tis safer to / Avoid what's grown than question how 'tis born' (430–1).

The machine set in motion by suspicion now starts to pick up speed. But these late Shakespeare plays – unlike the earlier comedies and tragedies – are never pure machines. The inexorable forward motion is abruptly halted by a scene which appears to exist out of time. It does not, naturally, for in the course of the banter among Mamillius, his mother and the ladies-in-waiting Mamillius is reminded that 'The queen, your mother, rounds apace', and we can, indeed, see the evidence before us. Yet when Hermione asks her son to tell a story we do, momentarily, move into the timelessness of old tales. What kind does she want? he asks, merry or sad? And when she says merry he comes back with 'A sad tale's best for winter', and then plunges into it at once, in the age-old style: 'There was a man . . . dwelt by a churchyard —' He drops his voice: 'I will tell it softly; / Yond crickets shall not hear it.' (Crickets in winter? we wonder, then realise he must mean the ladies-in-waiting.) Come on then, responds his mother, whisper it in my ear. (II.i.25–32)

But not even Hermione is destined to hear the story. *That* tale will never be told. Leontes rushes in, madder than ever, having heard that Camillo and Polixenes have escaped, which seems to confirm his suspicions. For him, as for Swift, happiness now seems to be merely the state of being well deceived:

> There may be in the cup
> A spider steeped, and one may drink, depart,
> And yet partake no venom, for his knowledge
> Is not infected; but if one present
> Th' abhorred ingredient to his eye, make known
> How he hath drunk, he cracks his gorge, his sides,
> With violent hefts. I have drunk, and seen the spider.
>
> (II. i. 39–45)

Antigone insists that Hermione is innocent, that Leontes has been 'abused and by some putter-on / That will be damned for't' (140–1). But there is no Iago here; it is all the work of Leontes' own abusive imagination. He now makes a show of reason, sending to enquire of the oracle of Apollo, since 'in an act of this importance 'twere / Most piteous to be wild' (181–2). But before the answer from the oracle arrives we learn that Hermione has been delivered of a girl in the prison where he has incarcerated her. Burn the bastard! screams Leontes, and when his courtiers plead with him he yields to the extent of instructing Antigonus to take the child to a desert

island and there abandon her. This is not a variant of Viola's or
Jacob's trust in time to do its work but an abdication of responsibility — 'where chance may nurse or end it' (II. iii. 182). The
heralds arrive with the message of Apollo's oracle. Leontes accuses
Hermione and she replies, in words which sum up the play so far:

> You speak a language that I understand not,
> My life stands in the level of your dreams,
> Which I'll lay down.
>
> (III. ii. 79–81)

The oracle is read out: 'Hermione is chaste; Polixenes blameless;
Camillo a true subject; Leontes a jealous tyrant; his innocent babe
truly begotten; and the King shall live without an heir, if that which
is lost be not found' (131–4). But suspicion of this kind cannot be
so easily cured: 'There is no truth at all i'th'oracle!' asserts Leontes.
'The sessions shall proceed. This is mere falsehood' (137–8). Words,
even those from an oracle, will not suffice to jolt Leontes out of his
fantasies. What is needed is for the world to deal him a blow, and
this it proceeds to do at once. A servant rushes in to tell him his son,
Mamillius, is gone. 'How?' says Leontes, thinking of Camillo and
Polixenes. 'Gone?' 'Is dead.'

That is enough. 'Apollo's angry', Leontes says at once, 'and the
heavens themselves / Do strike at my injustice' (144–5). The queen
faints and her maidservant Paulina points an accusing finger at him:
'This news is mortal to the queen. Look down / And see what death
is doing' (146–7). She will recover, Leontes says, more in hope than
expectation,

> I have too much believed mine own suspicion.
> Beseech you, tenderly apply to her
> Some remedies for life.
>
> (149–51)

Then, when she is carried out he, like David when the story of his adultery with Bathsheba and of his implication in Uriah's death comes out, throws himself on the mercy of the higher powers: 'Apollo, pardon.' But by the time his plea is over Paulina has returned with the news that Hermione is indeed dead. For fifty lines or more she rails against Leontes and his folly. 'Go on, go on', he replies, 'Thou can'st not speak too much. I have deserved / All tongues to talk their bitt'rest' (212–14). At this point Paulina recovers her own balance: 'He is touched / To the noble heart. What's gone and what's past help / Should be past grief.' And Leontes vows to visit every day the chapel where lie the bodies of his wife and son, 'and tears shed there / Shall be my recreation' (237–9).

But life is not a machine, even if jealousy sets a destructive machine in motion within a man's life. Just as the scene with Mamillius and the ladies-in-waiting brought another world, the world of once upon a time, into the world of jealousy and suspicion into which Leontes had turned the Sicilian court, so now we enter the world of pantomime and clowning. Many of the characters are new as well, but not all, for we start with Antigonus and the baby girl he has promised to leave on a desert island. 'And, for the babe / Is counted lost for ever, Perdita, / I prithee call it' (III. iii. 31–2), her mother had instructed him, and now, as a storm gathers, he lays her on the ground with a scroll and a box of gold and jewels and prepares to return to the ship. But, before he can do so, a bear erupts on to the stage and chases him off. That, at least, is what we must assume, since the enigmatic stage direction, probably Shakespeare's most famous, simply reads: 'Exit, pursued by a bear.'

There has been much debate about whether or not a real bear was used. It seems to me that it has to be a pantomime bear. We are no longer in the world of *Othello*, or even of *A Comedy of Errors*. We are in the world of story-telling, which in one sense is much more realistic than the other. For in story-telling the teller does not seek to efface himself, as does the novelist; and in pantomime there is no pretence that what we see is anything other than what play-wright and actors are putting on before us as a show. This is the kind of pact Shakespeare enters into with his audience in these late plays, and it is important to bear this in mind when reading them, for much more hangs on this pact than is usual in tale-telling or pantomime.

No sooner has the bear erupted on to the stage and chased off Antigonus than an old shepherd enters and finds the child, followed by his son, described as a 'clown' in the list of characters. He describes how he saw Antigonus eaten by the bear as the storm raged and the boat sank off-shore with all its crew crying out in despair: 'how the poor souls roared, and the sea mocked them, and how the poor gentleman roared and the bear mocked him, both roaring louder than the sea or weather'. 'But look thee here, boy', replies the shepherd, 'Now bless thyself! thou mettest with things dying, I with things new-born' (III. iii. 94–107).

It's not enough to say that this symbolises the passing of the old order of winter and suspicion and the birth of the new order of spring and trust. The events we have seen and the way they are pre-sented to us bear exactly as much relation to death-and-resurrection symbolism as the mechanicals' play of Pyramus and Thisbe bears to the moralised Ovid's interpretation of that story as symbolic of the Passion – which does not mean none at all, but does mean that we must be aware of the central importance of *tone* in both instances.

And the tone of *The Winter's Tale* is maintained in the next scene. Time enters, as Chorus, and we begin to grasp how non-naturalistic theatre, by stressing its theatricality, can do things that the naturalist theatre never can. For time, we now realise, is the pre-siding spirit of this play, as Iago was of *Othello*. We have already seen how neither Leontes nor Polixenes was willing to accept time, preferring the absolutes of Eden and Hell. And Leontes, for all his change of heart, is still unable to recognise it, merely thinking of it as the tedious interval between now and death in which he will fulfil his vow to visit the graves of his wife and son each day. But here is Time, in person, as real and unreal as the bear, addressing us.

Pandosto, Shakespeare's source, suggests that time triumphs by revealing all. But Shakespeare is no longer interested in revelation, in time as the untier of knots, as he was in *The Comedy of Errors* and even in *Twelfth Night*. Time is rather life itself, and he is inter- ested in showing what happens when we try to defeat time by stalling or trying to forestall it. In that way he hopes to make time palpable to us, to make us feel what it is really like to live in time. In that sense *The Winter's Tale* re-applies the lesson of Dante's *Commedia*: we cannot run straight up the mountain, we must always go the long, slow, tortuous and painful way round, and Perdita, even when she is found, retains her name: the lost one. For time is precisely that which we do not know, it is 'what happens to us' in the course of our lives, it is Hermione's swelling stomach and the birth of Perdita and the death of Mamillius. Autolycus, as we will see, is its instrument. Time here as in the Hebrew scriptures is not so much what is eventually *revealed* as what *unfolds*. To trust in it is to trust in life itself.

When Time appears in person before us he starts by telling us that he is the one who, though he pleases some, tries all. It is in his power, he says, 'To o'erthrow law and in one self-born hour / To plant and o'erwhelm custom' (IV. i. 8–9). Time is precisely that which is unexpected, that which figures in no law and flouts the cus- tomary. That is why Time says he will not prophesy, 'but let Time's news / Be known when 'tis brought forth' (26–7). And, addressing us, the spectators, he reminds us that we too are immersed in time, that it is time which we are spending here as we watch this play unfold before us with all its surprises. What is to come, he concludes,

> Is th' argument of Time. Of this allow
> If ever you have spent time worse ere now;

If never, yet that Time himself doth say
He wishes earnestly you never may.

(29–32)

Sixteen years have passed. Time has just told us that. Camillo begs
Polixenes to allow him to return to Sicily, for he wishes to die
there and his old master, now so penitent, has sent for him.
Polixenes refuses and instead asks him what he knows of his
son, Florizel, who, he suspects, is in love with a simple shepherdess.
The two of them disguise themselves and set out to spy on the
young couple.

And now in comes Autolycus, singing. There are three interrup-
tions in the forward momentum of this play: the story-telling of
Mamillius, cut short before it has even got under way; the songs of
Autolycus; and the mysterious wordless music of the last scene. And
just as Cordelia and the Fool have struck some viewers of *Lear* as
being in some way aspects of the same person, the latter disap-
pearing when the former returns, so, it seems to me, there is a deep
link between the innocent boy who promised so much and whose
death is announced in Act III, and Autolycus, the cunning trickster,
who appears for the first time in Act IV.

Autolycus's first song makes the connection and helps explain the
title of the play:

When daffodils begin to peer,
    With heigh! the doxy over the dale,
Why, then comes in the sweet o'the year,
    For the red blood reigns in the winter's pale.

(IV. iii. 1–4)

It has always been a puzzle as to why the play was called what
it was. After all, the only time the title appears in the play is in

Mamillius's 'A sad tale's best for winter', and the play cannot, taken in its entirety, be described as sad. I think, though, that we are meant to pick up the echo here: winter's tale / winter's pale. Autolycus's song suggests that even when the earth is covered in winter snow the red blood of spring is already racing in its veins. So it is not a sad play, but it is not a 'happy' play either. It is a play which brings out the way in which sadness and happiness are bound up with each other, in which the blood of life reigns in the dead of winter, and, of course, in which the whiteness of winter already reigns in the red blood of spring.

I suggested in discussing *A Midsummer Night's Dream* that the verbal and conceptual errors of the mechanicals had the effect of making us work to put them right. The errors of the mechanicals were very funny, and laughter is often the best way for such work to be generated. But it need not be. The play generated by the assonance winter's tale / winter's pale is not comic, but it has the same effect of making us feel between the words of our language, in the interstices of *grammatica*, as it were, the movement of reality itself.

We feel this subliminally. What we see on stage is a singer and what we hear is a song. Who is the singer? The *dramatis personae* tells us simply that Autolycus is 'a rogue', but Autolycus himself, having sung his song, gives a rather fuller account of himself. 'My traffic is sheets', he begins, suggesting both that he steals linen and that he works in the bedclothes, with the sexual desires of his clients. 'My father named me Autolycus', he goes on, 'who being, as I am, littered under Mercury, was likewise a snapper-up of unconsidered trifles' (IV. iii. 24–6). Now Mercury is the god of tricksters and cheats, but he is also the conveyor of souls, the Psychopomp as the Greeks call him. Autolycus, as we will see, conveys or helps to convey the very physical bodies of some of the key characters in this play from Bohemia to Sicily, where the dead will be discovered and come alive. In Greek legend, moreover, Autolycus is supposed to be none other than the grandfather of Odysseus, the greatest trickster and survivor of all.

True to his name, he promptly proceeds to fool and rob the Clown, asserting in the process that he himself has just been robbed by a rogue men call Autolycus, who 'put me into this apparel' (100–1). Like Odysseus with the Cyclops he is both nobody and very much himself – a person who can turn himself into anyone and everyone, and lie even as he tells the truth.

Autolycus leads us into the sheep-shearing scene. This is often taken by itself as the key to the play and the words of Polixenes and Perdita finely scrutinised to see what Shakespeare thought of art and nature and their interrelation; but its noble discourse must be taken in conjunction with the low cunning of Autolycus, just as the words of Theseus must be balanced against the play of the mechanicals. Perdita may dispense grace and welcome to all, but there is no grace without the kind of resourcefulness we have seen in Jacob and see now in Autolycus, and if Perdita is the one who is found as well as the one who is lost, Mamillius is lost for ever. Perdita may echo Proserpina but the play is not named after her or after Hermione: she is only part of the tale.

Mamillius was last seen telling a winter's tale; and a servant announces Autolycus by saying that 'He hath songs for man or woman, of all sizes', and that 'he sings several tunes faster than you'll tell money. He utters them as he had eaten ballads and all men's ears grew to his tunes' (IV. iv. 185–93). And now he enters, singing. Mopsa wants to buy ballads from him, holding that if they are printed they must be true. Mopsa's evident concern with truthfulness parallels the debate between Perdita and Polixenes about naturalness. When Autolycus offers her a ballad 'to a very doleful tune, how a usurer's wife was brought to bed of twenty money-bags at a burthen, and how she longed to eat adders' heads and toads carbonadoed', she asks, 'Is it true, think you?' 'Very true', answers Autolycus, 'and but a month old' (257–62). This is the criterion of truth which will drive the writing and purchase of novels, as Defoe well knew. We sense here that it is being contrasted with another kind of truth, one which will not require 'five justices' hands at it' and 'witnesses more than my pack will hold' (278–9) to guarantee its truth, but rather our sense of recognition: this is true because at some deep level we have always known it to be true.

As Autolycus gets the shepherds singing and proceeds to rob them, the plot closes in. But, in striking accord with the mode of the Hebrew scriptural narratives, and in contrast to Shakespeare's earlier plays, the plots men make and the plots in which they figure turn out to be very different. Nothing moves here towards a tidy solution. The young couple, to escape Florizel's angry father, turn to Camillo for help. He, wanting to get back to Sicily, persuades them to go there and take him with them. Instead of trusting your-selves to chance, he tells them, go to Leontes, ask for his help; that, he says, is 'A course more promising / Than a wild dedication of yourselves / To unpathed waters, undreamed shores, most certain / To miseries enough' (558–61). However, Autolycus, overhearing them, decides it is in his interest to tell the king: as in a Muriel Spark novel, things work out for the best precisely through the efforts of the evil characters to gain their own ends – or, as Autoly-cus puts it later, 'Though I am not naturally honest, I am so some-times by chance' (700–1). To himself he says: 'What a fool Honesty is! And Trust, his sworn brother, a very simple gentleman!' (588–9). But this is to think of Trust as Leontes did, as the naivety of the simple-minded. And now, in a further twist Camillo, discovering Autolycus, has the idea of dressing Florizel in his clothes – 'we'll make an instrument of this' (615), he says. Perdita, seeing what is required, now reveals herself as being in a sense akin to Autolycus – and of course to those earlier resourceful women, Rosalind and Viola: 'I see the play so lies / That I must bear a part' (644–5). Autolycus, left alone now in Florizel's clothes, utters his credo – but it need not be his alone; indeed it underlies the actions of both

Perdita and Paulina and in a sense prepares us for the last scene:
'I understand the business, I hear it. To have an open ear, a quick
eye, and a nimble hand is necessary for a cutpurse. A good nose is
requisite also, to smell out work for the other senses . . . Sure the
gods do this year connive at us, and we may do any thing extem-
pore' (660–3). Resourcefulness, resilience, the ability to improvise
– these are the very opposite of the desire to remain in Eden for
ever and, if Eden thrusts you out, to seek refuge in Hell. But, partly
through the unlikely agency of Autolycus, Leontes will be released
from his season in Hell.

We return to him now and find him still in it, unable to rid
himself of the memory of what happened, wallowing in guilt, just
as Achilles could not shake off the horror of Patroclus' death at the
start of *Iliad* XXIV. 'Forget your evil; / With them forgive yourself',
Cleomenes urges him. But Leontes cannot do that:

> Whilst I remember
> Her and her virtues, I cannot forget
> My blemishes in them, and so still think of
> The wrong I did myself, which was so much
> That heirless it hath make my kingdom and
> Destroyed the sweet'st companion that e'er man
> Bred his hopes out of.
>
> (V. i. 5–12)

Paulina drives home the lessons of reality:

> There is none worthy,
> Respecting her that's gone. Besides, the gods
> Will have fulfilled their secret purposes;
> For has not the divine Apollo said,
> Is't not the tenor of his oracle,
> That King Leontes shall not have an heir

Till his lost child be found? Which that it shall
Is all as monstrous to our human reason
As my Antigonus to break his grave
And come again to me . . .

(34—43)

It would be monstrous to human reason, yet surely less monstrous
than the stories recounted in Autolycus's ballads and attested by
innumerable witnesses; as monstrous as the dead returning to life,
which, as we will see, can in some sense happen. But Antigonus will
not return, he has been eaten by the bear, and Mamillius will not
return, he is dead and rotting in his grave.

The discovery, in the next scene, of who Perdita is, happens off-
stage and is merely reported. It would, of course, have made the
coming to life of Hermione in the following scene an anti-climax,
which Shakespeare could not afford. It allows us, too, to cast our
minds back to the opening scene of the play, which also featured
two courtiers talking. It is a nice irony, too, that the news should be
broken to Autolycus, the peddler of wildly improbable ballads. 'They
looked', the First Gentleman says, talking of Camillo and Leontes,
'as they had heard of a world ransomed, or one destroyed' (V. ii.
14—15). 'The oracle is fulfilled', the Second Gentleman announces.
'The king's daughter is found. Such a deal of wonder is broken out
within this hour that ballad-makers cannot be able to express it.'
'This news', he goes on, 'which is called true is so like an old tale
that the verity of it is in strong suspicion.' (22—9) The Third
Gentleman, asked what became of Antigonus, takes up the theme:
'Like an old tale still, which will have matter to rehearse, though
credit be asleep and not an ear open. He was torn to pieces with a
bear.' (59—60) When such things are found to be, he suggests, suspicion is shown up as merely human limitation, for in 'every wink
of an eye some new grace will be born' (105—6).

The last scene of the play will demonstrate this to the spectators, both those who gather on stage and we who sit in the auditorium. As Paulina unveils the statue of Hermione she says: 'I like your silence; it the more shows off / Your wonder' (V. iii. 21–2). Wonder, which has appeared as a motif throughout the play, is beginning to take on firm outlines. It is the response we give to the world when we have overcome suspicion; not the response of the fool and the gull, which is the response of Mopsa, who would ask at every stage, Is it true? Is it true? And not the response of Leontes to the assertion that his wife is innocent when his suspicions tell him she is guilty. But the response of those who have experienced suspicion and learned how it distorts and falsifies.

'Does not the stone rebuke me / For being more stone than it?' (38–9) asks Leontes, and we sense that he too is beginning to accept the possibility of wonder. An aspect of wonder is that what we give up of ourselves in entering that state is given back to us with interest. We too, who sit in the dark and watch, see only stone, yet if we are prepared to respond to 'an old tale' it may yet come alive. Paulina, though, keeps our feet firmly on the ground: 'My lord's almost so far transported that / He'll think anon it lives' (69–70). Leontes, she is suggesting, is in danger of falling into another kind of folly, the folly of idolatry, and she makes to pull the curtain to, but both Leontes and Perdita restrain her: 'No, not these twenty years', he says, and she: 'So long could I / Stand by, a looker on' (84–5). In that case, says Paulina, 'Either forbear, / Quit presently the chapel, or resolve you, / For more amazement. If you can behold it, / I'll make the statue move indeed, descend / And take you by the hand.' (85–9) By itself the statue cannot move, is not alive. We need a human ritual to bring it to life. But are such rituals not a sign that we are in league with the powers of darkness? Leontes is unconcerned: whatever you can make the statue do, 'I am content to look on'. Then, says Paulina, and we are moving now into the world of Kafka's parable of Ulysses and the Sirens, a world where to pretend to be innocent may itself be the sign of true innocence,

a world for which Shakespeare has prepared us by setting up the
absurd wonders of the ballads against the wonderful possibilities of
his art of truth,

> It is required
> You do awake your faith. Then all stand still;
> Or those that think it is unlawful business
> I am about, let them depart.
>
> (94–7)

These things do not simply exist or not exist; it is required of us that
we awake our faith in them. That does not require an effort of the
will but an openness to the new, to whatever time will bring. And
we can be helped. 'Music! awake her, strike!' cries Paulina. And now
we have reached the third stage: first we had Mamillius's aborted
tale; then Autolycus's songs; now music without words. Paulina
speaks over the music:

> 'Tis time; descend; be stone no more; approach;
> Strike all that look upon with marvel. Come,
> I'll fill your grave up. Stir, nay, come away;
> Bequeath to death your numbness, for from him
> Dear life redeems you. You perceive she stirs.
>
> (99–103)

And the statue moves.

Of course it is a trick. And it is not a trick. If it were Wagner it
would be a trick, a seduction of our rightful sense of suspicion by
means of art; but because we are in the world of tale-telling and
pantomime, a world where a stage is only a stage and a bear only
an actor in a bearskin, it is not a trick. 'O, she's warm!' Leontes
exclaims, touching her. 'If this be magic, let it be an art / Lawful
as eating.' (109–11) This is typical of the language of these late

plays. It is easy enough to paraphrase it roughly: 'Let this be white magic, not black!' But the words 'art', 'lawful' and 'eating' refuse to take their places docilely in the sentence, so to speak. Since when is eating lawful? Natural, certainly, but lawful? It is as though language itself is being transformed and the most ordinary words are being made to resonate with unexpected connotations. We think of the naturalness of the bear's eating Antigonus and the lawlessness unleashed by Leontes' jealousy and how Time boasted of his power to overthrow law and custom; we think perhaps of the mystery of the sacrament. What is important is that there is no attempt to dazzle us with language, as there is in the early plays and poems, or any sense of strain, as there is in the *Sonnets* and the middle-period plays. The language is ordinary and down to earth and yet utterly strange; as ordinary and as strange as Hermione's warmth.

'That she is living, / Were it but told you, should be hooted at / like an old tale' (115–17), says Paulina. And we see what is happening and we realise that Hermione must have been hidden all this while by Paulina (if we want Mopsa-like explanations), and we know that this is only an actress doing what the playwright and the director have told her to do, and at the same time we sense that we are witnessing a mystery, a cause for awe and wonder as great as we experience at the end of *Hamlet* or *Lear*.

Hermione speaks:

> You gods, look down,
> And from your sacred vials pour your graces
> Upon my daughter's head!
>
> (121–3)

And she goes on to explain the mystery. But the explanation is no simple dénouement: 'For thou shalt hear that I, / Knowing by Paulina that the oracle / Gave hope thou wast in being, have preserved / Myself to see the issue' (125–8). Only hope kept her alive.

The 'issue' is the result of the work of time, but it is also the child, Perdita. Yet the word forces us to recall that other symbol of hope with which the play began, that other issue, Mamillius, who will never be found in this life. The tale he started to tell is never told, and its never being told is one strand in that other tale which Shakespeare both tells and shows, a tale which helps us to experience the co-existence of the red blood and the winter snow in our own lives as well as in nature.

5 Romantic doubts

As to Poetry, I have altogether abandoned it, being convinced
that I never had the essentials of poetic Genius, and that I
mistook a strong desire for original power.

Coleridge

In 1851, some two and a half centuries after *The Winter's Tale* was
written, Baudelaire published the following sonnet:

Il est amer et doux, pendant les nuits d'hiver,
D'écouter, près du feu qui palpite et qui fume,
Les souvenirs lointains lentement s'élever
Au bruit des carillons qui chantent dans la brume.

Bienheureuse la cloche au gosier vigoureux
Qui, malgré sa vieillesse, alerte et bien portante,
Jette fidèlement son cri religieux,
Ainsi qu'un vieux soldat qui veille sous la tente!

Moi, mon âme est fêlée, et lorsqu'en ses ennuis
Elle veut de ses chants peupler l'air froid des nuits,
Il arrive souvent que sa voix affaiblie

Semble le râle épais d'un blessé qu'on oublie
Au bord d'un lac de sang, sous un grand tas de morts,
Et qui meurt, sans bouger, dans d'immenses efforts.

The sonnet is constructed in classical style, with the two quatrains of the octave setting up scenes and images which the sestet then undermines. It is, says the poet, both sweet and bitter to sit round a fire on a winter's night listening to memories rising up and mingling with the sound of church bells coming through the fog. Bitter because those times are gone for ever, sweet because the fire, the bells and the memories themselves, which rise up so impersonally in the midst of the company, link us to history and to the community of men. The mention of bells leads the poet to the thought that even old and worn bells keep ringing out the Christian message, and the first scene is brought back and enriched by the surprising comparison of the bells to a war veteran keeping watch in his tent — enriched because the community of the old and the community of Christians are now turned into the community of citizens whose bond is reinforced by their having fought for their country.

But then comes the turnabout. The poet identifies with the bell, but instead of ringing out loud and true his soul is cracked, and when he wishes to give vent to his sorrows he finds he cannot do so. Instead of a community of men gathered round a fire, instead of the veteran in his tent, there is only a heap of dead bodies by a pool of blood, and the poet's voice sticks in his throat like the death-rattle of a soldier who does not even lie, like Rimbaud's, under the stars, but suffocates, forgotten, beneath the pile of dead bodies and who, though he makes heroic efforts to call out, dies without managing to utter a word.

Baudelaire's magnificent poem, so classical, so controlled, and yet spelling out the death of classicism and control, is only the most compressed and extreme example of a common Romantic and post-Romantic theme. Why did that theme achieve such prominence in the nineteenth century and why does it still speak to us today?

We have to remember – and it may be a bit of an effort in the wake of 'La Cloche fêlée' – that the Romantic movement was in the first instance an expression of hope. Images of the bound made free, of the prisoner at last stepping out of the gloom of incarceration into the light of liberty, are rife, from Blake's *Jerusalem* to Shelley's *Prometheus Unbound*, from Beethoven's *Fidelio* to *The Communist Manifesto*. In the spheres of politics, of philosophy, of art, there was the same sense of liberation from the shackles of class, of prejudice, of diction and genre. For these are now seen to be not part of the natural scheme of things, but *impositions*, which no-one, having seen the truth, could ever submit to again. '*Sapere aude!*' urged Kant in his little 1784 essay, 'What is Enlightenment?', 'Dare to think for yourself!' And the implication is that if you will only do so you will see what lies had held you prisoner for so long.

Yet within a few years all that hope had turned to dust. Wordsworth, who had enthusiastically chanted that 'Bliss was it in that dawn to be alive', could write, hardly a decade later: 'We poets in our youth begin in gladness; / But thereof come in the end despondency and madness.' Hölderlin, who had begun by asserting that 'Holy vessels are the poets, / In which the wine of life, / The spirit of heroes is preserved', could write, again only a few years later: 'But, my friends, we have come too late. True, the gods are living, / But over our heads, above in a different world.' 'It seems to me often,' he goes on,

Better to sleep than like this to be quite companionless here,
Thus to wait, and what's to be done or said in the meantime,
I do not know, and what are poets for in a period of dearth?

In a *dürftiger Zeit*, an empty, waste, impoverished time. And, much later in the century, we have the poems of Baudelaire and the haunting figure of Melville's Bartleby, simply sidestepping life, refusing to work and in the end even to feed himself, for no other reason than that he would 'rather not'.

What was it that led to this remarkable transformation from hope to despair, from joy to melancholy? Two answers have, by and large, been given to this question, and both seem to me, though partly true, ultimately unsatisfactory.

The first is biographical and psychological. It is, the argument goes, in the private lives of individual artists that we will find the reasons for the change. And it has to be said that there is plenty of evidence that the writers themselves often took this view. Wordsworth lamented the irremediable break with childhood:

> There was a time when meadow, grove, and stream,
> 　The earth, and every common sight,
> 　To me did seem
> Apparelled in celestial light,
> The glory and the freshness of a dream.
> It is not now as it hath been of yore; —
> 　Turn whereso'er I may
> 　By night or day,
> The things which I have seen I now can see no more.

Coleridge accused himself of lack of will-power and admitted that he had been mistaken in his vocation: 'As to Poetry, I have altogether abandoned it, being convinced that I never had the essentials of poetic Genius, and that I mistook a strong desire for original power.' Hölderlin, Nerval and Nietzsche all went mad, and the personal problems of Baudelaire and Flaubert have been amply documented. Nevertheless, such explanations are less than wholly convincing for the simple reason that the pattern is too universal to blame on individual circumstances. Why, after all, did this sense of despair settle on so many nineteenth-century writers, affecting and infecting their work, and not on those of previous centuries? Swift and Dr Johnson, after all, were not the most cheerful of spirits, yet this does not seem to have affected their work as it did that of Coleridge and Baudelaire; Diderot's *Le Neveu de Rameau* seems as powerful an assault on the pretensions of reason as we find in the nineteenth century, yet it has a poise, a lightness of touch, a signal lack of melancholy, which it is difficult to find in its nineteenth-century counterparts.

The second answer is political. This comes in various guises, but essentially it is the suggestion that these artists, in their different ways, all felt profoundly betrayed by the French Revolution and its aftermath, or betrayed by what happened in France – and indeed in Europe – after the death of Napoleon. Again, there is plenty of evidence that this is what many artists did feel. Wordsworth and Blake are explicit about it, and both Stendhal and Dostoevsky suggest that with the passing of Napoleon the world has entered a stage of terrible ordinariness, has lost all grandeur and even all meaning, and that as a consequence living – and writing – is simply futile. Once again, though, it is the pervasiveness of the phenomenon that leads me to think that though this was undoubtedly a contributary factor, to take it as the sole explanation is to deflect understanding from the deeper changes that were taking place, changes instinctively grasped by the greatest artists, even if they were not always able to formulate them conceptually.

1637: Descartes begins his revolutionary *Discourse on Method* with an image: 'There is often less perfection in what has been put together bit by bit, and by different masters, than in the work of a single hand. Thus we see how a building, the construction of which has been undertaken and completed by a single architect, is usually superior in beauty and regularity to those that many have tried to restore by making use of old walls which had been built for other purposes.'

If we think of the churches we know we realise the extent of Descartes's iconoclasm, for they are, for the most part, built over earlier churches which were themselves built over still earlier ones which were often built on the site of a pagan shrine. All architectural historians will say is that there was a building on the site since earliest times. Often, of course, new parts of a church are added to an existing structure, so that diagrams have to be provided for modern tourists with the different strata marked in different colours.

It is clear that the building of churches was a part of what I have called a craft tradition; the break with the past involved in the Cartesian injunction to start afresh can therefore be seen as a monumental shift in attitudes. Of course Descartes would not have said what he did had he not felt, as Bacon felt before him and Kant would after him, that the craft tradition was dead and that attempts to perpetuate it were fatal to the life of the present. And I use the word 'iconoclasm' advisedly. For Descartes, like Bacon and Kant, is very much a product of post-Reformation thought. Just as the Reformers insisted that each of us must be free to decide for ourselves, that we cannot simply act on the say-so of Popes and Councils, so the Enlightenment insisted that each man must use his reason to decide for himself how he is to live and what he is to think. And just as the Reformation proceeded to demolish many of the great churches and images of medieval Christendom, so the Enlightenment proceeded to demolish many of the myths and customs which had existed for centuries, on the principle that these were barbaric superstitions designed only to maintain the status quo. That in both cases such attitudes would not only have been articulated but that they should have found support amongst the most acute thinkers of the time testifies to the fact that something had gone wrong, that what had once been taken for granted was coming more and more to be seen as arbitrary, unfair and unnecessary.

The French Revolution and its aftermath seemed to bring these ideas into the realm of tangible reality. Each man was now a citizen, with equal rights, and each man, no matter how humble his background, could rise through his own merits to the very top – to become Emperor was no longer the stuff of fairy-tales.

Dostoevsky's *Crime and Punishment* brings out the sting in the tail of this story of emancipation. If each man could be Napoleon, why, asks the desperate and penniless student Raskolnikov, am *I* not Napoleon? Why am I penniless and without power? What Nietzsche calls *ressentiment* begins to gnaw at the entrails of every petty clerk in government service, at every lazy yet intelligent inhabitant of the big cities that were multiplying throughout Europe. And the particular anxiety produced by *ressentiment* lies in the feeling that perhaps, just perhaps, it is not others who are to blame but I myself. Once, everyone had a place and knew it. It might be a lowly place, but it was yours: shoemaker, farmer, lawyer, playwright. But in the new climate of equality, in the huge sprawl of urban conglomerations, in the galloping spiral of capitalism, there was no longer any such thing as a place, a station. There was only the room you rented and the gnawing sense of ambition and *ressentiment*. No wonder that cog in the workings of Wall Street, Melville's Bartleby, wishes to have nothing to do with the new juggernaut which its apostles term Progress but which is felt by most as enslavement; no wonder he quietly asserts that he would 'rather not' do the job capitalism has assigned to him and enacts before the horrified gaze of his conventional employer a version of what Ghandi would later glorify as passive resistance.

In the arts we find the same ironic spiral. Poets emancipate themselves from patrons and from the worn-out forms of their predecessors. They will not speak a *poetic* language, but the language of ordinary men, to ordinary men. A composer like Beethoven will be beholden to no-one except himself, paying his way by selling his works and filling the halls where he performs them. Yet here too, when the dust has settled, the question comes to haunt poets and composers: is talking to all men not another way of saying that one is talking to no-one? When composers without Beethoven's towering self-belief seek to produce new works they can no longer rely on a craft tradition to see them through: each new work must be a masterpiece or it is nothing. Are they up to it? Can one even create with such thoughts in mind? Or does the idea not begin to take hold, so perfectly voiced by Coleridge, that perhaps they never had 'the essentials of poetic Genius', that they mistook 'a strong desire for original power'?

There are of course artists in the nineteenth century who seem unaffected by such feelings. Not only second-rate artists like Southey and the painter Benjamin Robert Haydon, but major ones like Dickens and Verdi. Indeed, Isaiah Berlin used precisely the Schillerian terms I deployed in my second chapter, *naive* and *sentimental*, to characterise Verdi as the last naive artist. Many today – especially in England – would rate Verdi and Dickens above Wagner and Melville, insisting that their essential naivety allowed them to tap resources closed off to more self-conscious artists such as Wagner and Melville. I have some sympathy with this position. But I think our love affair with the tremendous unself-conscious energy of the great mid-nineteenth-century artists, a love affair not confined to readers but frequently expressed by writers as well, is merely an index of our society's nostalgia and innate conservatism and – to put it in blunt Nietzschean terms – of its basic ill-health.

Rather than comparing Verdi and Dickens to those artists stung, as it were, by the serpent of Romantic self-doubt, compare them – I will not say to Homer, but – to Shakespeare and Mozart. Then the sentimentality, the frequent bathos, the overwhelming importance in their work of ludicrous plots developed without an ounce of irony, cannot but strike one forcibly. This is an impoverished art, all the poorer, Kierkegaard would say, for its failure to understand just how poor it is, in spite of its tremendous energy.

It is instructive to compare those two tales of heroic brigands, Scott's *Rob Roy* and Kleist's *Michael Kohlhaas*. Scott's story comes through as a tale for children, an innocent frolic, an excellent candidate for Hollywoodisation. Kleist's terrible tale, on the other hand, is based on the premise that we have grown up, that we know the world will never conform to our wishes and that the plottings of narrative are only the transference into adult life of the fantasies of childhood. All Kleist's stories gain their frightful beauty from the writer's recognition that he himself is implicated in the world he describes, and that to plot a story elegantly is to conspire with the powers of Progress to which he is so implacably opposed. At the climax of *Michael Kohlhaas* all is about to be revealed – and then this happens:

> Kohlhaas, striding up in front of the man with a suddenness that took his guard by surprise, drew out the capsule, removed the paper, unsealed it and read it through; and looking steadily at the man with the blue and white plumes, in whose breast fond hopes were already beginning to spring, he stuck the paper in his mouth and swallowed it. At this sight the man with the blue and white crest was seized by a fit and fell unconscious to the ground. Kohlhaas, however, while his dismayed companions bent over him and raised him from the ground, turned around to the scaffold where his head fell under the executioner's ax.

Another, shorter, perhaps less powerful but equally characteristic story, 'The Duel', takes up the themes I explored in connection with *Richard II*. A Duke has been killed by the arrow of an unknown assassin (we are in the fourteenth century). The finger seems to point at the Duke's half-brother, Count Jacob. Asked to defend himself, he admits that the arrow is his but claims he has no idea how the murderer came by it; he himself, on the night in question, was with a certain lady. Pressed to say who, he names Wittib

Littegarde von Auerstein. This lady, who had rejected the advances of many suitors to please her father and especially her brothers, who wished the inheritance to pass entire to their descendants, was known as a paragon of virtue. She denies the Count's slur, but the accusation kills her father and leads to her brothers throwing her out of their castle. A former suitor, Chancellor von Trota, takes her in and challenges Count Jacob to a duel to prove the lady's honour. After all, says the narrator, such a trial by combat is 'the sacred verdict of arms which unfailingly brought the truth to light'. Unfortunately, after wounding the Count very slightly, von Trota trips over his own spurs and falls. Count Jacob thrusts his sword into his side and, standing over him, proclaims himself the victor. Littegarde, now proved guilty beyond question, is thrust into prison. Surprisingly, though, her champion does not die, but recovers. He visits her in prison and their exchange forms the first climax to the story. The poor woman is convinced that she is guilty, since 'God is truthful and never errs', at the same time as she knows she is innocent, 'as innocent as a newborn baby's breast, as the conscience of a man who has just come from confession, as the corpse of a nun that died in the vestry while taking the veil'. 'Oh, merciful God!' exclaims von Trota, 'Your words make me live again.' 'Oh, you unhappy man!' responds Littegarde, recoiling from him. 'How can you believe a single word that comes from my mouth?' This is not like Oedipus' sense that he is both innocent and polluted. Littegarde's state of mind is closer to that of Shakespeare's Troilus when he discovers Cressida's perfidy: 'This is and is not Cressid.' She is broken on the back of the contradiction between her inner certainty and the objective facts.

Kleist wraps up the story with a piece of deliberately absurd plot-making. The lady's waiting-woman, it turns out, is the real culprit, for on the night in question she had dressed up as her mistress to entertain the Count. Thus both the Count and the lady are correct in thinking they are telling the truth. The Count, however, was not telling the full truth about the murder, for he had in fact ordered it to be carried out while his assignation with Littegarde provided him with the perfect alibi. Von Trota's apparently mortal wounds heal, while the slight scratch sustained by the Count early on turns septic and soon infects his whole body. God, it seems, does speak through the deeds of men, even if what He has to say is not always understood by men. The Count dies, the lady marries her suitor, and the Emperor has the statutes governing trial by combat, 'wherever it was assumed that guilt was immediately revealed', emended to read, 'if it should be the will of God'. Which is as much as to say that such a trial will tell us nothing.

To sum up so far: Romanticism, in its first phase, merely put flesh on the bones of Enlightenment ideas and aspirations; for the majority of readers and artists the Enlightenment and Romantic claims went on seeming self-evidently true – and still do today. But for a small but powerful number of artists and thinkers Enlightenment iconoclasm had destroyed far more than its advocates realised. At the same time they were perfectly well aware that it was impossible to return to the pre-Enlightenment world of hierarchy and tradition, and so could only articulate their despair in the hope that, as Kierkegaard put it, by keeping the wound of the negative open some sort of natural healing might take place.

These are difficult issues, doubly so for being still very much with us. What we have to do is to try to grasp as clearly as possible what it was that was lost when Descartes and Kant made their iconoclastic claims. This is a vast subject, and one that philosophers like Stanley Cavell and cultural critics like Richard Sennett have explored with great acumen. What I would like to do here is to cast just one beam of light upon it by taking a look at the difference between Romantic and more traditional views of Shakespeare and, in the wake of that, of biography. The two issues are bound up together and can be explored together if we focus on Dr Johnson as the spokesman for those more traditional views.

We have already examined Schiller's notion of Shakespeare as a naive artist, like Homer, and the contrast he draws between them and what he calls sentimental artists like himself and his contemporaries, Goethe excepted. Goethe himself was of the same opinion: '[Shakespeare] has . . . been recognised to belong not so much to the modern "romantic" poets but rather to the "naive" kind. . . . The value of his work rests on the reality of the present; barely at its most sensitive, most extreme point does it touch the emotion of desire for something other than this world affords.' This last phrase, 'the emotion of desire for something other than this world affords' is G. F. Parker's inspired paraphrase of the single German word *Sehnsucht*, and it brings out well the essential difference between Goethe and the Romantics on the subject of Shakespeare, and the perhaps surprising congruence of Goethe's views and those of Dr Johnson. For Johnson too Shakespeare was the poet of this world and this life, to be admired or criticised to the degree that he depicted it well or badly. When Johnson felt Shakespeare was being tiresome or actually weakening his effects, as in the excessive punning of *Romeo and Juliet*, he was not afraid to say so; when he was bowled over by something in Shakespeare, as by his creation of Falstaff, he was not afraid to admit to mixed and even contradictory responses.

In fact, for Johnson, the ability to evoke such mixed responses was precisely what made Shakespeare Shakespeare. Milton for him was the poet of the single powerful vision, which he would impose on the world: 'Reality was a scene too narrow for his mind,' is how Johnson tellingly puts it. Shakespeare, on the other hand, because he is the poet of reality, of our world, forces us to face the often uncomfortable fact that reality seldom fits in with what we would wish. Johnson's note on Falstaff brings this out admirably:

Falstaff is a character loaded with faults, and with those faults which naturally produce contempt. He is a thief, and a glutton, a coward, and a boaster, always ready to cheat the weak and prey upon the poor; to terrify the timorous and insult the defenceless. At once obsequious and malignant, he satirises in their absence those he lives by flattering ... Yet the man thus corrupt, thus despicable, makes himself necessary to the prince that despises him, by the most pleasing of all qualities, perpetual gaiety, by an unfailing power of exciting laughter, which is the more freely indulged, as his wit is not of the splendid or ambitious kind, but consists in easy escapes and sallies of levity, which make sport but raise no envy.

As Parker points out in his book on Johnson, Shakespeare and the Romantics, Johnson 'admires Falstaff's real abilities, but he does not esteem them'. And he goes on to make a crucial point: 'One might have supposed that a character whom one found despicable could hardly possess such irresistible and admirable power to please. This unexpectedness in Johnson's discriminations, together with the tone of delighted wonder with which he measures the solidity of Shakespeare's achievement against its theoretical improbability', suggests that Johnson trusts both his own mixed responses and Shakespeare's ability to depict what is there in the world.

Contrast this with the Romantic attitude to Falstaff as it comes through in some remarks of Schlegel's: 'Falstaff is the most agreeable and entertaining good-for-nothing ever depicted. His contemptible qualities are not disguised ... [Yet], despite all this, at no point does he arouse our indignation or dislike. We see that his tender care for himself is without any admixture of malice towards others.' These remarks could be replicated in a dozen other Romantic commentaries, and what they all give us is a sentimentalised Falstaff, a Falstaff who is rendered harmless and thus robbed of the real mystery of his attractiveness. Johnson is well aware that the man who is capable of recruiting the least adequate soldiers because the adequate ones have bribed him to let them off is a dangerous man; he is aware that Hal really does despise him; and at the same time he recognises that he has 'an unfailing power of exciting laughter' and that this makes him, for a while, necessary to Hal. Schlegel, on the other hand, in typically modern fashion, appears to be judiciously weighing up the man's character – 'His contemptible qualities are not disguised' – but then brushes aside everything that is negative with an airy 'despite all this' (compare the modern politician's 'having said that') – despite all this, he says, we love him because he is quite without malice.

A profound change has taken place between Johnson and Schlegel, as profound perhaps as the change between Homer and Plato. It comes out again in the difference between Johnson's response to the character of Hamlet and that of the Romantics.

Johnson feels that there is in Hamlet's sparing of Claudius at prayer 'something too horrible to be read or to be uttered', and he says firmly that he regards his treatment of Ophelia as 'useless and wanton cruelty'. One might accuse Johnson of being insensitive to the complexity of the play, and there is some truth in that: much of what we value in it seems to pass him by. But when one turns to Romantic discussions of Hamlet one feels that by responding so empathetically to the hero they completely lose sight of the jaggedness, the discomfort generated by the play as a whole, something which Johnson certainly responds to. For Coleridge Hamlet is a being who inhabits a world of the imagination far superior to our own, a world which can only come into being through the power of Shakespeare's imagination, but which we too can enter by identifying with Hamlet. Parker is very good on the way Coleridge slides from Hamlet to Shakespeare himself: 'For Coleridge,' he writes, 'that unusual activity of mind which he analyses in Hamlet seems to be continuous with the power of *Shakespeare's* poetic imagination, that "endless activity of thought, in all the possible associations of thought with thought, thought with feelings, or with words, or of feelings with feelings, and words with words", which Coleridge regards not as the restless working of a mind for which time is out of joint, a mind running too free and too fast to engage with the world in which it finds itself, but as the mark of power, life, and freedom of the mind generally.' Coleridge, in other words, like Barthes and Foucault, and unlike Kierkegaard and Mann and Perec, opts for the single vision and refuses to live with the play's contradictions.

If Hamlet the man is in a certain sense Shakespeare, then of course Prospero is even more so. Like Prospero, Shakespeare created whole worlds out of his imagination. Shakespeare, says Coleridge in a notebook entry, is the *demiourgos*, the creator, who takes the *hyle* or inchoate material of the universe and fashions it into something rich and strange. For Johnson Shakespeare bodies forth the contradictions of our world and so helps us face and understand them. For the Romantics Shakespeare is the quintessential artist who creates whole worlds which we can enter, leaving our own miserable and confused world behind. Johnson's Shakespeare, we can see, is close to the Mozart of *The Marriage of Figaro*, *Così* and *Don Giovanni*; the Shakespeare of the Romantics is not far removed from Wagner.

Interestingly, Schlegel, like Schiller before him, draws a contrast between the ancients and the moderns, but for him Shakespeare belongs firmly in the camp of the moderns, who are, as in Hegel, identified with Christianity: 'The old religion of the senses sought nothing higher than blessings of an external, transient kind', he says; 'immortality, insofar as it was believed in at all, was a dim and distant shadow, a dream faintly remembered in the sunny waking daytime of life.' Unlike Schiller, Kierkegaard and Nietzsche, who struggle in their discussions of the ancient Greeks to understand something powerful and alien, something they feel they have lost and so do not even have the words for, Schlegel here falls into all the traps of the historian of ideas, projecting a neat scheme upon the complexities of history. 'In the Christian perspective', he goes on, 'everything is reversed: the intuition of infinity has destroyed what is finite, and it is life which has become a world of shadow and darkness, while the eternal day of our real existence dawns only on a further shore. Such a religion necessarily brings into full consciousness the intimation sleeping in every sensitive heart, the intimation that we aspire to a happiness unattainable here, that no external object can ever entirely satisfy our souls.' And he concludes: 'The poetry of the ancients was that of enjoyment, and ours is that of desire.'

This explicitly Christian and Neoplatonic view of man's condition helps to explain why identification with character is so important to the Romantics, and why they felt that Shakespeare could never really come alive on the stage, only on the page. For Lamb, when we are in the theatre of our imaginations 'we see not Lear, but we are Lear, – we are in his mind, we are sustained by a grandeur which baffles the malice of daughters and storms'. Dr Johnson, on the other hand, far from identifying with Lear, finds him a 'poor crazy old man', and what moves him in the play are the sudden changes of fortune and the rapid succession of events which it presents to us, filling our minds with a perpetual tumult of indignation, pity and hope.

Johnson is thus much closer to Aristotle in this, as in so much else, than he is to the Romantics and to many of his contemporaries. For him as for Aristotle the play is a *mythos*, a pattern of events, which move us to pity and fear. Lamb and Hazlitt, on the other hand, though they do not realise it, talk about Shakespeare very much as Luther talks about the Bible. Luther responds passionately and personally to individual biblical episodes, identifying with the protagonist, often at the expense of the overall meaning of the story. Thus in writing about Noah, for example, he marvels at his having had the courage to believe in God's word and build an ark when there was no cloud in the sky. In Roland Bainton's paraphrase he remarks 'how his neighbours must have mocked him for constructing a sea-going vessel far from the coast! It was all the harder for Noah because he lived so long. Not only while the ark was under construction but for hundreds of years beforehand he must have endured the taunts of unbelievers.' 'If I had seen such men in the camp of the ungodly opposing me', Luther concludes, 'I should have thrown down my ministry in sheer desperation. Nobody knows how hard it is for one man to stand out against the consensus of all the other churches and against the judgement of his noblest and choicest friends.' Luther's own circumstances make it possible for him to empathise with Noah, even to identify with him; yet they also make him read the biblical story in a strangely distorted manner. Who would ever guess from his comments that there was absolutely nothing in the Bible either about Noah's courage or about the laughter and mockery of others. The Bible simply tells us that Noah 'found grace in the eyes of the Lord', and then, when God has told him how to build the ark, 'Thus did Noah; according to all that God commanded him, so did he' (Genesis 6:8, 22).

To identify with characters in narratives or plays is certainly better than to regard them with cold indifference. But to identify totally with them is to risk turning them into a version of ourselves. To see the Bible or Shakespeare wholly in terms of their characters is to lose the sense of *mythos*, of fable, and to miss the sense of awe and wonder at events which we witness but cannot fully comprehend.

It is easy to see how the Romantics could move from identification with Hamlet or Lear or Prospero to identification with Shakespeare as Hamlet or Lear or Prospero. This would never have entered Johnson's head. His attitude to biography is one with his attitude to Shakespeare: he stands back and tries to pronounce justly on the whole. This is sometimes seen as the attempt to fit the complexity of life into a rigid system of morals. Richard Holmes, a highly successful and accomplished modern biographer, famed in particular for his two-volume biography of Coleridge, has even written a whole book trying to persuade us that Johnson was unconsciously a modern biographer and only a moralist against the grain, as it were. He bases his case on a close examination of Johnson's first great Life, the *Life of Savage*. Johnson ends the book thus: 'This relation will not be wholly without its use if those who languish under any part of his sufferings shall be enabled to fortify their patience by reflecting that they feel only those afflictions from which the abilities of Savage did not exempt him; or those who in confidence of superior capacities or attainments disregard the common maxims of life shall be reminded that nothing will supply the want of prudence, and that negligence and irregularity long continued will make knowledge useless, wit ridiculous, and genius contemptible.' Holmes quotes the last part of this and asks: 'Is it, at the very last, a damnation?' No, he replies, for when Johnson was correcting his *Life* for the second edition, 'he wrote against that final, sad dismissive passage the one word: "Added". This', concludes Holmes, 'was not how he had originally intended to conclude his biography. It was a solemn, placatory afterthought; a conciliatory gesture to the forces of social opinion, which became so powerful in his own life.' The original edition, on the other hand, he suggests, 'defiantly evokes the world of Grub Street, his own world, and romantically challenges the reader to accept the conditions of Savage's existence. It urges empathy before judgement.'

This is the creed of the Romantic reader of Shakespeare as of the modern biographer. But is Holmes right? Taking a break in his two-volume biography of Coleridge to write his little book on Johnson and Savage, he is clearly trying to make of Johnson the patron saint or founding father of the genre to which he has committed himself. The failure of his enterprise helps us to understand why the very modern genre of literary biography is a child of Romanticism, and why, rather than the discovery of a new and deeper vision, it signals a narrowing of what is understood by human life.

'I believe that biography itself, with its central tenet of empathy, is essentially a Romantic form', asserts Holmes, 'and that Johnson's friendship with Savage first crystallised its perils and its possibilities.' By transforming his friendship with Savage into a *Life*, and by recognising how much of himself there was in Savage, Holmes argues, Johnson brought this new Romantic genre of biography into being. It was no longer based on classical models – Plutarch, Tacitus, Sallust – but on native English forms. (One is reminded here of the Romantic view of Chaucer as shedding those stiff French and Italian forms and finally finding himself in his full natural Englishness with *The Canterbury Tales*, a view which has thankfully long since been discredited.) 'In Johnson's hands', Holmes concludes, 'biography became a rival to the novel. It began to pose the largest, imaginative questions: how well can we know our fellow human beings; how far can we learn from someone else's struggles about the conditions of our own; what do the intimate circumstances of one particular life tell us about human nature in general?'

Holmes is absolutely right to see biography and the novel as developing together. But he is himself so imbued with Romanticism that he quite fails to see the force of Johnson's very different position. In an essay he wrote on epitaphs Johnson said: 'As honours are paid to the dead in order to incite others to the imitation of their excellencies, the principal intention of epitaphs is to perpetuate the examples of virtue, that the tomb of a good man may supply the want of his presence, and veneration for his memory produce the same effect as the observation of his life.' For Johnson the innermost recesses of a man's life are not what is important about him. What is important are his actions, how he has conducted himself in the course of his life in the community of men. Holmes is right to want to win Johnson over to his camp; were he to succeed he would be silencing one of the most powerful critics of the kind of work to which he has devoted his life. But Johnson will not be won over. His attitude embodies a long tradition which stands as a perpetual challenge to the assumptions of modern biography, of the classic novel, and of autobiography.

For that is the missing third element of Holmes's pantheon. Autobiography, as practised by Augustine, Rousseau and all who have followed him, is built on two planks, both of which can be traced back to St Paul. The first is the belief that, through an act of conversion, I can become transparent to myself; the second is apologetic: I have done wrong, but I believed it to be right at the time, and, anyway, my heart urged me; besides, confessing now in these pages, I am absolved. Johnson, like Aristotle, will have none of it; just as he criticised Falstaff and Hamlet, so he would criticise all such attempts at exculpation – while never for a moment, I am sure, denying the fascination of an Augustine, a Coleridge, a Michel Leiris.

We need to take Johnson and the tradition he represents seriously if we are to understand the paradoxes and doubts of Romanticism. The Romantic notion that we can enter into the life of another and live it, through imaginative empathy, and thus forgive any fault we find there, suggests that we will do the same with our own and would ask others to do likewise. Johnson, like Aristotle and Dante, wants to see individual lives within a larger rhythm and under a double perspective: infinitely precious to each of us but subject to laws which bind the rest of creation. The effect of this, as I suggested in an earlier chapter, is not to diminish us but, on the contrary, to give us back a sense of the wonder of life.

What happens when the social and ethical context in which such a view of existence can flourish breaks down? Then, for those who still hold the Johnsonian vision, the only thing left is to bring out into the open the extent of the breakdown. As Kierkegaard put it: 'It is necessary first of all to observe that [a thing] is lacking, and then in turn to feel quite vividly the lack of it.'

In the chapters that follow I will be looking at examples of artists and thinkers who, feeling the lack quite vividly, spent their lives trying to find the means of expressing this. Now, though, I want to return to that moment in English Romanticism when a space seemed to open up which allowed certain poets to write as no-one had ever written before and as only a few great poets were ever to write again.

What is moving about Wordsworth and Coleridge is not how well but how little they understood themselves. And how, understanding themselves so little, they were nevertheless able to trust their instincts.

The difficulty of trusting one's instincts when there seems to be no established language for what you want to say or any established set of social codes within which to place what you want to say is most obvious in Wordsworth's relation to his solitaries, all those beggars, wanderers, leech-gatherers, discharged soldiers, and boys and girls who died inexplicably young, who people his poems. Lewis Carroll, with his parodist's gift for going straight for the jugular and his parodist's love for his subject, put his finger on the problem: speech. What are these outcasts to say which will both fit in with what Wordsworth *wants* to say and not seem either flat or portentous?

Take the Leech-Gatherer. 'There was a roaring in the wind all night', the poem begins, and we are immediately immersed in the natural world. But it is an apocalyptic world, one where, after the storm, 'The sky rejoices in the morning's birth'. 'I was a Traveller then upon the moor', the poet tells us, and, unlike Baudelaire, he does not make the natural conditions a mere symbol of his own state of mind, but allows us to feel how each affects the other: 'I saw the hare that raced about with joy; / I heard the woods and distant waters roar.' But just as the stormy weather changes to fine, so joy turns to melancholy, suddenly, inexplicably, and the poet sinks into a dejection which is all the worse for being a kind of 'dim sadness' which cannot be named or placed. However, he does try to explain it, and comes up with the thought that it was brought about by brooding on all the wonderful poets whose youth began in gladness but who in the end succumbed to 'despondency and madness'. In this dream-like state, where we are not sure if our thoughts are giving rise to visions or visions to thoughts, he comes upon a strange sight: 'Beside a pool bare to the eye of heaven / I saw a Man before me unawares: / The oldest man he seemed that ever wore grey hairs.'

The point about this figure is that he is both human and a part of the landscape: 'As a huge stone . . . / Couched on the bald top of an eminence', or 'Like a sea-beast crawled forth', sunning itself on a shelf or rock – 'Such seemed this Man', says the poet, 'not all alive nor dead, / Nor all asleep – in his extreme old age.' As the poet draws near the old man remains 'Motionless as a cloud', 'That heareth not the loud winds when they call; / And moveth all together, if it move at all'.

Coming up to him the poet engages him in conversation, and at once the tone Lewis Carroll caught unfortunately emerges: 'This morning gives us promise of a glorious day', says the poet, for all the world as if he had simply met a passer-by on one of his walks. And he goes on to ask the old man what he does, like a keen young novelist with his ever-ready notebook. The old man obliges and explains that he is gathering leeches to earn his living. But even as he talks 'his voice to me was like a stream / Scarce heard; nor word from word could I divide; / And the whole body of the Man did seem / Like one whom I had met with in a dream'. His former deadening thoughts return, but the poet struggles free of them to ask again: 'How is it that you live, and what is it you do?' The old man repeats what he has already said, then gives a little history of leech-gathering. But again the poet's mind wanders, and 'In my mind's eye I seemed to see him pace / About the weary moors continually, / Wandering about alone and silently'. But, says the poet, the cheerfulness of the old man's speech and the warmth of his personality force him to see that despair cannot be the right response to life when it contains such examples of fortitude and uprightness:

I could have laughed myself to scorn to find
In that decrepit Man so firm a mind.
'God,' said I, 'be my help and stay secure;
I'll think of the Leech-gatherer on the lonely moor.

'You are sad', the White Knight says to Alice, 'let me sing you a song to comfort you.' 'Is it very long?' asks Alice. 'It's long', says the Knight, 'but it's very *very* beautiful. Everybody that hears me sing it – either it brings the *tears* into their eyes or else –' 'Or else what?' asks Alice. 'Or else it doesn't, you know', replies the White Knight. And he begins:

I'll tell thee everything I can;
 There's little to relate.
I saw an aged aged man,
 A-sitting on the gate.
'Who are you, aged man?' I said.
 'And how is it you live?'
And his answer trickled through my head
 Like water through a sieve.

He said, 'I look for butterflies
 That sleep among the wheat:
I make them into mutton-pies,
 And sell them in the street.
I sell them unto men,' he said,
 'Who sail on stormy seas;
And that's the way I get my bread –
 A trifle, if you please.'

But I was thinking of a plan
 To dye one's whiskers green,
And always use so large a fan

That they could not be seen.
So, having no reply to give
    To what the old man said,
I cried, 'Come, tell me how you live!'
    And thumped him on the head.

His accents mild took up the tale:
    He said, 'I go my ways,
And when I find a mountain-rill,
    I set it in a blaze;
And thence they make a stuff they call
    Rowland's Macassar Oil –
Yet twopence-halfpenny is all
    They give me for my toil.'

But I was thinking of a way
    To feed oneself on batter,
And so go on from day to day
    Getting a little fatter.
I shook him well from side to side,
    Until his face was blue:
'Come tell me how you live,' I cried,
    'And what it is you do!'

Alice, the narrative tells us, 'stood and listened very attentively, but
no tears came into her eyes'. On the other hand, 'Of all the strange
things that Alice saw in her journey through the Looking-Glass, this
was the one that she always remembered most clearly. Years afterwards she could bring the whole scene back again, as if it had
been only yesterday.' And that, I think, is how we respond to
Wordsworth's strange poem. As with most great works, readers are
divided as to its significance and effect. There are those who feel
that Wordsworth is here indeed wresting hope from an observed

social fact, and that what makes him so much greater than most
Romantic poets is precisely that he engages with the world around
him. And there are those who feel that Wordsworth, desperate to
make sense of his visionary intuitions, tried to give them a social
and moral grounding and fell when he did so into bathos. But
Carroll has got it exactly right: it brings no tears to our eyes, yet
we remember it long after more perfect poems have faded from
our minds.

A much shorter poem, like 'Animal Tranquillity and Decay', does
not pose the same problems. Wordsworth is here prepared to trust
his instincts and leave it at that, with the result that it is wholly free
of the bathos that engulfs the longer poem:

> The little hedgerow birds,
> That peck along the road, regard him not.
> He travels on, and in his face, his step
> His gait, is one expression: every limb,
> His look and bending figure, all bespeak
> A man who does not move with pain, but moves
> With thought. – He is insensibly subdued
> To settled quiet; he is one by whom
> All effort seems forgotten; one to whom
> Long patience hath such mild composure given
> That patience now doth seem a thing of which
> He hath no need. He is by nature led
> To peace so perfect that the young behold
> With envy, what the Old Man hardly feels.

The Old Man is a real old man, as the birds are real birds;
Wordsworth finds the language to convey what he sees. The poem
is visionary not because it deals with another world but because it
sees more of this world than most of us can. He stays with his
instinct, which tells him that, if we would only see it, the Old Man

is an emblem of our condition. Even the title reinforces our sense that here Wordsworth, like the Old Man, is 'insensibly subdued / To settled quiet': not the morally uplifting 'resolution and independence', but the painful yet wondrous sense that here we are faced with 'animal tranquillity and decay'.

It is the way in which these solitaries, deprived of nearly everything that makes us human, are thereby folded back into the larger rhythms of life, which is at the heart of the curious solace Wordsworth finds in them. Their immersion in the landscape is both what gives them dignity and what makes them ultimately unfathomable. But it is not just an immersion in physical nature – rocks and stones and trees; it is, since they are human beings like us, after all, a waking of ourselves to the Homeric and Sophoclean double vision: man is mortal, he will decay and die; but death is natural and life in its inherent tranquillity goes on. How strange and wonderful that the Homeric and Sophoclean note should sound again not in Milton and not in Goethe but in so intensely *local* and revolutionary a poet as Wordsworth! It is as though Romanticism, in its deepest currents, had rediscovered that ancient stream of song.

But this now has to be fought for and struggled with, 'imagined as an inevitable knowledge, / Required as a necessity requires', as Wallace Stevens put it in his very Wordsworthian 'The Plain Sense of Things'. No modern poet can stay with that for very long.

As has often been pointed out, there is a curious symmetry to both the achievements and the failures of Wordsworth and Coleridge. Wordsworth considered his greatest poem to be but a prelude to the real thing; Coleridge thought his finest piece of sustained criticism, the *Biographia Literaria*, to be a mere offshoot of his projected magnum opus. With hindsight we can see that each of them misunderstood not only the nature of his gifts but also the possibilities for art in his time.

It might seem to Wordsworth that *The Prelude* was only a clearing of the throat prior to embarking on his Miltonic epic, but
we can see that it is precisely the clearing of the throat that is
important: Proust would have no doubts about that. And the same
is true of Coleridge. It is extraordinary, given his criticism of
eighteenth-century modes of thought, that he could not see the
fallacy of the very idea of a magnum opus. And it is a nice irony,
but one which is to be found again and again in the art of the next
two centuries, that the poems he wrote as a way of expressing his
inability to write, the Dejection Ode and 'This Lime-Tree Bower
My Prison', should now be seen as perhaps his finest achievements.

But the misunderstanding persists with regard to Romantic art.
Thomas McFarland, the doyen of contemporary scholars of Romanticism, for example, argues in his *Romanticism and the Forms of
Ruin* that Keats should never have included the last stanza of his
'Ode to a Nightingale' in the finished work. Having quoted the
penultimate stanza, which ends with 'magic casements, opening on
the foam / Of perilous seas, to faery lands forlorn', he says: 'A more
absolute climax would be hard to conceive – it opens onto that
prospect of infinity cherished by Romanticism; and yet Keats, seemingly hypnotised by the word 'forlorn', extends himself into a last
stanza that carries within it ruinous circumstances:

> Forlorn! the very word is like a bell
> To toll me back from thee to my sole self!
> Adieu! the fancy cannot cheat so well
> As she is fam'd to do, deceiving elf . . .'

What McFarland fails to understand is that the 'ruinous circumstances', as he calls them, are a part of what the poem is *about*, not
a ruin of the poem. The Nightingale, as Gregory Nagy has recently
shown, is taken by the tradition that runs from the *Odyssey* through
the troubadours as the spirit of poetry. For Keats he is, in a sense,

both Homer and Shakespeare. He sings to the Romantic poet who can, momentarily, sing with him and make of his song his poem. But if the poet is to be true to the spirit of the nightingale he must accept that this can only be a momentary identification. And this truth, the truth of the desire for and the failure to live within that tradition, itself becomes the beautiful truth of the poem. It is a truth that will be most deeply mined in the work of Proust.

6 Proust and the face of true goodness

This talent, which I sought to discover outside the part itself, was indissolubly one with it.

Proust

In 1972 Paul de Man published an essay on Proust which is a fine example of suspicion in action. De Man focuses on just a few pages of *Combray*: the episode where the narrator recounts the child Marcel's pleasure in reading, and the episode immediately preceding this, where the kitchen-maid is compared to Giotto's Charity in the Arena Chapel in Padua. De Man's aim, however, is, as always, to demonstrate that attempts to read the entire work as a coherent whole founder on its profound internal contradictions.

De Man's argument, if I have understood it aright – for, as is often the case with him, while the thrust of the passage is clear enough, it is difficult to grasp precisely what is being said at any one time – consists of two central steps: first of all to cast doubt on Proust/Marcel's central assertion that by retreating into the comfort of his shaded room or some equally shaded bower in the garden in order to read, he was in fact more closely in contact with the world than if he had been engaged in some activity out in the open; and then to cast doubt on his interpretation of Giotto's figure which, he rightly senses, serves to underpin the argument about reading.

'The burden of the text, among other things', says de Man, 'is to reassure Marcel about his flight away from the "real" activity of the outer world . . . The guilty pleasures of solitude are made legitimate because they allow for a possession of the world at least as virile and complete as that of the hero whose adventures he is reading.' To back these assertions he seeks to show that the metaphors Proust uses to persuade us – and himself – are not really up to the task. 'In a passage that abounds in successful and seductive metaphors . . . persuasion is achieved by a figural play in which contingent figures of chance masquerade deceptively as figures of necessity.' Where Proust tries to seduce us aesthetically de Man resists temptation by focusing on Proust's rhetoric: 'The disjunction between the aesthetically responsive and the rhetorically aware reading . . . undoes the pseudo-synthesis of inside and outside . . . , motion and stasis, self and understanding, writer and reader, metaphor and metonymy, that the text has constructed . . . It . . . asserts the impossibility of a true understanding at the level of the figuration as well as of the themes.'

What de Man wishes to do is to show up the element of idealism and wish-fulfilment which imbues not only Proust's text but also the readings of that text by even such subtle and hard-headed critics as Gilles Deleuze and Gérard Genette. They argue, he suggests, that the novel is 'the allegorical narrative of its own deconstruction', and that it can thus be recuperated as a stable whole, aware of and in control of its thrust towards self-destruction. To clinch his case he moves to the second step of his argument, which is that the episode about reading is preceded by an episode about allegory which seeks to underpin the whole but is equally unconvincing. Here the kitchen-maid is compared, first by Swann and then by Marcel, to

Giotto's image of Charity in his great sequence of Virtues and Vices in the Arena Chapel at Padua, of which much is made in the course of the novel. Proust is here trying to ground his own use of allegory and symbolism in that of the medieval painter, 'but', says de Man, 'in allegory, as here described, it seems that the author has lost confidence in the effectiveness of the substitutive power generated by the resemblances', since he is forced to use 'a literal sign which bears no resemblance to that meaning', has, that is, to inscribe the word KARITAS above the image. 'The facial expression of the "heavy and mannish" matron painted by Giotto connotes nothing charitable', de Man points out, and he concludes by asserting that 'A literal reading of Giotto's fresco would never have discovered what it meant . . . We know the meaning of the allegory only because Giotto, substituting writing for representation, spelled it out on the upper frame of his painting.' In just the same way, de Man suggests, Proust has in effect inscribed the word LECTIO on his little episode of childhood reading in an effort to persuade us that this is really what he is describing. Following him, Deleuze and Genette are forced to *say* what cannot be *shown* (or, if shown, will reveal itself to be full of inner contradictions). The truth is, we are for ever barred access 'to a meaning that yet can never cease to call out for its understanding'.

Finally de Man notes that Proust, in the course of his narrative, uses the phrase 'plus tard je compris', 'later I came to understand', and he points out that this phrase, though seeming to promise total fulfilment and clarity whenever it is used in the novel (and it is very frequently used), in fact never fulfils that promise. De Man is implying that even at the end of the novel we are only left with another possible revelation round the corner, and that the view that Marcel has now, finally, reached the point when he can begin to write the novel we have been reading is as much the product of the wish-fulfilment of the narrator and the critic as anything guaranteed by the text. Truth, in effect, can never coincide with itself, it can only be gestured towards as a vague hope. '*A la Recherche du temps perdu*', de Man triumphantly concludes, 'narrates the flight of meaning, but this does not prevent its own meaning from being, incessantly, in flight.'

I have quoted at such length from what is, after all, only a minor article by a critic whose reputation, some may feel, is far in excess of his real merits, not only because it leads into the central issues connected with Proust with which I wish to deal, but because it is itself a perfect example of criticism as suspicion. Such criticism, as we will see, rests on a bedrock of Romantic assumptions which have passed into the common currency and are taken as self-evident by many intelligent and well-read people today. By an irony which would not have pleased de Man these are precisely the assumptions which Proust is concerned to show up as false and misleading in the passage in question.

At the heart of de Man's criticism, here as elsewhere, is the unquestioned assumption that if something does not yield up full meaning we have to despair of its yielding up any meaning at all. The fallacy of this view has often been exposed by philosophers in recent years, and I hope I have disposed of it in my discussion of the quarrel between Plato and Homer and Iago and Othello. But note the kind of language de Man uses: 'the burden of the text is to *reassure* Marcel'; 'the *guilty pleasures* of solitude are *made legitimate*'; '*seductive* metaphors'; *masquerade deceptively*'; '*pseudo-synthesis*'. This is Iago speaking. The manner is objective, almost scientific; the implication is that he, for one, is not going to be taken in by Proust's bluff. But I don't think I'm being perverse in detecting a mixture of arrogance and triumphalism in remarks like the following: 'By suggesting that the narrator, for whatever reason, may have a vested interest in the success of his metaphors, one stresses [note the impersonal pronoun!] their operational effectiveness and maintains a certain critical vigilance with regard to the promises that are being made.'

As I suggested in the opening chapter, such an attitude is understandable; it is a response to the sentimentality and gush of so much post-Romantic writing and of course of so much modern criticism, when literature and talk about literature have become a substitute for religion and theology. But, as I also suggested in that chapter, this attitude, understandable though it is, is itself also very much the product of Romanticism, of the very tendencies that Proust, in the passage under consideration, is at pains to combat. De Man's misreading of Proust, I want to argue, is a typical example of suspicion at work; but Proust, far from being the naive proponent of a set of attitudes which such suspicion is right to want to deconstruct, is in fact the sophisticated proponent of an attitude to trust which recognises the power of suspicion but sees that it is both the product of specific historical forces and inadequate to the task of coming to terms either with the world of men and women, the world in which we live, or with the greatest works of art of the past and the present.

Let's begin then with the first episode with which de Man concerns himself, that of the pregnant kitchen-maid. A correct understanding of what is at issue here will bring with it an equally correct understanding of the episode of childhood reading and even, as de Man sensed, of the entire novel.

The kitchen-maid is introduced, as de Man correctly notes, as a figure of continuity, of permanence in change: 'The kitchen-maid was an abstract personality, a permanent institution to which an invariable set of functions assured a sort of fixity and continuity and identity throughout the succession of transitory human shapes in which it was embodied; for we never had the same girl two years running.' That year, the narrator tells us, she was a poor sickly creature, heavily pregnant, who 'was beginning to find difficulty in bearing before her the mysterious basket, fuller and larger every day, whose splendid outline could be detected beneath the folds of her ample smock'. It is this garment which reminds Swann of Giotto's allegorical figures and leads him always to enquire after her with the phrase: 'Well, how goes it with Giotto's Charity?' (I, 79 / I, 94).

However, the narrator, as usual, looks more deeply than Swann. The latter is merely pleased with his witty *aperçu*. For Marcel, on the other hand, there is a more profound sense in which the kitchen-maid resembles Giotto's Charity:

> For just as the figure of this girl had been enlarged by the additional symbol which she carried before her, without appearing to understand its meaning, with no awareness in her facial expression of its beauty and spiritual significance, as if it were an ordinary, rather heavy burden, so it is without any apparent suspicion of what she is about that the powerfully built housewife who is portrayed in the Arena Chapel beneath the label 'Caritas' . . . embodies that virtue, for it seems impossible that any thought of charity can ever have found expression in her vulgar and energetic face.
>
> (I, 80 / I, 95)

Like Rilke, Marcel is drawn to the mysteries of our relation to our bodies, of the way the body knows better, as it were, than the mind or the soul, and of the way we, as sentient and rational beings, are always at a loss to make sense of our bodies. And, like Rilke, he understands that it is in special circumstances, in pregnancy, in death, that this separation is most clearly manifested. But, like Rilke too, he faces this mystery *as* a mystery, something to be reached out to rather than neatly explained. Indeed, the role of art, in both writers, is in large part that of gradually homing in on the mystery rather than simply resolving it. Much of *Combray* and this episode in particular, consists of Marcel's growing awareness of the mystery, his cautious circling round it in an effort to grasp its dimensions, rather than in any attempt to resolve it. In this instance that circling round is directed at and inspired by the images of Giotto.

He thus goes on to describe the image of Charity, drawing on Ruskin's description of her, but adding his own hilarious, yet apt, final twist:

> By a fine stroke of the painter's invention she is trampling all the treasures of the earth beneath her feet, but exactly as if she were treading grapes in a wine-press to extract their juice, or rather as if she had climbed on to a heap of sacks to raise herself higher; and she is holding out her flaming heart to God, or shall we say 'handing' it to him, exactly as a cook might hand up a corkscrew through the skylight of her basement kitchen to someone who has called down for it from the ground-floor window.

It is the same, he says, with the figure of Envy, who 'should have had some look of envy on her face', but who is so obviously struggling with the snake which fills her mouth 'that the muscles of her face are strained and contorted, like those of a child blowing up a balloon, and her attention – and ours too for that matter – is so utterly concentrated on the activity of her lips as to leave little time to spare for envious thoughts' (I, 80 / I, 95).

Charity and Envy

Despite Swann's admiration for these images, says the narrator, it took *him* a long time to appreciate this Charity devoid of Charity and this Envy who 'looked like nothing so much as a plate in some medical book'. His initial response, in other words, is very like de Man's, the natural response of someone who has been brought up on Romantic and post-Romantic art and criticism. But, he says, 'in later years I came to understand that the arresting strangeness, the special beauty of these frescoes derived from the great part played in them by symbolism, and the fact that this was represented not as a symbol (for the thought symbolised was nowhere expressed) but as a reality, actually felt or materially handled, added something more precise and more literal to the meaning of the work, something more concrete and more striking to the lesson it imparted' (I, 81 / I, 96).

De Man is right in saying that the phrase 'in later years I came to understand' does not mean that we have finally arrived at the truth. The way this novel is constructed always leaves open the possibility that today's understanding will itself be overturned by tomorrow's experience. But it is also often the case that the pattern is simply binary: an initial misunderstanding leaves Marcel puzzled and confused, but that puzzlement is then resolved by a new episode. This, we shall see, is the case with Marcel's visits to see Berma acting in Racine, and it is the case here. 'Later I came to understand', in other words, should alert us in this case to the importance Proust places on what is understood. Let us try and make sense of it.

Unlike Swann, who is satisfied by the play of wit which discerns in Odette a Botticelli and in the kitchen-maid a Giotto, Marcel is puzzled by his own reaction. These figures are in a sense repulsive, they do not fit in with his expectations, yet they have an 'étrangeté saisissante', an arresting strangeness, and a special beauty. He struggles to explain this by saying that the thought symbolised in the figures is not expressed but that the symbol – Charity – is somehow made real. We would say that they are typical of a very medieval notion of allegory, one which is still to be found in Spenser but which goes out of fashion by the seventeenth century and is dismissed as wooden and mechanical by the Romantics. This is de Man's attitude: an allegory of this kind, he says dismissively, needs prior knowledge in order to decode it, while symbolism expresses concretely what is symbolised.

But are the Romantics right? The main reason why Proust, when he first discovered Ruskin, felt at once that Ruskin was capable of helping him understand what he had darkly sensed but been unable to articulate, was that Ruskin, in his description and analysis of medieval art, had been able to go behind this simple Romantic contrast and to rediscover in medieval allegory a deeper truth. Ruskin does not do this like, say, the great twentieth-century American scholar, Rosamond Tuve, by parading before us a wealth of scholarship; he does it rather by looking hard and responding with greater openness and generosity of spirit than any of his contemporaries and immediate predecessors. And of course he has looked at a vast range of medieval art and looked at it with passion and an awareness of the religious basis of the iconography. In *The Stones of Venice*, for example, he spends several pages drawing up a list of parallels between some of the great medieval series of Virtues and Vices, such as Orcagna's in Florence, Giotto's in Padua, those in the Ducal Palace in Venice, and those of Dante and Spenser. Proust, as we have seen, follows him faithfully in his description of Charity, only adding an image that the high-minded Ruskin might have found a little shocking; and now, in his further meditation on the image, he remains very much within Ruskin's ambiance.

What is it that makes these superficially unattractive figures so moving? In the case of the kitchen-maid, with whom, after all, the meditation began, one's attention is constantly drawn to her belly by the weight which drags it down; 'and in the same way again', Proust says, 'are not the thoughts of the dying often turned towards the practical, painful, obscure, visceral aspects, towards that "seamy side" of death which is, as it happens, the side that death actually presents to them and forces them to feel, and which far more closely resembles a crushing burden, a difficulty in breathing, a destroying thirst, than the abstract idea to which we are accustomed to give the name of Death? (I, 81 / I, 96). And indeed later, in describing the death of his grandmother, the narrator will recount how, at the end, the old lady seems to have turned away from the loving family at her bedside and to be struggling in a private duel with an impersonal enemy only she can see.

In other words the pregnant kitchen-maid and Giotto's Charity, far from being abstractions, cerebral allegories which cannot be understood without reading the superscription, are figures which draw us *in* to reality and make us understand that it is we who, in our normal lives, maintain purely abstract and unrealistic notions of what charity or death or pregnancy might be; and it is artists like Giotto – and Proust – who are the true realists, uncovering and giving us the chance to share with them the insight into the actual fact of charity and death and pregnancy.

The reason why Charity does not look charitable or Envy envious is not that the painter or the tradition substitutes the idea for the thing, but rather that they recognise that human beings are always more than their thoughts or their feelings, that they are embodied and active in the world. What Giotto's images do is to relate Charity and Envy to all the other images and activities we can imagine of Charity and Envy, and to guide us in this exploration by the choice of attribute given to them. I suspect that this is also why Giotto's figures always step partially out of their frames: we are shown Charity in action, not someone who has a charitable disposition, Envy in action, not one who has an envious disposition. Allegory is perhaps the wrong word; it sets up a resistance in us and makes us incapable of responding to these figures. Let us say rather that Giotto has compressed into one image a whole state of being, just as Erich Auerbach suggested that Dante's characters, presented to us so briefly and so powerfully, are conceived by the poet in their otherworldly state: a compression and summation of their earthly existence. But this is no mere medieval vision, to which we need to make a purely historical response. Does not Mallarmé make the same point in the opening line of his great funeral sonnet for Edgar Allan Poe: 'Tel qu'en Lui-meme enfin l'éternité le change.' ('As into himself eternity finally transmutes him.') In our daily life we are too busy, in too much of a hurry, to respond fully to people or places; it takes death to jolt us out of our abstraction, to make us realise what the person really was in the fullness of their being. Death or art.

And *that* is what is at the heart of Marcel's subsequent meditation on reading. Sitting in his room, protected from the glare of the sun outside, yet pleasantly aware of the humdrum daily activities going on, entering the world of the book, which in fact means the world of himself, but always aware of himself reading, of the thought of the delicious lunch to come, he seems to be able to catch the totality of the day in a way he never could were he out there and engaged in some singular activity, 'like a hand reposing motionless in a stream of running water', which sustains 'the shock and animation of a torrent of activity (I, 82 / I, 98). De Man reads this as a protective fantasy; but his suspicion blinds him to its profound relation to what has come before.

And de Man omits the paragraph that concludes the meditation on Giotto's Charity, because, I suspect, he does not know what to do with it. But that paragraph is the key to the whole section, and, indeed, to the ethical scheme of the whole novel. 'Quite possibly', says the narrator – for Proust is never dogmatic, especially where his most important insights are concerned –

quite possibly, this lack (or seeming lack) of participation by a person's soul in the virtue of which he or she is the agent has, apart from its aesthetic meaning, a reality which, if not strictly psychological, may at least be called physiognomical. Since then,

whenever in the course of my life I have come across, in convents
for instance, truly saintly embodiments of practical charity, they
have generally had the cheerful, practical, brusque and unemo-
tional air of a busy surgeon, the sort of face in which one can
discern no commiseration, no tenderness at the sight of suffering
humanity, no fear of hurting it, the impassive, unsympathetic,
sublime face of true goodness.

(I, 81 / I, 96–7)

The face of true goodness is *antipathique* (rather different
from 'unsympathetic': the French implies someone who arouses no
sympathy, the English someone who lacks sympathy for others) and
sublime: 'le visage antipathique et sublime de la vraie bonté'. It
is only bad novelists and their readers who believe that people are
wholly one thing or the other, or perhaps that they are *essentially*
one thing though they may *appear* to be another. Shakespeare,
Dr Johnson and Proust know better: Falstaff is cowardly, mean and
vindictive, but also great fun to be with; Mlle Vinteuil's lover
encourages her to desecrate the photo of her dead father but she is
also responsible for getting the old composer's last score into a per-
formable state; Françoise is cruel, sentimental and foolish, but she
is also loyal and has a kind of incorruptible innocence about her
which makes her more precious to Marcel than all his high-born
friends. This is the error of the modern biographer, the Romantic
whose creed is empathy: by empathising with his subject he reads
that subject's life in his own terms; but our lives are always more
and other than we understand them to be. This and not the crazy
wish to see all life in terms of a strict set of moral principles is what
lies behind Dr Johnson's very different attitude to biography and
what links him at once with Sophocles and with Proust.

Both the kitchen-maid and Giotto's Charity, says de Man, are
characterised by *non-understanding*, they display features 'without

seeming to understand their meaning', and both, he says, 'seem to be condemned to the same dyslexia'. But why these negative terms? One could with more justice say that for both meaning 'shows itself' rather than being understood. The maid carries her pregnancy before her, like a burden. The nun and the surgeon are too busy doing good to try to look good. There are not many characters in Proust's novel who display these qualities. Indeed, perhaps there are only two: the narrator's mother and his grandmother. By contrast, the vast majority of characters seem perpetually to be seeking to convince those in whose company they find themselves that they *are* good, or intelligent, or sensitive, and they do that by trying to embody those qualities in their expressions.

Mme Verdurin is only the most conspicuous example. 'If the pianist suggested playing the Ride of the Valkyries or the Prelude to *Tristan*, Mme Verdurin would protest, not because the music was displeasing to her, but, on the contrary, because it made too violent an impression on her. Then you want me to have one of my headaches? You know quite well it's the same every time he plays that. I know what I'm in for. Tomorrow, when I want to get up – nothing doing!' ('Je sais ce qui m'attend! Demain quand je voudrai me lever, bonsoir, plus personne!') (I, 186 / I, 226). When her husband announces that the pianist is going to play a certain sonata she screams: 'No, no, no, not my sonata! . . . I don't want to be made to cry till I get . . . neuralgia all down my face, like last time. Thanks very much, I don't intend to repeat that performance.' 'This little scene', says the narrator, 'which was re-enacted as often as the young pianist sat down to play, never failed to delight her friends as much as if they were witnessing it for the first time, as a proof of the seductive originality of the 'Mistress' and of the acute sensitiveness of her musical ear.' Just the *andante* then, suggests her husband. 'Just the *andante*! That really is a bit rich!' cries Mme Verdurin. 'As if it wasn't precisely the *andante* that breaks every bone in my body. The Master is really too priceless! Just as though, in the Ninth, he said: "We'll just hear the *finale*", or "just the overture" of the *Mastersingers*' (I, 203 / I, 247).

Mme Verdurin even goes to the extreme of dislocating her jaw in her attempt to convey the raptures into which music puts her; but she is not alone in feeling that she must somehow convey in her expression and gestures what music is doing to her. At the Marquise de Sainte-Euverte's musical gathering Swann's gaze falls on two ladies, no longer young, sitting side by side:

Filled with melancholy irony, Swann watched them as they listened to the pianoforte intermezzo (Liszt's 'Saint Francis preaching to the birds') which had succeeded the flute and followed the virtuoso in his dizzy flight, Mme de Franquetot anxiously, her eyes starting from her head as though the keys over which his fingers skipped with such agility were a series of trapezes from any one of which he might come crashing a hundred feet to the ground, stealing now and then a glance of astonishment and unbelief at her companion, as who should say: 'It isn't possible, I'd never have believed that a human being could do that!', Mme de Cambremer, as a woman who had received a sound musical education, beating time with her head, transformed for the nonce into the pendulum of a metronome, the sweep and rapidity of whose oscillations from one shoulder to the other (performed with that look of wild abandonment in her eye which a sufferer shows when he has lost control of himself and is no longer able to master his pain, saying merely 'I can't help it') so increased that at every moment her diamond earrings caught in the trimming of her bodice, and she was obliged to straighten the bunch of black grapes which she had in her hair, though without any interruption of her constantly accelerated motion.

(I, 322 / I, 395)

Were this a Kingsley Amis novel that would be the end of that. The absurdity of the two women would be implicitly or explicitly contrasted to the sturdy common sense of the hero, and his aesthetic and moral superiority would be confirmed. But Proust will not let it rest there. He senses that though the two women *are* absurd, their attitudes are only our own carried to ridiculous lengths and perceived by an implacable viewer. For they are not just trying to show *others* how sensitive and musical they are; they are also trying to *persuade themselves* that what they are hearing means something to them, that they are engaged in more than a meaningless social ritual. And this is something we all need to do, indeed something we all do most of the time. Most of us are content to reach for the first phrase that comes to mind to explain our feelings to ourselves, 'wonderful music'; or 'fantastic performance!'; or, like Swann reviewing his passion for Odette: 'To think that I gave up the best years of my life for a woman who was not my type.'

But Marcel differs from us, and from Swann, as I have said, in his unwillingness to be fobbed off by such ready-made phrases. This leads to frustration, of course, as when, unable to convey his feelings about the beauty of the day to himself in any coherent fashion, he is driven to striking the ground with his umbrella and crying out: 'Zut, zut, zut, zut!' Or it leads to the slightly more concerted attempt to overcome his frustration by writing about it, as with the puzzling experience of the three spires. Often it leads to a simple conflict within him which he seems unable to resolve until the experience is repeated and we realise that *now* he is starting to understand precisely because he has never quite let the puzzling experience go.

This comes out very clearly in the two visits made by the young Marcel to the theatre in order to see la Berma acting in *Phèdre*. Marcel has been burning with desire to see the great actress in the greatest play in the French language, and eventually his parents give in and let him go. He is in a state of high excitement: 'What I demanded from this performance – as from the visit to Balbec and the visit to Venice for which I had so intensely longed – was something quite different from pleasure: verities pertaining to a world more real than that in which I lived, which, once acquired, could never be taken from me again by any trivial accident ... of my otiose existence' (I, 434 / II, 15). Needless to say, he is profoundly disappointed. While the two actresses who precede Berma do give some hint of what he has been looking for, she herself delivers the great declaration of love to Hippolyte 'so rapidly that it was only when she had come to the last line that my mind became aware of the deliberate monotony which she had imposed on it throughout' (I, 441 / II, 23). However, when the audience erupts in frenzied applause 'I mingled my own with theirs, endeavouring to prolong it so that Berma, in her gratitude, should surpass herself, and I be certain of having heard her on one of her great days'. And the more he applauds the better, it seems to him, has Berma been acting. A woman sitting next to him whispers: 'Now I really call that acting, don't you?' and Marcel, 'happy to find ... reasons for Berma's superiority', drinks in her words. Nevertheless, when the curtain does finally fall he cannot hide from himself a certain feeling of disappointment (I, 442 / II, 24).

That evening, though, the great diplomat, M. de Norpois, has been invited to dinner by his parents, and, when Marcel's father proudly tells him that his son has been to see Berma in *Phèdre* that afternoon, Norpois grandly pronounces: 'I have never seen Mme Berma in *Phèdre*, but I have always heard that she is excellent in the part. You were charmed with her, of course?' A man as intelligent and cultured as M. de Norpois, thinks Marcel, 'must know that hidden truth which I had failed to extract from Berma's playing, and would reveal it to me'. To his father's horror he admits to having been disappointed. Norpois takes this in his stride and, turning to Marcel's mother, explains to her the reasons for the actress's greatness. Of course his speech is nothing but a string of platitudes: 'The perfect taste that she shows in her choice of roles'; 'brings the same good taste to the choice of her costumes' as to her acting; 'her admirable voice', on which she plays as on a musical instrument; etc., etc. Nevertheless, it suffices almost to persuade Marcel: 'It's true!' he thinks, 'what a beautiful voice, what an absence of shrillness, what simple costumes, what intelligence to have chosen *Phèdre*! No, I have not been disappointed' (I, 448–9 / II, 31–2).

But Marcel goes on turning over his experiences of that afternoon, his personal disappointment constantly coming up against the view of Berma held by the world. And it is this refusal to yield to the pull of one side or the other, his personal impressions and what the world says, his need to bring the two into harmony rather than allowing one to triumph over the other, which characterises Marcel and will in the end make it possible for him to write the book he had always obscurely felt he had it in him to write. The next time he sees Berma on stage he understards what it was he had missed the first time, and the reason why he had, as well as finding the real reasons for her greatness to replace the clichés used by others. This second visit to the theatre, it will be noted, has nothing of Barthes's attitude to re-reading. It is not that, disappointed the first time, Marcel now decides to amuse himself 'against the grain' of the performance. On the contrary, he goes reluctantly, expecting little, and is overwhelmed by the truth.

The two pages which describe the effect on Marcel of this second visit to the theatre are among the richest in the entire novel, and need to be read with as much care as those concerned with Giotto's Charity. 'Miraculously', the narrator says,

> like those lessons which we have laboured in vain to learn overnight and find intact, got by heart, on waking up next morning, and like those faces of dead friends which the impassioned efforts of our memory pursue without recapturing and which, when we

are no longer thinking of them, are there before our eyes just as they were in life, the talent of Berma, which had evaded me when I sought so greedily to grasp its essence, now, after these years of oblivion, in this hour of indifference, imposed itself on my admiration with the force of self-evidence.

Formerly, he says, he had tried in some way to subtract *Racine*'s effect from that of the actress so as to discover in the surplus what was the essence of her genius.

But he says, this talent, which I sought to discover outside the part itself, was indissolubly one with it. So with a great musician . . ., his playing is that of so fine a pianist that one is no longer aware that the performer is a pianist at all . . . because his playing has become so transparent, so imbued with what he is interpreting, that one no longer sees the performer himself – he is simply a window opening upon a great work of art.

Before, he had contrasted Berma's diction unfavourably with that of the actresses playing Aricie and Ismène, because they at least seemed to convey a little of what one might expect from great acting. But now he understands that Berma's genius resides precisely in *not* allowing anything 'actressy' to intervene between her and her role. Like Giotto's Charity, like the nun and the surgeon evoked by Proust in connection with her, Berma is wholly subsumed into her role, while the other two, a little like Mme Verdurin or the two ladies at the concert, are concerned to let the audience know how deeply they are feeling:

Berma's voice, in which there subsisted not one scrap of inert matter refractory to the mind, betrayed no visible sign of that surplus of tears which, because they had been unable to soak into it, one could feel trickling down the voice of Aricie or Ismène, but had been delicately refined down to its smallest cells like the instrument of a master violinist in whom, when one says that he produces a beautiful sound, one means to praise not a physical peculiarity but a superiority of soul . . .

And it is the same with her movements and even with the white veils in which she is draped:

All these, voice, posture, gestures, veils, round this embodiment of an idea which a line of poetry is (an embodiment that, unlike our human bodies, is not an opaque screen, but a purified, spiritualised garment), were merely additional envelopes which, instead of concealing, showed up in greater splendour the soul that had assimilated them to itself and had spread itself through them . . . So Berma's interpretation was, around Racine's work, a second work, quickened also by genius.

Instead of asking the audience to respond to the depth of her feeling or the brilliance of her technique, la Berma loses herself in the role. Or rather, she finds herself in the role, making it live again as she incarnates it.

Marcel now understands that his initial mistake was to confront the performance with 'a pre-existent, abstract and false idea of dramatic genius', committing the same mistake as he had made in his encounter with Gilberte in the Champs-Elysées: 'I had come to her with too strong a desire.' Moreover, in both cases –

we have brought with us the ideas of 'beauty', 'breadth of style', 'pathos' and so forth which we might at a pinch have the illusion of recognising in the banality of a conventional face or talent, but our critical spirit has before it the insistent challenge of a form of which it possesses no intellectual equivalent, in which it must disengage the unknown element. It hears a sharp sound, an oddly interrogative inflexion. It asks itself: 'Is that good? Is what I am feeling now admiration? Is that what is meant by richness of colouring, nobility, strength?' And what answers it again is a sharp voice, a curiously questioning tone, the despotic impression, wholly material, caused by a person whom one does not know, in which no scope is left for 'breadth of interpretation'. And for this reason it is the really beautiful works that, if we listen to them with sincerity, must disappoint us most keenly, because in the storehouse of our ideas there is none that responds to an individual impression.

(II, 347–52 / III, 46–9)

We thus see here the same pattern at work as in Marcel's love affairs and in the episode of the pregnant kitchen-maid and Giotto's Charity: an initial disappointment, as Marcel tries to read the play or painting in a certain way, to read it to conform with his prior imaginings and with the way he has been brought up to do; and then a dawning understanding of a new mode of reading, forced on him by his greater experience and by the work or person themselves, which leads him to understand what Giotto and la Berma were up to. In both cases we could say that a post-Renaissance way of reading, certainly a post-Romantic one, which he had taken to be the natural one, a reading in terms of psychology and individuality, is replaced by a different mode. We could call these the medieval and the Symbolist, but such terms only set up another screen in place of the first. Better to say that in both cases Marcel discovers a human truth which is not so much psychological as physiological, a truth about the way men and women really are in the world, not as they (we) imagine they are.

What both Giotto's Charity and la Berma's acting reveal to Proust eventually is that the face of true goodness is the face of one totally caught up in a selfless activity, giving themselves up to it and becoming one with it. But Marcel's insight is not simply an ethical one. If he as a writer is to be true to it he will have to find a way of presenting human beings, as Homer does, as Giotto and Dante do, as part of a larger whole, making their way through life only partly consciously and only partly in control of their destinies. To do this will require not just understanding, not just vision, but the forging of an appropriate style.

This is what Proust has been groping for all his adult life. His dissatisfaction with *Jean Santeuil*, with his Ruskin translations and prefaces, with his delightful set of pastiches and his profound and moving essays on writers, painters and composers, with his critique of Sainte-Beuve, was at heart a dissatisfaction with himself. But work on all these led inexorably, as we can see in retrospect, to *A la recherche*, which embodies elements of all these past works, but takes them up into a fictional narrative which moves beyond each and every one of them. In this narrative form and content at last become one, as they do for Giotto and the Middle Ages, and as they do for la Berma.

Proust's style is often admired or derided in itself, but it should be seen as part of his quest for truth, part of his effort to move, as it were, from Mme de Verdurin, or at least Swann, to Giotto's Charity, to la Berma, to Vinteuil and Elstir, to his grandmother and mother.

Just before the description of the two ladies listening to Liszt in the music-room of the Marquise de Sainte-Euverte, the narrator describes, again through Swann's eyes, but moving well beyond Swann's vision, three men, all characterised by their monocles. The last of these is M. de Palancy:

> Meanwhile, behind him M. de Palancy, who with his huge carp's head and goggling eyes moved slowly through the festive gathering, periodically unclenching his mandibles as though in search of his orientation, had the air of carrying about upon his person only an accidental and perhaps purely symbolic fragment of the glass wall of his aquarium, a part intended to suggest the whole, which recalled to Swann, a fervent admirer of Giotto's Virtues

and Vices at Padua, that figure representing Injustice by whose
side a leafy bough evokes the idea of the forests that enshroud
his secret lair.

(I, 322 / I, 394)

Injustice

Giotto's mode need not be confined to the Middle Ages, Proust
discovers; it is up to the contemporary artist to find the equivalent
for himself. And this is possible, for it is not just a convention, a trick
of style, but rather the expression of a vision which grasps the fact
that human beings are more and other than what they imagine, and
that to capture this we must escape from the merely psychological
and biographical. What I said earlier about the Giottos holds good
for M. de Palancy: it is not allegory but the compression into one
image of a whole state of being which will emerge in our ways of
moving, of eating, of dressing, of dying, as well as in what we think
and feel.

M. de Palancy makes another appearance in the novel, this time
in the theatre just before Marcel's revelation about la Berma's
acting. This is not surprising as the entire theatre, which Marcel is
observing with much more interest than he will show in the start
of the performance, is described entirely in terms of marine life,

which is the appropriate setting for its centrepiece, the queen of marine life, the Princesse de Guermantes.

The Marquis de Palancy, his face bent downwards at the end of his long neck, his round bulging eye glued to the glass of his monocle, moved slowly around in the transparent shade and appeared no more to see the public in the stalls than a fish that drifts past, unconscious of the press of curious gazers, behind the glass wall of an aquarium. Now and again he paused, venerable, wheezing, moss-grown, and the audience could not have told whether he was in pain, asleep, swimming, about to spawn, or merely taking breath. No one aroused in me so much envy as he, on account of his apparent familiarity with this box and the indifference with which he allowed the Princess to hold out to him her box of sweets.

(III, 41)

[Par moments il s'arrêtait, vénérable, soufflant et moussu, et les spectateurs n'auraient pu dire s'il souffrait, dormait, nageait, était en train de pondre ou respirait seulement. Personne n'excitait en moi autant d'envie que lui, à cause de l'habitude qu'il avait l'air d'avoir de cette baignoire et de l'indifférence avec laquelle il laissait la princesse lui tendre des bonbons.

(II, 343)

This is very funny, but again, though it may remind us of certain English satirists, or even of a master of the grotesque description such as Dickens, the effect in Proust is neither temporary nor local, but in keeping with the whole novel: it reveals to us a truth which habit and our conventional ways of thinking would have kept hidden from us had not Proust, through his vision and his style, uncovered it for us, 'expressing', as he puts it in a general comment about the role of art, 'the essence of the impression that something produces, an essence which remains impenetrable by us so long as genius has not unveiled it'.

In this sense Proust's novel does what he suggests the music of Vinteuil and the paintings of Elstir do: not lift us into a higher world of Beauty and Truth, but reveal to us what we had always known but could not articulate, and so in a sense did not know at all. But there is of course a sense in which Proust's novel is utterly different from the works of Elstir and Vinteuil, Giotto or Bonnard. For it not only presents us with M. de Palancy and Mme Verdurin, it also shows us Marcel moving from incomprehension to understanding (in the case of Giotto's Charity or la Berma's acting), and from frustration and silence to speech and release (in the case of his own art).

Like Coleridge, Marcel comes to see that though he may dream of becoming a famous writer, this is perhaps the result of self-delusion, that he had perhaps mistaken 'a strong desire' for 'original power'. As a child he daydreams of sauntering hand in hand with the Duchesse de Guermantes in the grounds of her property, while she begs him to tell her what he hopes one day to write. 'And these dreams', he says, 'reminded me that, since I wished some day to become a writer, it was high time to decide what sort of books I was going to write. But as soon as I asked myself the question, and tried to discover some subject to which I could impart a philosophical significance of infinite value, my mind would stop like a clock, my consciousness would be faced with a blank, I would feel either that I was wholly devoid of talent or that perhaps some malady of the brain was hindering its development.' But, unlike Coleridge, Proust / Marcel does not accept this state of affairs. In a volte-face which seems like a sudden flash of insight but is in fact the fruit of a lifetime's patient probing, he comes to understand that this very problem is to be the theme of his novel. This insight is strictly comparable to the one which led Freud to advance to his true vocation by grasping that what was important was not whether his patients had indeed been molested by their fathers when they were young, only that they had imagined that they had; and to the one which led Wittgenstein to grasp that the proper business of philosophy is not the unveiling of some Great Truth about the limits of our language but the patient unravelling of the intricate steps of confusion and self-misunderstanding by which we come to persuade ourselves of the existence of such a Great Truth. Suddenly, what had been holding Proust back becomes the very thing that impels him forward; trusting fiction at last, after having, like Dante, flirted for a decade with ideas, and trusting that fiction, if undertaken with enough openness and patience, will lead him by way of error to the truth, he begins, in 1907–8, to write the book he will never stop writing till his death.

In the book as we have it we begin by seeing the world, first of Marcel's childhood, and then of his adolescence and young manhood. But as the book progresses, describing for us one sentimental and literary setback after another, something else begins to thrust itself into the frame. It is not Marcel's psyche or character, for as I hope I have made sufficiently plain, Proust's whole enterprise is profoundly inimical to autobiography and memoir – but himself in his whole being, swimming through the sea of life like M. de Palancy, his eye fixed on the object like the nun and the surgeon evoked in connection with Giotto's Charity: a being existing in time, fulfilling to the best of his abilities what he had it in him to do, with no more thought than Dante's Virgil for the glory his work might bring him, but concerned simply to do it well and to go on doing it till death should come to claim him.

7 Franz Kafka: the innocent pretence

Everyone on earth feels a tickling at the heels, the small chimpanzee and the great Achilles alike.

Kafka

Amongst the little group of aphorisms or meditations which Kafka wrote down as a sequence some time between October 1917 and February 1918 is one which reads: 'A stair that has not been deeply hollowed by footsteps is, from its own point of view, merely something that has been bleakly put together out of wood.' The general sentiment reminds us of innumerable Romantic and post-Romantic writers, such as Hölderlin, Rilke and Heidegger, but only Kafka would have had the wit and empathy with the victim to see things from the point of view of the poor modern staircase, with no past to give it dignity and meaning and therefore in a sense no present and no future either.

There is little doubt that Kafka identified with the poor modern staircase. A year or two later he was to write to Milena: 'Nothing is granted to me, everything has to be earned, not only the present and the future, but the past too – something after all which perhaps every human being has inherited, this too must be earned, it is perhaps the hardest work.' And if we feel that here, as everywhere in these terrible letters, there is more than a touch of self-pity and even of masochism, the same cannot be said for the aphorism. Indeed, the phrase 'from its own point of view' suggests that others might not notice *and would be right not to notice* the difference between this staircase and other, longer-lived, more footworn ones. It is even possible to read the aphorism as suggesting that it is in the nature of newly erected staircases to see themselves in this light, to idealise older ones and despise themselves.

But the argument cuts both ways: if the wise older staircase can amusedly note that the newly built one is not, after all, so different from itself, that it only imagines that it is, then it may be that the older staircase too retains a memory of itself as having been 'bleakly put together out of wood', of being a construction, and a rather haphazard one at that, rather than a fact of nature. Another, rather longer piece from a group Kafka wrote down in his diaries in 1920, and to which Max Brod gave the collective title 'He', brings out the ambiguity rather more clearly:

He remembers a picture that represented a summer Sunday on the Thames. The whole breadth of the river was filled with boats, waiting for the lock-gate to be opened. In all the boats were gay young people in light, bright-coloured clothing; they were almost reclining there, freely abandoned to the warm air and the coolness of the water. They had so much in common that their convivial spirit was not confined to the separate boats; joking and laughter was passed on from boat to boat. He now imagined that in a meadow on the bank . . . he himself was standing. He was contemplating the festival, which was not really a festival at all, but still one could call it that. He naturally had a great desire to join in, indeed he longed to do so, but he was forced to admit that he himself was excluded from it, it was impossible for him to fit in there; to do so would have required such great preparation that in the course of it not only this Sunday, but many years, and he himself, would have passed away; and even if time here could have come to a standstill, it would still have been impossible to achieve any other result; his whole origin, upbringing, physical development would have had to be different. So far removed, then, was he from these holiday-makers, and yet for all that he was very close to them too, and that was the more difficult thing to understand. They were, after all, human beings like himself, nothing human could be utterly alien to them, and so if one were to probe into them, one would surely find that the feeling which dominated him and excluded him from the river party was alive in them too, but of course with the difference that it was very far from dominating them and merely haunted some darker corners of their being.

We are all of us subject to such a feeling, this suggests, but for most of us it remains at the outer corners of our being and does not totally dominate us. For the observer, unfortunately, because of his origin, upbringing and physical development, it is absolutely central and could never be eradicated even if he were to live a thousand years, even if time were to stand still. In other words it is not a question of a difference which might be resolved by an adjustment over time but an ontological difference: the others seem to find life natural, they appear to be 'inside' it, trusting it completely and drawing their strength and their happiness from such trust, while he, for whatever reason, lacks that trust and can only look in on life from the outside with longing and despair. And yet the word 'haunted', like the word 'bleakly' in the first piece, troubles the surrounding phrases. On the one hand, it suggests, though we are all of us dimly aware of such feelings of exclusion, they do not occupy the centre or our being; but perhaps, precisely because that is the case, we are even more in thrall to them, haunted by them, than he who faces them head-on every day. Kierkegaard suggested as much when he said that the first stage of despair is not to know that you are in despair, for then you are perpetually dragged down by it, whereas if you acknowledge it you may be on the road to overcoming it. So is the watcher on the bank not perhaps really happier than the laughing youths in the boats? Or at least one stage further along the road out of unhappiness? Kafka, much less confident than Kierkegaard, certainly much less polemical, would certainly not go so far. He might even suggest that that kind of thought is precisely what would occur to a watcher on the bank and be simply further evidence of his exclusion. And yet the hint is there, troubling the picture and the apparently simple schema.

Kafka seems always to have been in the grip or this sense of being excluded from what comes naturally to others. A passage in his early, unfinished and discarded novel, *Description of a Struggle*, sounds the theme distinctly: 'Once when I was a child and just waking up from a short afternoon nap, still half asleep, I heard my mother calling down from the balcony in the most natural voice: "What are you doing, my dear? It's so hot." And a woman answered from the garden: "I'm having tea on the lawn." She said it quite simply and without insistence, as if it were to be taken quite for granted.' But nothing, it seems, could be taken for granted in this way by the young Kafka.

The reasons for this state of affairs have been extensively rehearsed: the sensitive only son of a loutish, bullying, self-made businessman; the German-speaking Jew in a Prague beginning to stir with Czech nationalism; the sickly employee of an insurance firm whose only desire is to have time enough to get on with his writing, who discovers, in the course of his life, that that writing excludes not only the possibility of regular office hours but also any sort of normal life, including marriage. Everything, it seems, has conspired to isolate him: his upbringing; his ambiguous relation to that ambiguous condition, Jewishness; his body. But what complicates the picture where Kafka is concerned is that he comes to discover that it is not a question of his writing versus the claims of the world but that for his writing to make any sense at all it has itself to spring from the naturalness he so admires in others, even though he so signally lacks it himself: in the young people boating on the Thames, in the woman in the garden, in his active and aggressive father, in those who marry and settle down, in Felice and Milena and all the other women he so disastrously fell in love with.

Where, for Proust, life was moulded by his gentle and loving mother, for Kafka it was moulded by his father's sheer size, brutality, coarseness and zest for life: 'I was, after all, depressed even by your mere physical presence', he writes in the enormous letter he wrote to his father in 1917 but, typically, never sent. He goes on:

> I remember, for instance, how often we undressed together in the same bathing-hut. There was I, skinny, weakly, slight, you strong, tall, broad. Even inside the hut I felt myself a miserable specimen, and what's more not only in your eyes, but in the eyes of the whole world, for you were for me the measure of all things. But then when we went out of the bathing-hut before the people, I with you holding my hand, a little skeleton, unsteady, barefoot on the boards, frightened of the water, incapable of copying your swimming-strokes, which you, with the best of intentions, but actually to my profound humiliation, always kept on showing me, then I was frantic with desperation and all my bad experiences in all spheres at such moments fitted magnificently together.

The tone here is characteristic of the letter as a whole: Kafka manages to convey both a deep resentment at the way his father treated him, humiliated him, made him loathe his body, and a profound admiration for this man who was everything he could never be. And not just for his physical presence, but for everything he had achieved: 'Marrying, founding a family, accepting all the children that come, supporting them in this insecure world and even guiding them a little as well is, I am convinced, the utmost a human being can succeed in doing at all.' So far so clear. But then, as always with Kafka, come the qualifications: 'That seemingly so many succeed in this is no evidence to the contrary, for, first, there are not many who do, in fact, succeed, and secondly these not-many don't "do" it, it merely "happens" to them.' The ambiguity of his response rises to the surface and is held there in the constantly shifting emphases of the language: does the fact that things 'merely happen' to others while for himself everything has to be 'done' damn the others or himself?

Part of the problem lies in the two radically different views of his father which co-exist in Kafka. On the one hand Hermann Kafka stands for normality, for what is natural, for family life. His own father had been a butcher in a village in Southern Bohemia. He had got to Prague by dint of hard work and he was determined that his children would not have to experience the poverty and degradation he had known in his native village, but would absorb the dominant German culture and move ever upwards in the world. One can sympathise with these ambitions. But for Kafka his father was at the same time someone who had made his way in the world by crushing all who stood in his path, who behaved with rudeness and even brutality to his own employees, and who was determined to put the *shtetl* and its traditions for ever behind him. One can imagine the father's horror at finding his son reluctant to follow in his footsteps and even consorting with Jews of the very type he had striven to escape from all his life. No wonder he remarked bitterly to his son on discovering the closeness of his ties with the actor Yitzhak Löwy, 'He who lies with dogs picks up fleas.' And no wonder his son resented this and condemned his father's purely social Judaism and his dismissal of forms of life which seemed to him so rich in meaning and spirituality.

The ambiguities surrounding his relations to his father were reproduced in his relations to marriage. On the one hand marriage and the nurturing of children would allow him to enter the world of normality; but on the other hand it was a way of turning into his father and a part of him could not stomach that. Thus 'the plans to marry became the most large-scale and hopeful attempt to escape, and then the failure was on a correspondingly large scale, too'. For Kafka his father and fatherhood were inseparable. Marriage for him only made sense if it was the prelude to fatherhood; yet could he lend himself to this act, which had perhaps once been sanctioned by sacrament but now seemed merely a 'happening'? Others seemed to act and live as though all they did they did by natural birthright, but, for Kafka, the very thought of this was sickening. Perhaps this was the result of his profound awareness of the nature of sacrament and thus his horror at not merely the fact of its absence in modern life, but at the fact that nobody seemed to notice its absence. Or perhaps it was the result of his own unnatural hatred of the body. All he could tell was that birth aroused in him a peculiar horror: 'The sight of the double bed at home, the used sheets, the night-shirts carefully laid out, can exasperate me to the point of nausea, can turn me inside out; it is as if I had not been definitely born, were continually born anew into the world of that stale life in that stale room, had constantly to seek confirmation of myself there, were indissolubly joined with all that loathsomeness, in part even if not entirely, at least it still clogs my feet which want to run, they are still stuck fast in the original shapeless pulp.'

This is so powerful, so violent, that we may be tempted to give it a purely private meaning, to seek the roots of it in Kafka's private life and in his unique relations with his parents. But it is worth remembering that the horror of childbirth is to be found expressed by a number of modern writers. 'What finished me was birth', says the narrator of Beckett's novella, *First Love*, as he prepares to decamp from the flat he has been sharing with a woman on learn-

ing that she is about to give birth to their child. 'Mirrors and copu-
lation are abominable', says Borges more than once, 'because they
increase the number of men.' It is not that Beckett and Borges hate
humanity but that they sense that fatherhood is the attempt by
humankind to make nature and meaning converge, to create not in
the full awareness of what you are doing but out of a mixture of
chance and erotic desire. Perhaps because they feel that they themselves were so conceived they feel that they have not been fully born
and so are not fully alive.

How to overcome this feeling of not having been definitely born?
For Kafka, as for Beckett and Borges, the only hope seems to lie in
the one thing they find they really want to do: write. 'It is easy to
recognise a concentration in me of all my forces on writing', Kafka
confides to his diary on 3 January 1912.

> When it became clear in my organism that writing was the most
> productive direction for my being to take, everything rushed in
> that direction and left empty all those abilities which were
> directed towards the joys of sex, eating, drinking, philosophical
> reflection, and above all music. I atrophied in all these directions.
> This was necessary because the totality of my strengths was so
> slight that only collectively could they even half-way serve the
> purpose of my writing. Naturally, I did not find this purpose inde-
> pendently and consciously, it found itself, and is now interfered
> with only by the office, but that interferes with it completely
> . . . I need only throw my work in the office out of this complex
> in order to begin my real life in which, with the progress of my
> work, my face will finally be able to age in a natural way.

Looking back from the end of his life to that golden year of promise,
1912, we can see that Kafka is being wildly romantic in his belief
that only the office lies in the way of the natural growth of his

writing and his life. What the next few years will teach him is that the problem lies in writing itself – but that discovery is still some way away.

What is in no doubt is that from the start words had for him an extraordinary physical reality. In only the second sentence of the diaries he jots down a phrase he has overheard and comments on it: ' "If he should forever ahsk me." The *ah*, released from the sentence, flew off like a ball on the meadow.' (' "Wenn er mich immer frägt." Das ä, losgelöst vom Satz, flog dahin wie ein Ball auf der Wiese.') In 1911 he notes: 'I live only here and there in a small word in whose vowel ("thrust" in the above sentence, for instance) I lose my useless head for a moment. The first and last letters are the beginning and end of my fish-like emotion.'

Words make such a profound and immediate impression that 'when I arbitrarily write a single sentence, for instance, "He looked out of the window", it already has perfection.' But by the same token there are other times when nothing he writes down has any value at all: 'The tremendous world I have in my head. But how to free myself and free it without being torn in pieces? And a thousand times rather be torn in pieces than retain it in me or bury it. That, indeed, is why I am here, that is quite clear to me.' This is the predominant mood of those early diary entries: he feels he has so much to say but everything he puts down is a travesty and a mockery of that feeling. 'I can't write', he tells Brod in 1910, 'I haven't written a single line that I can accept, instead I have crossed out all I have written – there wasn't much – since my return from Paris. My whole body puts me on my guard against each word; each word, before even letting itself be put down, has to look round on every side; the phrases positively fall apart in my hands, I see what they are like inside and then I have to stop quickly.'

'How is it possible to write at all if one has so much to say and knows that the pen can only trace an uncertain and random trail through the mass of what has to be said?' he writes to Felice. What he is after in his writing, he notes in January 1911, is 'a description in which every word would be linked to my life, which I would draw to my heart and which would transport me out of itself'. 'Wrote badly', he notes in October of that year, 'without really arriving at that freedom of true description which releases one's foot from the experienced.' The dream he has of writing is of something in which every word is linked to his life and yet where the whole would release him from the drudgery and horror of life. It is surely no coincidence that the image used here is the same as that brought on by the sight of the unmade bed at home, whose loathsomeness 'still clogs my feet which want to run, they are still stuck fast in the original shapeless pulp'.

If words are like bodies, banging against each other, flying apart from each other, then the body is very like an unruly sentence, filled with violent and contradictory impulses which cannot easily be harnessed. The sign of this is the gesture. 'It is so easy to be cheerful at the beginning of summer', he writes in a letter to Brod in August 1904. 'One has a lively heart, a reasonably brisk gait, and can face the future with a certain hope. One expects something out of the Arabian Nights, while disclaiming any such hope with a comic bow and bumbling speech . . . And when people ask us about the life we intend to live, we form the habit, in spring, of answering with an expansive wave of the hand, which goes limp after a while, as if to say that it was ridiculously unnecessary to conjure up such things.' This is the world of Kafka's febrile line drawings, which show ludicrously tall or squat people stretching, twisting, leaning towards or away from one another, in what would be grotesque if it were an attempt at realism but which instead conveys perfectly how we sometimes feel, both constrained in our bodies and lunging free, both playing a game and close to desperation. The early diaries are full of detailed descriptions of gesturing, which seems to be a sign of frustration when it is he himself who is doing the gesturing, but is clearly also as much a part of his extreme sensitivity to others as his response to words.

In a late diary entry (24 January 1922) Kafka, looking back at his life, quite specifically linked his writing with such gesturing: 'Childish games (though I was well aware that they were so) marked the beginning of my intellectual decline. I deliberately cultivated a facial tic, for instance, or would walk across the Graben with arms crossed behind my head. A repulsively childish but successful game. (My writing began in the same way . . .)' Yet in those early years he is less hard on himself, aware that his attitude to gestures, like his attitude to words, is a gift as well as a curse. On 30 September 1911 he notes in his diary: 'Szafransky, a disciple of Bernhardt's, grimaces while he observes and draws in a way that resembles what is drawn. Reminds me that I too have a pronounced talent for metamorphosing myself, which no one notices. How often I must have imitated Max. Yesterday evening, on the way home, if I had observed myself from the outside I should have taken myself for Tucholsky.'

The problem is that he doesn't seem to know what to do with this talent, as with his extreme sensitivity to words. On 5 November 1911 he records his bitterness and sense of isolation as Max Brod reads out to a group of friends 'my little motor-car story': 'The disordered sentences of this story with holes into which one could stick both hands; one sentence sounds high, one sentence sounds low, as the case may be, one sentence rubs against another like the tongue against a hollow or false tooth; one sentence comes marching up with so rough a start that the entire story falls into sulky amazement.' He dreams then of being able one day to write 'something large and whole, well shaped from beginning to end', feeling that the story would then be able to detach itself from him 'and it would be possible for me calmly and with open eyes, as a blood relation of a healthy story, to hear it read'.

We don't know what the 'little motor-car story' was, but there are

several examples in the diaries of fragments of narrative followed
by Kafka's caustic comments on them. On 10 March 1912, for
example, he tries out the following:

> He seduced a girl in a small place in the Iser mountains where
> he spent a summer to restore his delicate lungs. After a brief
> effort to persuade her, incomprehensibly, the way lung cases
> sometimes act, he threw the girl – his landlord's daughter, who
> liked to walk with him in the evening after work – down in the
> grass on the river bank and took her as she lay there unconscious
> with fright. Later he had to carry water from the river in his
> cupped hands and pour it over the girl's face to restore her. 'Julie,
> but Julie', he said countless times, bending over her. He was ready
> to accept complete responsibility for his offence and was only
> making an effort to make himself realize how serious his situa-
> tion was. Without thinking about it he could not have realized it.
> The simple girl who lay before him, now breathing regularly
> again, her eyes still closed because of fear and embarrassment,
> could make no difficulty for him; with the tip of his toe, he, the
> great, strong person, could push the girl aside. She was weak and
> plain, could what had happened to her have any significance that
> would last even until tomorrow? Would not anyone who com-
> pared the two of them have come to this conclusion? The river
> stretched calmly between the meadows and fields to the distant
> hills. There was still sunshine on the slope of the opposite shore.
> The last clouds were drifting out of that clear evening sky.

Here too his comment follows immediately: 'Nothing, nothing.
This is the way I raise up ghosts before me. I was involved, even if
only superficially, only in the passage, "Later he had" . . . mostly in
the "pour". For a moment I thought I saw something real in the
description of the landscape.' This is very revealing. Kafka is trying
to write conventional narrative and his heart isn't in it. The act does

not involve him, only its aftermath, because, we might speculate, the act is so arbitrary and brutal, mirroring the writer's act in inventing and putting down this anecdote. Once the deed is done, however, the reactions of his protagonist quicken his interest, and then the landscape, which has witnessed these goings on and will witness many more, becomes something he can feel excited about conveying.

Despite his own self-criticism, or perhaps because of it, Kafka, like every artist, wants the world to confirm his sense that he has a very special talent, wants the world to convince him that he is wrong to be so critical. A diary entry for 19 January 1911 brings out what is at stake:

> Once I projected a novel in which two brothers fought each other, one of whom went to America while the other remained in a European prison. I only now and then began to write a few lines, for it tired me at once. So once I wrote down something about my prison on a Sunday afternoon when we were visiting my grandparents and had eaten an especially soft kind of bread, spread with butter, that was customary there. It is of course possible that I did it mostly out of vanity, and by shifting the paper about on the tablecloth, tapping with my pencil, looking around under the lamp, wanted to tempt someone to take what I had written from me, look at it, and admire me. It was chiefly the corridor of the prison that was described in the few lines, above all its silence and coldness . . . Perhaps I had a momentary feeling of the worthlessness of my description, but before that afternoon I never paid much attention to such feelings when among relatives to whom I was accustomed (my timidity was so great that the accustomed was enough to make me half-way happy), I sat at the round table in the familiar room and could not forget that I was young and called to great things out of this present tranquillity. An uncle who liked to make fun of people finally took the page that I was

holding only weakly, looked at it briefly, handed it back to me, even without laughing, and only said to the others who were following him with their eyes, 'The usual stuff', to me he said nothing. To be sure, I remained seated and bent as before over the now useless page of mine, but with one thrust I had in fact been banished from society, the judgement of my uncle repeated itself in me with what amounted almost to real significance and even within the feeling of belonging to a family I got an insight into the cold space of our world which I had to warm with a fire that first I wanted to seek out.

This stands, along with M. de Norpois's equally dismissive response to the young Marcel's literary efforts, as one of the key moments of modern literature. It is not an episode Dante or Shakespeare or Dr Johnson would have made much sense of, I suspect, for in their day it would have been pretty obvious if a young man was gifted or not, and 'the usual stuff' would have been exactly what would be expected of him, the only question being whether he had turned it out elegantly or not. In our world though – and in this respect Proust and Kafka inhabit our world – matters are different: few can spot what is truly original when it first appears, and the burden on the artist is for that reason much greater: should he trust his instincts, which have so often let him down, or the judgement of others, which seems so massively authoritative? Moreover, though he feels that writing is the only thing that can warm the coldness of the world, his own feelings about the writing he manages to produce only too often coincide with the judgement of others: 'The usual stuff'.

What makes the moment so important in both Kafka and Proust is not only that they had the ability to describe it, but that they had the resources of character to react to it, not by dismissing the judgement out of hand but by incorporating it into their work, thus both accepting and overcoming it.

Two and a half years after that terrible Sunday afternoon, on 24 May 1913, Kafka noted in his diary: 'In high spirits because I consider "The Stoker" so good. This evening I read it to my parents, there is no better critic than I when I read to my father, who listens with the most extreme reluctance. Many shallow passages followed by unfathomable depths.'

'The Stoker' is also a story about seduction, but the event is never described, only its aftermath. And it is also about imprisoning walls and a young man who goes to America, but this time we are dealing not with two brothers but with a single son. And now Kafka does not wait for someone to wrench the page from him and look at it. He has grown in confidence to such an extent that he actually reads it out loud to the sternest of judges, his father. And though as he reads he recognises that there are 'many shallow passages' in the story, he also notes that these are followed by 'unfathomable depths'. What has happened to change things to such an extent?

The brief answer is: two interrelated events, the meeting with Felice Bauer at Max Brod's in August 1912 and the experience of the night of 22 September 1912.

He had met Felice when she was on her way to Budapest from Berlin. On 20 September he wrote to her for the first time:

Dear Fraulein Bauer, In the likelihood that you no longer have the remotest recollection of me, I am introducing myself once more: my name is Franz Kafka, and I am the person who greeted you for the first time that evening at Director Brod's in Prague, the one who subsequently handed you across the table, one by one, photographs of a Thalia trip, and who finally, with the very hand now striking the keys, held your hand, the one which confirmed a promise to accompany him next year to Palestine.

Felice, a little taken aback, responded, releasing a torrent of letters. Kafka had made his choice and he was determined that Felice would lead him into the promised land of normality. In June of 1913 he proposed and she accepted him.

Meanwhile, on 23 September 1912 Kafka wrote a short story down in his diary and then commented:

> This story, 'The Judgement', I wrote at one sitting during the night of 22–23rd, from ten o'clock at night to six o'clock in the morning. I was hardly able to pull my legs out from under the desk, they had got so stiff from sitting. The fearful strain and joy, how the story developed before me, as if I were advancing over water. Several times during this night I heaved my own weight on my back. How everything can be said, how for everything, for the strangest fancies, there waits a great fire in which they perish and rise up again. How it turned blue outside the window. A wagon rolled by. Two men walked across the bridge . . . The appearance of the undisturbed bed, as though it had just been brought in. The conviction verified that with my novel-writing I am in the shameful lowlands of writing. Only *in this way* can writing be done, only with such coherence, with such a complete opening out of the body and the soul.

All his life Kafka was to look back to this night as the moment when his dream of writing was fulfilled. Here he had written the whole story in one go and it had satisfied his deepest desires. As a sign of that there was the bed, undisturbed, 'as though it had just been brought in', with no evidence of the insomniac's tossing and turning and no sign of that other use to which beds are put, that 'night work' as he calls it elsewhere, which leads to the birth, in that same bed, of children.

'The Judgement' opens with Georg Bendemann sitting at an open window from which, as from Kafka's own window, a bridge can be seen, daydreaming and writing a letter to a friend in far-off Russia. This is an image of the writer, in his room, with time on his hands to think and scribble, but who is cut off from the world by the pane in his window. Now, by bringing this image *into the story*, by presenting us in a story with the birth of stories, so to speak, Kafka suddenly finds a way forward. Just as his story of the two brothers had been dismissed in a single sentence by the 'Urteil des Onkels', the 'judgement of my uncle', so now both letter and daydreams and Georg himself are dismissed by Georg's father. The aged, enfeebled man, who is looked after by his strong young son in his widowhood suddenly rears up in bed where Georg had solicitously – as he no doubt put it to himself – tried to cover him up, and issues a judgement on the writer and dreamer: 'An innocent child, yes, that you were, truly, but still more truly have you been a devilish human being! – And therefore take note: I sentence you now to death by drowning!'

The terrible sentence is a strange kind of release for both Georg and the narrative: 'Georg felt himself urged from the room, the crash with which his father fell on the bed behind him was still in his ears as he fled . . . Out of the front door he rushed, across the roadway, driven towards the water.' The force which drives him makes all hesitation, all dreaming on his part a thing of the past. He swings himself over the side of the bridge, 'like the distinguished gymnast he had once been in his youth, to his parents' pride', and then lets himself drop. 'At this moment an unending stream of traffic was just going over the bridge.'

The indifferent landscape of the fragment about the rape has turned into an image of the world going on its way as Georg's life comes to an end. In the earlier fragment the narrator had been guilty but had seemed incapable of recognising his guilt; here he is guilty of no single evil act yet accepts his father's judgement and so brings his life and the story to its end. But it is as though the acceptance of that judgement had allowed a new kind of writing to be born, one where even the sense of excessive gesturing finds its place in the ludicrous but somehow melancholy phrase about him swinging over the side of the bridge 'like the distinguished gymnast he had once been'. A comic tone, quite foreign to his earlier writing, has been born out of the recognition that the most terrible things can be said.

Two days later 'The Stoker' was written. Karl Rossmann, as the long first sentence tells us, is being packed off to America by his parents for having got a servant girl with child, and the ship he is on has now entered New York harbour. But if America stands – as it has for so many immigrants and writers – for freedom, for the chance to forge ones own life, ones own narrative, in the wide open spaces and bustling cities, then the story promptly turns its back on it. Realising that he has left his umbrella 'down below', Karl turns back and, descending into the bowels of the ship, finds, in those narrow corridors and boiler-rooms, the space where Kafka's narrative feels most at home. Though he would try to write a complete novel about America, he never finished it, while stories about underground tunnels and burrowing moles proliferated in the years that followed.

Two months after writing 'The Judgement' and 'The Stoker' Kafka completed the greatest of his early works, 'Metamorphosis', and a year or so later the last of his early masterpieces, 'In the Penal Colony'. But if his writing had suddenly blossomed, his marriage plans had not. 'The Judgement' was dedicated to 'F', but Kafka soon found that Felice understood his work no more than his parents. Did that matter? Perhaps he had fallen in love with her precisely because she did not, because she was the image of solidity and down-to-earthness. Be that as it may, though they were first engaged in June 1913, in September he seems to have suffered some sort of breakdown and rushed off alone to a sanatorium in Riva where he had a brief affair with a young Christian girl. However, the engagement was renewed in January 1914 and in May Felice arrived in Prague to help him look for a flat for them to move into after their marriage. In June Kafka travelled to Berlin with his father for the official engagement; on 12 July there took place in the Hotel Askanischer Hof in Berlin the episode Kafka refers to as the 'tribunal', following which the engagement was again broken off. In August the war broke out, but by January 1915 Kafka and Felice had met again; in May he went on holiday with her and her friend, the enigmatic Grete Bloch (who later claimed to have had a child by Kafka); and in July 1916 he spent an extraordinarily happy fortnight in Marienbad with her. A year later they were once more officially engaged, but in August he had his first haemorrhage and wrote to her saying he would never see her again.

These facts suggest that Kafka's sense that marriage would be his salvation, his way of entering the world of ordinary humanity, met with an equally strong and even more primitive sense that when it came to it he could not go through with it. And it was to be the same with his writing: the great hope that flared up in him when he wrote 'The Judgement' was to be gradually tempered by the sense that writing was the ultimate snare, the devil's own way of destroying him. But that was still some way away. The failure of his quest for love and marriage and the outbreak of the war, though, may have coincided with a feeling that the four great early stories had perhaps been a little too Romantic in their embrace of death, a little too absolute in their endorsement of the judgement of the father. Whatever the reason, in the stories and parables he wrote from 1914 to 1920 a new spirit seems to take hold, one which seems to say: life is unbearable but we can bear it, and perhaps it is not so bad after all, perhaps, indeed, it is our human condition. These pieces constitute the most extensive fictional exploration of the nature and limits of trust known to me.

'We have a new advocate, Dr. Bucephalus', begins the first story in the collection Kafka painstakingly put together in 1919, *A Country Doctor*. 'There is little in his appearance to remind you that he was once Alexander of Macedon's battle charger. Of course, if you know his story, you are aware of something.' But even the usher at the law courts, who is presumably no classicist, though a keen race-goer, finds himself 'running an admiring eye over the advocate as he mounted the marble steps with a high action that made them ring beneath his feet'. However, this high-stepping urge is now kept well under control, for 'nowadays . . . there is no Alexander the Great'. Of course, even in Alexander's day 'the gates of India were beyond reach, yet the King's sword pointed the way to them'. Today, however, no-one even points the way – for in which direction would he point? It is true that many still carry swords, 'but only to brandish them, and the eye that tries to follow them is confused'. So, 'perhaps it is really best to do as Bucephalus has done and absorb oneself in law books. In the quiet lamplight, his flanks unhampered by the thighs of a rider, free and far from the clamour of battle, he reads and turns the pages of our ancient tomes.'

A terrible loss has been incurred, yet the last paragraph is neither pathetic not anguished, merely resigned: 'Perhaps it is really best to do as Bucephalus has done.' His flanks at least are unhampered by the thighs of any rider – yet we recall the high action of his legs as he strides up the staircase of the law courts, and feel the waste: a rider pressing him on to a specific goal would have made use of those marvellous attributes. As it is, he consoles himself by poring over ancient law books, though whether he does this out of a sense of duty or desire or merely in order to pass the time, the story does not say.

Resignation and its cost is also the theme of the last story in *A Country Doctor*. In 'A Report to an Academy' an ape addresses a distinguished academic gathering, explaining how he dragged himself by sheer will-power out of his simian condition and to his present exalted position in the world of men. The reason he has done this, he explains, is not from any innate desire on the part of apes to achieve the level of man but rather that, having been captured by men and shut up in a tiny cage, he understood that his only chance of escape lay in imitating those he could see walking about in freedom in front of his cage.

He cannot, he explains, really comply with the wishes of the academy which has so kindly invited him to speak and recount his life as an ape, for that life closed behind him the moment he was captured and was lost to sight for ever when he decided to transform himself. He can only recount the stages of his transformation: 'I could never have achieved what I have done had I been stubbornly set on clinging to my origins, to the remembrances of my youth', he explains, easily slipping into the tone of countless self-made men, Kafka's father among them. 'In revenge, however, my memory of the past has closed the door against me more and more.' As he grew increasingly at ease in the world of men, he goes on, 'the wind that blew after me out of my past began to slacken; today it is a gentle puff of air that plays around my heels'. 'To put it plainly', he tells his audience, 'your life as apes, gentlemen, insofar as something of that kind lies behind you, cannot be further removed from you than mine is from me.' And yet, 'everyone on earth feels a tickling at the heels; the small chimpanzee and the great Achilles alike'.

He has transformed himself, he explains, because he simply had no option. Not in order to find freedom, that is too large a word, but simply in order to find a way out of his horrible predicament as a captive. It is solely for that reason that he has learned to imitate the ways of men. As a result of this single-minded effort he is now able to command the best hotel suites and address such gatherings as the present one. And 'when I come home late at night from banquets, from scientific receptions, from social gatherings, there sits waiting for me a half-trained little chimpanzee and I take comfort from her as apes do'. And yet, 'by day I cannot bear to see her; for she has the insane look of the bewildered half-broken animal in her eye; no one else sees it, but I do, and I cannot bear it'.

So, like Alexander's horse, he has managed to accommodate himself to new conditions without nostalgia and without recrimination. It is a decent enough life, even, perhaps, in the eyes of some (the animal in his cage at the zoo for instance, or the soldier at the front), an enviable one. But it entails a hardening of oneself, a willed denial of the breeze licking about ones heels, of the look in the eyes of the half-broken animal one loves.

The richest story in the collection is the title one. It is clearly by the same author as wrote 'Metamorphosis', yet shows the distance Kafka has travelled from his early masterpieces. 'I was in great perplexity', it begins, 'I had to start on an urgent journey.' The journey is to a seriously ill patient in a village ten miles away, and the reason for his perplexity is that it is snowing heavily and his horse has died in the night. But it is also the writer's journey to the goal of his work, now that all the signposts on the terrain have been obliterated and he has no craft tradition on which to ride.

What is he to do? He kicks at the dilapidated door of an old empty pigsty and the door flies open, letting out the steamy smell of horses. A man crawls out on all fours, asking if he should yoke up. Two enormous horses follow him, 'with powerful flanks, . . . their legs tucked close to their bodies', their heads lowered as they squeeze out into the open. Soon they are standing before him and he orders the servant girl to help the groom. But before she can move the groom grabs hold of her and embraces her. She leaps away, revealing on her cheek the marks of two rows of teeth. Clearly the energy that has been unleashed is a dangerous one. The groom in fact orders him into the carriage, claps his hands and the horses fly off, while in his ears there sounds the shriek of the servant girl as she tries to barricade herself in against the groom. But though the doctor knows that her fate is sealed, a kind of sacrifice to his mission, he is already on his way, in fact has already arrived. The peasants drag him to the child's bedside, but though the patient whispers in his ear, 'Doctor, let me die', the doctor can at first find nothing wrong with him. He feels he has been called out needlessly once again and at the back of his mind is the thought that he must get back to help Rose, the servant girl. But as he examines the boy quickly one last time he suddenly realises that he is ill after all: 'In his right side, near the hip, was an open wound as big as the palm of my hand. Rose-red, in many variations of shade, dark in the hollows, lighter at the edges, softly granulated, with irregular clots of blood, open as a surface mine to the daylight.' But that is not all. As he looks at it closely he finds 'another complication. I could not help a low whistle of surprise. Worms, as thick and long as my little finger, themselves rose-red and blood-spotted as well, were wriggling from their fastness in the interior of the wound toward the light, with small white heads and many little legs. Poor boy, you were past helping. I had discovered your great wound; this blossom in your side was destroying you.'

Rose-red, like the name of the servant girl, this blossom is at once life and death. It is death because it is alive, like the story itself. But the horror does not overwhelm the story as it would have done the early ones. For no apparent reason the family and the village elders strip the doctor of his clothes while a school choir stands before the house, chanting

Strip his clothes off, then he'll heal us,
If he doesn't, kill him dead!
Only a doctor, only a doctor.

He is laid down next to the boy, against the wall, on the side of the wound, then everyone leaves and the door is shut. The singing stops; the whinnying horses thrust their heads in at the open windows. ' "Do you know," said a voice in my ear, "I have very little confidence in you. Why, you were only blown in here, you didn't come on your own feet. Instead of helping me, you're cramping me on my deathbed." ' He has not come here the way he should have and so cannot help. It is as though Dante had managed to get to the top of the mountain the first time and then had found that because he hadn't taken the long journey round he had no right to be there; it is as though, lacking any tradition to guide him on his journey into a story, only being able 'to trace an uncertain and random trail through the mass of what has to be said', he is bound to be shown up sooner or later as a sham and a fraud even if he does manage to reach his destination. He grabs his clothes and without waiting to dress leaps into his gig. But this time the horses do not race, the return is as protracted as the outward journey was quick: 'Like old men, we crawled through the snowy wastes; a long time echoed behind us the new but faulty song of the children:

> O be joyful, all you patients,
> The doctor's laid in bed beside you!'

'Never shall I reach home at this rate', he feels, 'my flourishing practice is done for, my successor is robbing me, but in vain, for he cannot take my place; in my house the disgusting groom is raging; Rose is his victim; I do not want to think about it any more.' He has been betrayed: 'A false alarm on the night bell once answered – it cannot be made good, not ever.'

This terrible story of horror and helplessness, of what happens when you decide to heed a call and how little use you in fact are to others, is balanced in the collection by one of the shortest stories, 'The Troubles of a Householder', or perhaps 'The Cares of a Family Man' – both titles have been used by translators. The problem is that *Hausvater* is untranslatable, suggesting as it does bourgeois solidity, ownership of property, family values. Into this *Hausvater*'s house comes Odradek, not exactly an object and not exactly a living creature, with a name which is not quite Slav and not quite German, shaped like a spool in the form of a star with little wooden crossbars attached. It is not that Odradek once had some sort of intelligible shape and is now only 'a broken-down remnant'; Odradek always looked like that, and perhaps it is we, with our notions of organic wholeness, who cannot make sense of him. He lurks in stairs and garrets and when you ask where he lives he squeaks: 'No fixed abode', and laughs – 'but it is only the kind of laughter that has no lungs behind it'. Naturally he gets on the nerves of the narrator. Is he always going to be rolling down the stairs 'before the feet of my children and my children's children?'

Where Kafka had once dreamed of a story as an organic whole with a life of its own, quite separate from the slime of himself, now he has come to accept that this may have been a mistake, a remnant of an old Romantic dream. A story is only an Odradek, able to move itself and us, able to speak, but it would be absurd to ask more of it. So long as Kafka believed in the Romantic idea that art would help him enter a more meaningful life, so long as he imagined that the test of the quality of his art was the amount of unbroken work he could put into it, it was inevitable that he would turn on himself and his surroundings in bitterness and frustration: he was lazy, he was weak, he was unhealthy, his family was suffocating him, his bachelorhood was crippling him, the office was destroying him, marriage would be the end of him. But now it is as though he had come to accept the Romantic folly of such dreams and such despair. Let him be satisfied with what he can do and accept that if it is not what he had dreamed of it is something.

But this is a precarious balance. Kafka is not embracing a post-Modernist *insouciance*, rejoicing simply in his ability to make. For the problem remains: such making is useless. We set out we know not where and even if we arrive at our destination we do not understand how we got there and so are of no use. Traditions, which once gave us the possibilities of life and art, have ossified and though we keep turning to them for guidance they only reflect our own bewilderment. Kafka warns against forgetting, but he does so by making us understand that remembering is no longer an option. For a tradition that needs to be remembered is no longer alive.

And yet one could look at it another way: perhaps it is possible to overcome the spirit of suspicion by simply imitating innocence. The clearest exposition of this cluster of themes is the little parable entitled 'The Silence of the Sirens'. The first paragraph tells us that it is going to be about 'proof that inadequate, even childish measures may serve to rescue one from peril'. Ulysses, as Homer tells us, filled his ears with wax and had himself bound to the mast of his ship. Actually, Homer tells us nothing of the sort. He tells us that Ulysses had the sailors' ears filled with wax and himself bound to the mast. Like that he would be able to hear the song of the sirens but not be dragged to his death by it while the sailors would row on unawares. In Kafka's version we are told that actually the song of the sirens can easily pierce through wax and that their song makes men so desirous of getting to them that mere chains will never hold them back. But innocent Ulysses does not know this and is pleased with his stratagem. However, the fable goes on, stronger even than their song is the silence of the sirens. Men may perhaps escape from their song but from their silence never. When Ulysses approached they did not sing. But Ulysses did not hear their silence, since his ears were filled with wax. 'He thought they were singing and that he alone did not hear them.' As he fixes his gaze firmly on the distance the Sirens vanish from his sight and mind. And they suddenly no longer desire to allure him, 'all that they wanted was to hold as long as they could the radiance that fell from Ulysses' great eyes'. Had they possessed consciousness they would have been annihilated at that moment; but as it is nothing happens except that Ulysses escapes them.

Now, says the tale, a codicil has been added to the foregoing. 'Ulysses, it is said, was so full of guile, was such a fox, that not even the goddess of fate could pierce his armour.' Perhaps he did notice that the sirens were silent, 'and held up to them and to the gods the aforementioned pretence merely as a sort of shield'. But here, says the story, 'human understanding is beyond its depth'.

This little story encapsulates most of what I have been trying to say in the course of this book. It tells use about the lightness of Homer and his heroes, a lightness which understanding cannot penetrate. And it tells us how innocence can overcome even the most powerful forces ranged against it, and how the cunning pretence of innocence is sometimes the same as innocence. But it also shows how the post-Romantic artist can be true to the world yet not broken on the contradiction between desire and achievement. He too requires an innocence, a primal innocence, an innocence which is indistinguishable from guile; if he possesses that precious gift it may be that his work will be able to travel safely across the page. But such innocence is not his as of right; it only becomes manifest in the act of writing.

The balance that Kafka achieved in the work he wrote between 1914 and 1920 could not be maintained. In a terrible letter to Brod of 5 July 1922 all the old demons of the pre-1912 period re-surface, but this time made more dreadful by the knowledge that if he could not achieve what he had dreamed of it was not his fault but inherent in the act of writing itself.

Last night as I lay sleepless and let everything continually veer back and forth between my aching temples, what I had almost forgotten during the last relatively quiet time became clear to me: namely, on what frail ground or rather altogether non-existent ground I live, over a darkness from which the dark power emerges when it wills and, heedless of my stammering, destroys my life. Writing sustains me, but is it not more accurate to say that it sustains this kind of life? By this I don't mean, of course, that my life is better when I don't write. Rather it is much worse then and wholly unbearable and has to end in madness . . . But what about being a writer itself? Writing is a sweet and wonderful reward, but for what? In the night it became clear to me, as clear as a child's lesson book, that it is the reward for serving the devil. This descent to the dark powers, this unshackling of spirits bound by nature, these dubious embraces and whatever else may take place in the nether parts which the higher parts no longer know, when one writes one's stories in the sunshine. Perhaps there are other forms of writing, but I know only this kind . . . And the diabolic element in it seems very clear to me. It is vanity and sensuality which continually buzz about one's own or even another's form – and feast on him . . . Sometimes a naive person will wish, 'I would like to be dead and see how everyone mourns me.' Such a writer is continually staging such a scene: He dies (or rather he does not live) and continually mourns himself. From this springs a terrible fear of death, which need not reveal itself as fear of death but may also appear as fear of change . . . The reasons for this fear of death may be divided into two main categories. First he has a terrible fear of dying because he has not yet lived. By this I do not mean that wife and child, fields and cattle are essential to living. What is essential to life is only to forgo complacency, to move into the house instead of admiring it and hanging garlands around it . . . The second réason – perhaps it is all really one, the two do not want to stay apart for me now – is the belief: 'What I have playacted is really going to happen. I have not bought myself off by my writing. I died my whole life long and now I will really die. My life was sweeter than other peoples' and my death will be more terrible by the same degree.'

To go into the house instead of admiring it and wreathing it with garlands. Once Kafka had imagined that writing would be a way of entering, now he feels that it is precisely writing that is keeping him outside. At the same time literature helps him live and keeps madness at bay. What is he to do? He had put it in a different way in a diary entry for 19 September 1917:

Have never understood how it is possible for almost everyone who writes to objectify his sufferings in the very midst of undergoing them: thus I, for example, in the midst of my unhappiness, in all likelihood with my head still smarting from unhappiness, sit down and write to someone: I am unhappy. Yes, I can even go beyond that, and with as many flourishes as I have the talent for, all of which seems to have nothing to do with my unhappiness, ring simple, or contrapuntal, or a whole orchestration of changes on my theme. And it is not a lie, and it does not still my pain; it is simply a merciful surplus of strength at the moment when suffering has raked me to the bottom of my being and plainly exhausted all my strength. But then what kind of a surplus is it?

Four years later, on 20 December 1921, he returns to the subject and expresses it in a more enigmatic and compressed fashion: 'Undeniably there is a certain joy in being able calmly to write down: "Suffocation is inconceivably horrible." Of course it is inconceivable – that is why I have written nothing down.' But of course he *has* written something down. And the puzzle remains: is the ability to write down that you are in despair a merciful surplus of strength or the final lie? Kafka, as always, leaves it as a question.

In 1846 the prolific painter Benjamin Robert Haydon, once the friend of Keats and now of, amongst others, Elizabeth Barrett who would soon elope with Robert Browning, hired the famous Egyptian Hall in Picaddilly as the site for an exhibition of his latest work. This was a critical moment for Haydon, whose self-belief had never wavered but who was finding it more and more difficult to sell his work or support his family. Downstairs in the same splendid building the American impresario Thomas Barnum was exhibiting a midget, 'General Tom Thumb'. All of London came to see the General, including Dickens and Carlyle, but hardly anyone bothered with Haydon's show. Two months later, in the middle of the exceptionally hot month of July, Haydon took his own life.

In the final year or so of *his* life Kafka wrote a number of stories, including 'The Hunger Artist'. As the hunger artist lies dying in the cage in which he has been 'performing' in his last years, the over-seer bends over him and listens to what he has to say. 'I always wanted you to admire my fasting', says the hunger artist. 'We do admire it,' says the overseer. 'But you shouldn't', says the hunger artist. 'Well then we don't', says the overseer. 'But why shouldn't we admire it?' 'Because I have to fast, I can't help it.' 'What a fellow you are', says the overseer, 'and why can't you help it?' 'Because I couldn't find the food I liked', says the hunger artist. 'If I had found it, believe me, I should have made no fuss and stuffed myself like you or anyone else.' With these words the hunger artist dies. The overseer has the cage cleaned out and installs a young panther in it, an animal whose 'noble body . . . seemed to carry freedom around with it too'. The sight of the beast is almost too much for the onlookers, 'But they braced themselves, crowded around the cage, and did not want ever to move away.'

It is instructive to compare the two stories, the one concerning real people, the other a fiction which could be read as a kind of confession. Haydon's story could be the illustration of a Victorian maxim about the folly of men, who would rather flock to see a deformed human being than an uplifting masterpiece, and whose crass materialism leads a lonely genius to take his own life. Certainly that was Haydon's own feeling about the affair which finally broke his hitherto indomitable spirit. To us, as perhaps even to his con-temporaries, it was not quite so simple: Haydon's painting was incompetent, his subject matter *passé*; why waste one's time with it when there was something more amusing in town? Kafka's story tells us that Kafka's sad and lonely life was not in any sense chosen by him; he could not even claim the virtue of determination, even quixotic determination. He had starved himself of the fruits of life, bringing sorrow to his parents and Felice, not in order to utter prophetic words, or even words of surpassing beauty, but simply because he could not feed on the diet so naturally eaten by other human beings; his work had met with no success not because of the originality of his vision but because he found it impossible to write like his contemporaries. Given this, it is a relief for him as for everyone else that he should finally die.

The irony is that Kafka was correcting the proofs of this story even as he lay dying of tubercular laryngitis in a country sanatorium: it was to be part of a new book consisting of four recent stories. Clearly, writing it must have given him pleasure and the desire to bring it before the public was just as great as it had been when he allowed his uncle to have a look at the story he was writing all those long years before. And is Kafka really the hunger artist? Is he not rather the maker of this story, before whose work, more perhaps than before that of any other writer of our time, we brace ourselves and do not want to move away? For the radiance that played around Ulysses' eyes and so overwhelmed the sirens seems to emanate from his writings as from no other's, making him, as Auden rightly said, the Dante, the Shakespeare, the Goethe of our time.

8 'Dear incomprehension!': Beckett and trust

Dire je. Sans le penser.

Beckett Samuel

With Kafka and Beckett we have reached the extreme edge of our subject. In both writers suspicion runs so deep as almost to paralyse the creative impulse; yet both produced a large and varied body of work which must figure as among the most important of this century. If we are to understand the nature of suspicion and its force, and if we are to understand how trust and suspicion fight each other, intertwine with each other, outwit each other and help each other, we will have to face up to the difficult and problematic work of both writers.

There are, as I see it, three phases in Beckett's writing life: in the first suspicion of writing and the need to write fight an exhausting and desperate battle in which neither side wins; in the second he suddenly finds a way to harness the two, and the great breakthrough works, the Trilogy, *Godot* and *Endgame*, are written; in the third, as with Shakespeare and Beethoven, a new voice makes itself heard, a new and unexpected harnessing of the two warring elements takes place.

Let me turn to the first phase.

'Monologue? What's that? Something to eat?' asks one of the women in Beckett's first novel, *Dream of Fair to Middling Women*, written in his early twenties and never published in his lifetime. And the answer comes back: 'Oh . . . , words that don't do any work and don't much want to. A salivation of words after the banquet.' The implication is that the words we use in daily life do honest work: I ask for an apple and you know what to give me; I thank you and so seal our transaction. But what of words in novels? For all fiction is monologue, words put down by the writer in the solitude of his room, even if he then allocates them to different characters. What kind of work do they do? What reasons do they have for existing? Are they not simply *pretending* to be working, rather as the maid in the play pretends to be dusting the furniture? Far from providing nourishing fare the writer's monologue merely fills the reader's mouth with something unwanted, 'a salivation of words after the banquet'.

This sense of horror and disgust at the uselessness and dishonesty of words in literature is not of course unique to the young Beckett. We have seen it in Hölderlin and Baudelaire and it is the main theme of Kafka's diaries. And it is not just words but the nature of narrative itself which makes these writers despair. When I tell myself or others the story of my life the narrative falls into a linear sequence: 'And then . . . and then . . . and then . . .' This is the pattern we are familiar with from novels and autobiographies and it is the one we naturally slip into when we start to write a novel or an autobiography ourselves. But when we are not telling or writing that story our lives do not seem to be like that at all. Far from falling into a simple linear pattern, a clear series of anecdotes, they remain dark and confused, without discernible shape and barely amenable to words.

From one point of view this is a state of weakness and even of anxiety, from which we need to escape as quickly as possible, perhaps precisely by turning to writing. But from another point of view it is the stories I tell about myself which seem false and misleading. I feel that as soon as I start to write I am moving away from rather than towards myself, and then the very reason why I turned to writing in the first place, in order to bring clarity to what was dark and confused, is felt obscurely to be that which is hindering any possibility of eventual clarity.

Clov and Hamm, in *Endgame*, wind up the alarm clock and then listen to it ringing. When it stops Clov says: 'The end is terrific!' 'I prefer the middle', replies Hamm. This is both funny and disturbing. Funny because Hamm and Clov, by treating the undifferentiated sound of an alarm clock as they would a piece of music, make fun of concert-goers. It is disturbing because it suggests that everything is really the same, that our distinctions between beginnings, middles and ends are merely the result of our human hopes and illusions. Listening to an alarm clock ringing we may even come to believe that the end *is* different from the middle, so strong is our need for endings, our horror at the thought that we might be living in a perpetual middle. Hamm and Clov, though, are not really taken in, they are only playing the social game called 'listening to music'. 'What's happening, what's happening?' Hamm asks in anguish at one point. 'Something is taking its course', Clov answers. Something, somewhere, is taking its course, but not only is it not amenable to our words and formulations, such attempts to make sense of it, to humanise it, are laughable because so pathetic, an example of what the French call tickling oneself to make oneself laugh.

What is happening is that our bodies are slowly moving towards decay and dissolution. Trying to make sense of life, as of history, is not simply misguided, it is a way of avoiding this central truth. Nietzsche and Kierkegaard, we saw, suggest that precisely this avoidance is a feature of our age: 'Man would sooner have the void for his purpose than be void of purpose', is how Nietzsche concluded his *Genealogy of Morals*, and Kierkegaard, less rhetorically: 'It is one thing that a life is over and a different thing that a life is finished by reaching a conclusion.' The writer who writes in conclusions thereby shows that he is no writer, for 'If he had been thoroughly aware of the inappropriateness of the third part – well, one may say, *si tacuisset, philosophus mansisset.*'

That is all well and good, but what happens when someone finds himself in the grip of what Beckett calls *cacoethes scribendi*, the incurable passion for writing? Beckett's early titles, *Dream of Fair to Middling Women, More Pricks than Kicks*, might easily be mistaken for undergraduate humour, but in reality they have a savage, self-critical edge, they imply: Here, take this if you really want to, but don't think you're going to get any profound spiritual insights out of me! No wonder his deeply bourgeois parents were appalled; it was bad enough their son's giving up a promising academic career to write, but then at least let him be a grave and distinguished writer like Mr Yeats.

Nor was Beckett's haughty disdain for the reader and disgust at the very task he was engaged in likely to win him many fans in the decade of Auden and Malraux and Sartre. For what was the reader to make of this, for example, in the masterpiece of those early years, the story 'Dante and the Lobster': 'Let us call it Winter, that dusk may fall now and a moon rise.' Doesn't the guy *know* if it was winter or not? And if he doesn't, what is he setting himself up as a writer for? Again, in *Watt*, written fifteen years later, but still locked in the same contradictions as the very early work, a young woman is described as 'a fine girl but a bleeder', and a footnote informs us that 'Haemophilia is, like enlargement of the prostate, an exclusively male disorder. But not in this work.' What's all this about prostates and haemophilia? the reader will ask. And what does it mean, not in this work? Have I spent valuable money and time on this book just to be laughed at and insulted like this?

Partly, of course, it is himself, the demon in himself which needs to write, that Beckett is laughing at and insulting. But partly too he is, like Kierkegaard and Nietzsche, trying to get the reader to wake up. But wake up to what? And why should he wake up at all? William Empson puts the case against Beckett with his usual witty common sense:

Mr. Bagby was quite right, I think, to point out the radical ambiguity of *Waiting for Godot*, but not all ambiguity is good. Here it expresses the sentiment: We cannot believe in Christianity and yet without that everything we do is hopelessly bad. Such an attitude seems to be more frequent in Irish than either English or French writers, perhaps because in Ireland the religious training of children is particularly fierce. A child is brought up to believe that he would be wicked and miserable without God; then he stops believing in God; then he behaves like a dog with his back broken by a car, screaming and thrashing on the public road, so that a passer-by can only wish for it to be put out of its misery. Surely we need not admire this result; the obvious reflection is that it was a very unfairly risky treatment to give to a child.

Unfortunately this Johnsonian attitude merely brings out that Empson is no Dr Johnson but the victim himself of his very English upbringing, his deeply ingrained suspicion of anything he thinks of as pretentious. For what is at issue here is not Christianity but authority of any kind. Empson here is like the George Eliot Nietzsche was so scathing about: he thinks he is a free spirit because he no longer believes in the Christian God, but he has simply replaced that God with the God of Reason and Common Sense.

The irony is that Empson would surely have approved of Belaqua's horror, in 'Dante and the Lobster', of, as he puts it, having 'conversational nuisance committed all over him'. Were Empson to be a little less supercilious, a little less suspicious, he would see that he and Beckett were really on the same side. For what is 'Dante and the Lobster' about? Teasing the reader? Feeling miserable without God? No. Like all Beckett's work it is about death and the lies we tell ourselves about it. Belaqua Shua, an intellectual Dublin layabout whose 'reality' is cast into doubt even as his essential character is brought into Dantean or Giottesque focus by being given the same name as the indolent spirit met by the pilgrim Dante on the lower slopes of Mt Purgatory – Belaqua Shua is first seen reading Dante, then making his lunch, meditating on the newspaper photo of a murderer who is to be hanged at dawn, buying a lobster for his aunt, going to his Italian lesson, then arriving at his aunt's. He hands her the lobster and she lays it out on the kitchen table:

'They assured me it was fresh,' said Belaqua.
　Suddenly he saw the creature move, this neuter creature. Definitely it changed its position. His hand flew to his mouth.
　'Christ!' he said, 'it's alive.'

Unperturbed, the aunt bustles off to the pantry and returns with an apron on and her sleeves rolled up. ' "Well," she said, "it is to be hoped so, indeed." '

'All this time,' muttered Belaqua. Then, suddenly aware of her hideous equipment. 'What are you going to do?' he cried.
　'Boil the beast,' she said. 'What else?'
　'But it's not dead,' protested Belaqua.

Gently she explains to him that lobsters are always boiled alive. 'They must be.'

She caught up the lobster and laid it on its back. It trembled. 'They feel nothing,' she said.
　In the depths of the sea it had crept into the cruel pot. For

hours, in the midst of its enemies, it had breathed secretly. It had survived the Frenchwoman's cat and his witless clutch. Now it was going alive into scalding water. It had to. Take into the air my quiet breath.

Belaqua looked at the old parchment of her face, grey in the dim kitchen.

'You make a fuss,' she said angrily, 'and upset me and then lash into it for your dinner.'

She lifted the lobster clear of the table. It had about thirty seconds to live.

Well, thought Belaqua, it's a quick death, God help us all.

It is not.

The aunt's attitude suggests a callous refusal to open oneself to another's suffering; yet does Belaqua's vague feeling of pity for the lobster, as for McCabe the murderer earlier in the story, do anything for them? Has the aunt not got a point? Belaqua's pity may be worse in fact than the aunt's realism, for he wishes to salve his conscience, yet accepts without demur the workings of criminal justice and, when it is ready, will tuck into the lobster.

And is Belaqua's attitude any different from that of the writer? By imaginatively conveying the lobster's agony the writer puts himself on the side of honesty, sympathy and truth. But is this sympathy not bought too cheaply? Does he in fact really understand the agony of McCabe or the lobster? Is there not even a monstrous presumption in imagining that he does? For he can empathise with their plight yet will himself always be able to turn away, live another day, empathise with another victim; whereas for McCabe and the lobster there is no other day.

We are back with Adorno's dictum that after Auschwitz there can be no lyrical poetry, and with my comment on it, in the opening chapter, that 'Auschwitz' is merely the most monstrous example of something felt by writers since the time at least of Keats, and felt, certainly by me, every time I read about another 'powerful and compassionate' novel concerning the plight of Rwandan refugees or the homeless or whatever.

It has been an unquestioned axiom, since the time of the Romantics, that empathy is good and lack of it bad. I had something to say about that in my chapter on the Romantics. What Beckett is suggesting here is that empathy is the final soothing lie; it protects us from recognising that 'something is taking its course', that for us and our loved ones too, as for McCabe and the lobster, one day there will be no tomorrow. Beckett thus tries to use the imagination against the imagination, writing against writing. But each time we grasp his point, each time we say, 'I see', he has failed. Each time he has to add an 'It is not', as it were. But then that too becomes a part of what we understand and he has to start all over again, fail again, as he says, fail better.

But that remark lies in the future. At the time of 'Dante and the Lobster' there seems to be only *cacoethes scribendi* and despair at what it yields. He can alleviate it by doing the conventional thing better than any of his contemporaries: 'A plug of moustache cowered at his nostrils like a frightened animal.' (Graham Greene and P. G. Woodhouse would go on polishing such similes all their writing lives. Not Beckett.) He can articulate his disgust with the whole business of fiction, beginning a novel (a *novel*, that which is new) with the sentence: 'The sun shone, having no alternative, on the nothing new.' But nothing will hide from him the fact that the whole enterprise is corrupt, and when he writes at the end of *Watt* that only 'fatigue and disgust' prevented him from incorporating into the body of the work material relegated to an appendix, we sense that he means it. Rabelais and Sterne could play games with the reader and with the forms of fiction out of a feeling of the absurdity of the task they were engaged on, but underlying their work is the sense that through these games they feel they can reach out and find common ground with their readers. The feeling of a common ground is lacking in Beckett as it is in Kafka.

Beckett could have gone on in this vein for the rest of his life, much as Flann O'Brien did, producing work of great interest and humour. But he didn't. His dissatisfaction with what he was doing was so deep that at times it affected his sanity. It was so deep that it had to find a resolution or he would have collapsed under its weight. However, three things combined at the end of his fourth decade, around 1946, to make a kind of resolution possible. First, on returning to Dublin early in 1946 to see his dying mother he had what can only be called a visionary experience, traces of which can be found in that most autobiographical of his later works, *Krapp's Last Tape*: 'Spiritually a year of profound gloom and indigence', Krapp records, 'until that memorable night in March at the end of the jetty, in the howling wind, never to be forgotten, when suddenly I saw the whole thing. The vision at last . . . What I suddenly saw then was this, that . . . the dark I have always struggled to keep under is in reality my most —'

Of course Krapp is overdramatising. Having listened to the tape on which he has recorded this, the old Krapp comments: 'Just been listening to that stupid bastard I took myself for thirty years ago, hard to believe I was ever as bad as that. Thank God that's all done with anyway.' But there can be no doubt that something happened to Beckett that night on the jetty in the storm, for he was later to say to Ludovic Janvier that the 'dark he had struggled to keep under' until then he now saw as the source of his creative life, and that he conceived '*Molloy* and what followed the day I became aware of my stupidity. Then I began to write the things I feel.'

This discovery was inseparable from two other, more technical decisions. On settling back in Paris after the war Beckett, who had failed to find an English publisher for *Watt*, had begun to try his hand at writing in French. His early efforts, *Mercier et Camier* and three stories, he put aside as soon as they were written, sensing that they were nothing more than a flexing of the muscles, and only allowed to be published after the success of *Godot* and the Trilogy. Nevertheless, they were crucial. Working in a language not his own made the words seem more solid, more 'other' than his native English. At the same time the combination of the French language, with its in-built bias towards abstraction, its wearing of *grammatica* on its sleeve, as it were, combined with Irish names and landscapes, gave his new work a strangeness which made it less necessary for the author to have to remind his reader at every turn that what he was reading was what someone had written, not 'reality'.

The second decision was even more vital. Beckett had always avoided first-person narration precisely because that seemed to close the gap between fiction and memoir – the very reason, of course, why it was chosen by Defoe. But suddenly, in the *nouvelles*, Beckett saw that the error lay only in creating a first-person narrator with the clarity and control of a third person. But what if one were to start with a first-person narrator who was as confused and incoherent, as 'stupid' as the author himself felt, who needed to speak and yet had no clear story to tell, and who, far from trying to overcome this situation, would accept it and speak precisely in order to try, by speaking, to cast some light on it? In Dantean terms, the very clash between *grammatica* and the individual need to speak would make manifest our situation in the world. The important thing would be simply to keep going. If he came to a dead end he would simply shift his ground and carry on in a different direction.

Beckett began working on *Molloy* with an intensity and a belief in himself he had never previously experienced. No longer worrying about the need to tell a coherent story and his visceral loathing of the falseness of it all, trusting only in his ability to keep going, he wrote *Molloy* in a few months at the end of 1947 and plunged at once into *Malone Meurt*. When that was finished, in the summer of 1948, he took three months off to write *En Attendant Godot*, then settled into the long haul of *L'Innommable*, which he finished early in 1950. To his old friend McGreevey he wrote: 'I see a little more clearly at last what my writing is about and fear I have perhaps ten years courage and energy to get the job done. The feeling of getting oneself in perfection is a strange one, after so many years of expression in blindness.'

Of course Beckett went on, energy undimmed, till the ill-health of his last years brought his production more or less to a stop, producing in thirty-eight years plays for stage, radio, film and television and works of fiction without parallel in literary history. The bouts of drinking and depression and of physical and mental illness which had dogged the first half of his life were never to recur, though he remained conscious to the end of his ineptitude and despaired of ever achieving anything of real value. It is as though, facing the suspicion which had been there from the start, he was able to use it and, by an act of trust in the sheer fact of writing, of moving the hand that holds the pen across the blank page, to turn it to his own purposes. It is, in a sense, a modern fairy-tale.

'Je suis dans la chambre de ma mère. C'est moi qui y vis maintenant. Je ne sais pas comment j'y suis arrivé (7). ('I am in my mother's room. It's I who live there now. I don't know how I got there' [7].) The tone is factual, reportorial even. There is no attempt to impress or startle, as there was in the earlier novels. Yet the gap between the second and third sentences impels the story forward. How did Molloy get to where he is? Where is his mother? What is the nature of their relationship? We read on, as with any good novel, in order to find out.

But this is not Defoe or Dickens. Molloy seems to know so little about his past and even about the present. He tells us that he has been asked to write his story and that a man comes to take away the pages he has written and gives him money in exchange. But it is not money he writes for. For what then? 'I don't know. The truth is I don't know much' (7). He has even forgotten his mother's name and 'how to spell too, and half the words' (8). He can't see and hear too well either, it turns out, and wonders if he is going blind and deaf. It is as though we were overhearing one of Wordsworth's solitaries talking, and the message was not resolution and independence but animal tranquillity and decay. What he would have liked, Molloy says, would have been to 'speak of the things that are left, say my goodbyes, finish dying' (7). But how is that to be done? What does it mean to say ones goodbyes? How does one ever know in this life what are the things that are left? And how can one say one's goodbyes, one's own unique goodbyes, in the language of others?

Molloy recounts in his rambling manner how he came to the city in search of his mother, tangled with the police, ran over a dog with his bicycle, moved in with its owner, left with some of her cutlery, roamed the countryside, found himself starting to lose his toes and was eventually reduced to dragging himself along the forest floor till he found himself finally at the edge of the forest. Thus summarised, it sounds like a picaresque novel, but the experience of reading the book is quite unlike reading any other work of literature. In a picaresque novel the adventures are the thing. Here we can never be sure if Molloy is remembering correctly, misremembering, or making it all up as he goes along. Yet there is none of the defiance attached to this that there had been in the earlier, third-person narratives. The whole thing is strangely calm even though it is at the same time quite desperate.

We have the feeling that Molloy's gradual physical deterioration is in some ways one with the gradual running out of steam of the narrative. This does not mean that one is an allegory of the other, rather that Beckett's discovery of a voice and a persona is carrying him forward into the terrain for which he had been looking all his writing life.

Everything tells Molloy that lying still is better than moving, silence better that speech, death better that life. 'Unfortunately there are other needs than that of rotting in peace, it's not the word, I mean of course my mother whose image, blunted for some time past, was beginning to harrow me again' (75). Yet 'when I was with her . . . I left her without having done anything. And when I was no longer with her I was again on my way to her, hoping to do better next time.' Thus he seems condemned by a deep desire to advance for ever towards a goal which recedes even as he moves towards it, yet which he can never abandon without feeling that he is abandoning himself. We leave him, not writing his memoirs but lying at the edge of the forest, still as far from finding the words to say his goodbyes as he was at the start.

However, if Molloy cannot find himself, for finding the right words would be to find himself, perhaps someone else can. A new start is made, a new report set before us. 'My name is Moran . . . I remember the day I received the order to see about Molloy' (92). Where Molloy tried to find his way by letting himself drift, by regressing towards a primal stage of childhood, Moran, the only one of Beckett's later characters to have a first name, is the very embodiment of the repressive superego. He is a sadist, delighting in the physical and mental pain he inflicts on his son and his servant and punctilious in his outward observation of social and religious custom. Like those Nazis Hannah Arendt described in terms of the banality of evil, Moran is absorbed by detail but happy to leave the problem of meaning and value to others. The result though is a fissure in his consciousness, which he at first refuses to recognise but which betrays itself in his opening words: 'My name is Moran, Jacques . . . I am done for. My son too' (92). His report is thus a mixture, at once hilarious and repugnant, of precision and vagueness: 'Molloy, or Mollose, was no stranger to me . . . Mother Molloy, or Mollose, was not completely foreign to me either . . . Of these two names, Molloy and Mollose, the second seemed to me perhaps the more correct. But barely' (113). Having been instructed to find Molloy he spends the rest of the day making detailed plans of the clothes he and his son will wear and of their means of transport, while refusing to face the fact that he has no idea where to find Molloy or what to do with him if and when he does find him.

But if Moran is the type of the functionary he is also the type of the writer-as-detective, the writer as third-person novelist. 'Perhaps I invented him', he concedes, 'I mean found him ready-made in my head' (112). Had he had friends and colleagues to talk things over with it might have been easier, he admits, but he has none, only instructions from above. 'Ah', he laments, 'those old craftsmen, their race is extinct and the mould broken' (115).

Like the novelist Moran is alone, without any tradition to rely on, only confused instructions from above and his own limited imagination. He tries to imagine Molloy, to feel him living inside him, as the novelist tries to feel his characters, but he is forced to admit that a gap always remains between the Molloy of his imagination and the real one. Not surprisingly, things quickly start to go wrong. A sudden pain in his knee leads to a stiffening of his leg and soon he too is in need of crutches and a bicycle. Far from finding Molloy, he seems to be turning into Molloy before our eyes. And inside his head things are not much better: 'What a rabble in my head . . . Murphy, Watt, Yerk, Mercier and all the others . . . Stories. Stories. I have not been able to tell them. I shall not be able to tell this one' (138). Soon he experiences 'a crumbling, a frenzied collapsing of all that had always protected me from all I was condemned to be' (149).

Having lost his son, his money and his bicycle, and realised he was never going to find Molloy, he receives new instructions to return home. But when he gets there he finds his bees and hens have died of neglect in his absence and the electricity has been cut off. A sense of hopelessness and rebellion takes hold of him: 'I shall not put up with it any more, I shall not try any more' (176). But a voice instructs him to write his report, and, dutiful functionary to the last, he complies and writes the narrative we have been reading. It ends: 'Then I went back into the house and wrote, It is midnight. The rain is beating on the windows. It was not midnight. It was not raining' (176).

In earlier Beckett this would have been spoken by the author/narrator and aimed at the reader. That is how it is usually read. But that is to misread. What is happening here is that Moran is making a pathetic attempt to assert his independence of Gaber and Youdi and the unknown voice. What he actually does, though, is to exile himself finally not only from his home but also from himself. He whose only reason for living was to protect what he possessed and to obey orders, who had always feared that if he let go of *grammatica* he would be letting go of his reason for living, had also always known that if all else failed there was always suicide. Now, in effect, he commits it. With those two 'nots' Moran has killed himself.

Molloy has failed. Moran has failed. It seems the self cannot be reached either by giving in to its own whims or by rigorously controlling it. But the fact that Moran has followed Molloy (as Swann's story followed the account of Marcel's childhood in Proust's novel) allows the writer to accept that the new failure is only temporary. A sequence has been set up. Now it is possible to go on, with a new voice, a new name, a new quest. Instead of the resigned voice of Molloy and the angry and frightened voice of Moran, this one is both light and firmly focused: 'Je serai quand même bientot tout à fait mort enfin' (7). ('I shall soon be quite dead at last in spite of all' [179].) The sentence acquires more and more limbs yet never seems to falter or deviate from its course, as though simply settling into a space that had been prepared for it since the beginning of time. We are worlds away from the self-destructive opening of *Murphy*.

Both Molloy and Moran were engaged in writing their memoirs; Malone is going to write only of what is happening to him in the present. If necessary, to pass the time, he will tell a few stories, but the anecdotes will be only aspects of the present, a passing of the time till he can die.

Yet for Malone even more than for Molloy the time passing while
he waits is counterpointed with a quite different order of time:
'Perhaps I shall survive Saint John the Baptist's Day and even the
Fourteenth of July, festival of freedom', he says. 'Indeed I would not
put it past me to pant on to the Transfiguration, not to speak of the
Assumption' (179). And just as figures from Beckett's earlier writing
had floated into Moran's confused brain, so Malone's mind seems
strangely porous as he vaguely recalls walking in a forest, and
wonders whether he is not already dead and in a vault of some kind,
and admits to feeling that 'I shall never get born and therefore never
get dead . . . I shall go on doing as I have always done, not knowing
what it is I do, nor who I am, nor where I am, nor if I am . . . , not
knowing what my prayer should be nor to whom' (226).

At first, though, as with Moran, everything is clear: he will tell
himself four stories, make an inventory of his possessions, then die.
But no less than Moran's, his plans come quickly unstuck. 'What
tedium!' he exclaims shortly after embarking on his first story. 'This
is awful', he notes a little later. 'Can't do it', he concludes. And the
reason he can't, as I pointed out in the opening chapter, is that 'the
wild beast of earnestness' will not let him. 'I was born grave as
others syphilitic. And gravely I struggled to be grave no more, to
live, to invent . . .' (195).

Yet, unlike Molloy and Moran, he does sometimes surprise
himself. 'That's it. Reminisce . . . That's it Babble' (201–2). He
starts to see that perhaps it doesn't matter if he cannot go on in one
vein, all he has to do is slip into another (Beckett has projected on
to him the lesson he learned by having Moran follow Malone). 'For
Sapo – no, I can't call him that any more, and I even wonder how I
was able to stomach such a name till now. So then for, let me see,
for MacMann, that's not much better but there is no time to
lose' (229–30).

The tone has changed. It is no longer a question of four clearly
defined stories followed by an inventory and then death. For it is

becoming increasingly clear both that there is no time to lose and that death will not come, or at least come as a Kierkegaardian conclusion. But − the old Beckettian comic sting − 'one must not be greedy', for what could one expect? Once, of course, much more, when Christ's Incarnation and Passion were guarantors of meaning for every Christian, but that day has long gone, if it ever existed, and the Church's feast-days are without significance, even if the calendar, like language itself, still pays lip-service to them. Yet why be discouraged? Life may have no more shape than the ringing of an alarm clock but only those who expect more will be disappointed.

Yet indifference is not an option for Malone any more than staying put was for Molloy. To that extent Empson may be right: something, perhaps his upbringing, has made Beckett too 'grave' for post-Modernist *jouissance*. 'Something is taking its course' and while he can he needs to try and speak of what that is.

He doesn't succeed, of course. And yet in a way he does. The book ends not with Malone on his bed but with a new story, a story of mayhem and destruction as a warder called Lemuel takes his charges on an outing on 'the Easter week-end, spent by Jesus in Hell' (282), and then turns on the other warders with a hatchet. We are no longer, as in the early novels, dealing with either reality or mere imaginings, for this story, told by Malone but now occupying the whole canvas, is in a sense the story of Malone and of the book we have been reading and of its end, a final letting go, not in frustration but in a kind of peace, as Lemuel

raises his hatchet on which the blood will never dry, but not to hit anyone, he will not hit anyone, he will not hit anyone any more, he will not touch anyone any more, either with it or with it or with it or with or

or with it or with his hammer or with his stick or with his fist or in thought in dream I mean never he will never

or with his pencil or with his stick or
or light light I mean
never there he will never
never anything
there
any more

(289)

We have travelled a long way from the first sentence and reached
a place and a tone of which the start knew nothing. But it is not a
place or a tone on which, for the moment, anything new can be
built. It is time to leave it and start again, with a new voice, a new
tone: 'Où maintenant? Quand maintenant? Qui maintenant? Sans
me le demander. Dire je. Sans le penser' (7). 'Where now? Who now?
When now? Unquestioning. I, say I. Unbelieving' (293).

With the advent of this new voice, as we leave Malone/Lemuel
behind and start to read *The Unnamable*, it suddenly strikes us
forcibly that something else has been going on, but at a more primitive level than that of plot and narrative, anecdote and character,
something much more immediate and yet much more difficult to
describe. It is at this moment that the musical analogy can no longer
be repressed: *Molloy* was the first of a three-movement concerto or
symphony, *allegro assai*, a movement retaining the ghost of sonata
form, with its first and second subjects and massive development,
though the development comes to nothing and there is no coda;
Malone Dies was a quiet middle movement, *adagio*, mysterious and
otherworldly, like the middle movement of Bartók's Second Piano
Concerto, coming to an ambiguous end, hovering, trembling, open.
Now the third and final movement has started, angular, fast, full of
desperate energy: 'Where now? Who now? When now?' For now
there can no longer be any prevarication. Everything must be faced,
even if that means total disaster: 'All these Murphys, Molloys and
Malones do not fool me. They have made me waste my time, suffer

for nothing, speak of them when, in order to stop speaking, I should have spoken of me and of me alone . . . There will be no more about them' (305–6).

They are figments of the speaker's imagination, ghosts coming between him and his reality. But who is he? Who is it who writes: 'Where now? Who now? When now?' Like Descartes in his room by his stove, Beckett knows that if he is to advance he will have to understand the basis on which he is advancing. He will be able to take nothing on trust, except the need to keep going: 'The fact would seem to be, if in my situation one may speak of facts, not only that I shall have to speak of things of which I cannot speak, but also, which is even more interesting . . . that I shall have to, I forget, no matter. And at the same time I am obliged to speak. I shall never be silent. Never' (294).

As he chases each of his previous personas down, and even the new ones his imagination keeps throwing up, he knows both that it is 'of me I must speak now' and that when he speaks 'it is not I, about me, it is not about me' (291). 'Is there a single word of mine in all I say?' he wonders, thus turning upside down the entire basis of autobiography and the Kantian Enlightenment notion that as free beings we must speak what we think. And then, in a rush of understanding, the words open up for him: 'Dear incomprehension, it's thanks to you I'll be myself in the end' (327). We will never know the right words, or perhaps simply the words 'it behoved one to say', but that is precisely why one must go on, not in disgust, like the author of *Watt*, not in despair, like Malone, but in a spirit of grateful acceptance.

Without our realising it, this sense of acceptance has brought with it a new note, plangent, sustained, strangely comforting, as the Unnamable finds himself speaking of having 'no memory of anything, no hope of anything, no knowledge of anything, no history and no prospects . . . , saying any old thing, your mouth full of sand . . .' (393).

Out of the initial short sharp anguished questions a kind of understanding is beginning to emerge, an understanding which is one with the release of speech: 'I can't say why I should have liked to be silent a little before being dead . . . no, I don't know, it's simpler than that, I wanted myself, my own land, for a brief space, I didn't want to die a stranger in the midst of strangers, a stranger in my own midst, surrounded by invaders, no, I don't know what I wanted . . . I must have wanted so many things, imagined so many things . . .' (400). My own land. Not 'the Molloy country', not Moran's fortress house, not Malone's room, not Ireland or France, but the place where these words are spoken, a place which exists while the words are spoken, here, now, as the ever-expanding sentences float free of their origins and of any concern with closure or endings.

To ask for more than this temporary accommodation is to fall into the old traps of truth versus lies, fact versus fiction, the old traps of *I* and *you* and *he* and *they*. 'Mercier never spoke, Moran never spoke, I never spoke, I seem to speak, that's because he says I as if he were I . . . perhaps it's not he, perhaps it's a multitude, one after another, . . . someone says you, it's the fault of the pronouns, there is no name for me, no pronoun for me, all the trouble comes from that, that it's a kind of pronoun too, it isn't that either, I'm not that either, . . . he, I, no matter, the man on duty speaks of himself, it's not that, of others, it's not that either, . . . no, I can't speak of anything, yet I speak . . .' (407–8). Pronouns are not place-holders for proper names but way-stations for passers-by, temporary shelters which become prisons when we try to make them permanent. Understanding that migration, not rootedness, is our promised land, I can enter the land at last and cease to be a stranger to myself.

There is a final fleeting glimpse of the kind of novel Beckett might have written had the spirit of suspicion, so destructive yet ultimately so productive, not gnawed away at him, the kind of novel published week after week to great acclaim: 'They love each other,

marry, . . . he goes to the wars, he dies at the wars, she weeps, with
emotion, at having loved him, at having lost him, yep, marries again,
in order to love again . . . , he comes back, . . . from the wars, he
didn't die, . . . she goes to the station, to meet him, he dies in the
train, of emotion, at the thought of seeing her again, having her
again, she weeps . . .' (410).

For the last time too he laments: 'If only I knew if I've lived,
. . . impossible to find out . . .', and then, in one great rolling period
which carries through a dozen pages, the voice reaches its end, the
redeeming word still unfound, or perhaps not, 'perhaps it's done
already, perhaps they have said me already, perhaps they have
carried me to the threshold of my story, before the door that opens
on my own story, that would surprise me, if it opens, it will be I, it
will be the silence, where I am, I don't know, in the silence you don't
know, you must go on, I can't go on, I'll go on' (418).

What happened when Beckett started *Molloy* in French, in the first
person, was the realisation of his visionary discovery that he could
perhaps make use of 'the dark he had struggled to keep under'. In
fiction this led to the Trilogy. In the theatre to *Godot* and *Endgame*.
In a sense the effect of his discovery was even more direct and
powerful in the theatre. For there people have gathered. To pass the
time. To be instructed. To have sense made of their lives. And
Beckett doesn't disappoint. But the sense he conveys is that there
is no sense, there is only living. That the time we spend in our seats
is exactly as long as the time spent on stage by the actors. That
as we have gone to the theatre to distract ourselves with fictions,
so they have found themselves in this place and similarly try to
distract themselves.

But again Beckett is careful not to become a positivist of the negative. Just as we reach towards meaning because that is part of what
being alive means, so the plays themselves reach towards it, then
fall back. Godot is not quite God, Hamm is not quite Hamlet or a

ham actor or a hammer. 'There is no longer any substantive, affirmative metaphysical meaning that could provide dramatic form with its law and its epiphany', Adorno writes in a fine essay on *Endgame*. Beckett wants, like Kierkegaard's essential philosopher, to make us feel this fact in our bodies. 'Moment upon moment, pattering down, like the millet grains of . . . [*he hesitates*] . . . that old Greek, and all life long you wait for that to mount up to a life.' So Hamm, to himself, to us. And again: 'Do you believe in the life to come?' 'Mine was always that.'

Yet 'something is taking its course', for Hamm and Clov, for us. We cannot focus directly on it, but the dramatist can make us feel it, and this dramatist does so as powerfully as Aeschylus and Sophocles ever did. If we will give up our dreams of domination, of understanding, of fulfilment, of progress, our dreams even of the absurdity of life, then we will be able to attend to that. *Godot* and *Endgame* lead us there.

Once he has discovered the theatre Beckett is able to move from stage to page as he had moved from Molloy to Moran, and back again, simply in order to keep moving, to go on embracing his 'dear incomprehension'. And it pays off. The change from the Trilogy to the later prose works, *Company*, *Ill Seen Ill Said*, *Worstword Ho*, and from *Godot* to *Footfalls* and *Rockaby*, is as great as the change from *Othello* to *The Winter's Tale*, from the Fifth Symphony to the late quartets of Beethoven.

Now there is no desperation, only an internal rocking that contains elements that would previously have fallen apart, only 'dire stroms of silence, in which has been engulfed the hysteria that he used to let speak up, pipe up, for itself', as Beckett described the last works of Beethoven back in 1927 in his first, unpublished novel.

'A voice comes to one in the dark. Imagine.' The voice speaks, tells stories, but 'only a small part of what is said can be verified'. All that can be asserted is that someone is lying on his back in the dark and that to this someone comes a voice, telling him stories. 'Use of the second person marks the voice. That of the third that canker-ous other. Could he speak to and of whom the voice speaks there would be a first. But he cannot. He shall not. You cannot. You shall not.' Of course it would be wonderful if he/you could. 'What an addition to company that would be! A voice in the first person singular. Murmuring now and then, Yes, I remember.'

The entire tradition of novel and autobiography depends on just this sleight-of-hand, a voice murmuring 'Yes, I remember'. But even the most truthful of autobiographers omits to ask himself: 'Even if the stories the voice tells me are familiar to me, how am I to know that they are stories about myself?' For what is a story about oneself? Is there a self there even?

This does not mean, as Barthes and Foucault seem to imagine, that there is no self, only that it is less an entity than a source of potential. For Beckett all that can be said is that the voice comes to one in the dark and that to listen to that voice is to acquire company. All that can be said is: 'Devised deviser devising it all for company. In the same figment dark as his figments.' And so a kind of pro-visional truth is arrived at: 'Huddled thus you find yourself imag-ining that you are not alone while knowing full well that nothing has occurred to make this possible. The process continues none the less lapped as it were in its meaninglessness. You do not murmur in so many words, I know this doomed to fail and yet persist. No. For the first personal and a fortiori plural pronoun had never any place in your vocabulary.'

Like any writer, and more than some, Beckett makes use of his own life and feelings. It is important to grasp this because critics have tended to talk about his work too much in terms of aesthetics and metaphysics and not to see what is before their eyes, the wonder that lies in the transformation into the public and communicable of that which is local and personal. We have glimpsed this in the way Beckett made use of his 'vision' in *Krapp's Last Tape*. That is perhaps the most personal of his plays; but *Footfalls* does not lag far behind. His biographers tell us that Beckett's mother used to walk about the house at night, unable to sleep. Another writer might have told the story of an old lady wandering about the house at night, unable to sleep. Or he might have used that to 'say something' about parents and children, or about guilt and the generations, as Joyce did in 'The Dead' and Yeats in *Purgatory*. That is not Beckett's way.

What Beckett seizes on is the element of repetition, which, in these late works, hovers between compulsion and release. As always, his stage directions are integral to the meaning: 'Pacing: starting with right foot (r) from right (R) to left (L), with left foot (l) from L to R. Turn: rightabout at L. leftabout at R.' Who is it who thus paces? Beckett does not say 'my mother' or 'a mother'. He does not say 'an actress'. 'Lighting: dim, strongest at floor level, less on body, least on head. Voices: both low and slow throughout.' Someone paces then, dimly lit, and a voice speaks. Let the one who paces be called May and the voice, Voice. Is the voice that speaks in May's head? Or is it that May is the projection of her mother's imaginings? What, in fact, are we seeing? There are five possibilities, at least: that Voice and May exist, as mother and daughter, and speak and move as we hear and see them; that voice is May's projection of a remembered or wished-for mother; that May is Voice's projection of a remembered or wished-for daughter; that May is Voice's projection of herself in childhood; that both are the projection of the author's remembered or wished-for or merely imagined mother and childhood.

The drama advances as May, released by the to-and-fro movement, starts to tell a story, the story of Amy, anagram for May, and *her* mother. But she cannot keep that up. Unlike Malone, however, this does not upset her, she simply allows the story to fade back into her own: 'Amy. [*Pause*] Yes, Mother. [*Pause*] Will you never have done? [*Pause*] Will you never have done . . . revolving it all? [*Pause*]

It. [*Pause*] It all. [*Pause*] In your poor mind. [*Pause*] It all. [*Pause*]
It all. [*Pause*]'

The light fades, then fades up a little. But there is no-one there.

Just as May and Voice are transmuted in May's story into Amy
and her mother, and then the effort to keep the story going proves
too much and we return to May and Voice, so Beckett can only speak
by creating May and Voice and then, after a certain time, the effort
proves too much and they vanish, and all vanishes, and we are back
to the silence and the next attempt to speak and once more to try
to allay the old ghosts.

Yet something has happened. As Wallace Stevens puts it: 'After
the leaves have fallen, we return / To a plain sense of things. It is
as if / We had come to an end of the imagination.' But to get there
we have been through something much more violent and painful
than we ever experience sitting through *A Long Day's Journey into
Night* or *Death of a Salesman*. For it is our own ghosts which have
been raised and given an airing and so exorcised, even if only tem-
porarily, by Beckett's human art.

These late plays and fictions move, as I have said, from repetition
as compulsion to repetition as release, testing out the ground, no
longer concerned to separate the one firmly from the other. As we
ourselves are lapped in the rhythm of repetition we sense that the
work only exists, that we only exist, within the folds of that repetition, within the rhythm of that rocking. We sense then that if we
exist it is less as the subject of a story or a clear set of memories
than as precisely that, a rhythm, which in the end may simply be
the rhythm of our breathing. But just as May can only start to
approach herself by telling the story of Amy, so we may start to
approach ourselves, our own unique rhythms, by seeing *Footfalls*, by
reading *Company*. Dear Beckett, it's thanks partly to you that I am
a little more myself. In the end. Perhaps.

9 Kinetic melodies

> It is not a kind of *seeing* on our part; it is our *acting*, which lies at the bottom of the language-game.

> Ludwig Wittgenstein

Ever since the Romantics we have dreamed of lightness, of a grace beyond gravity or of a grace so deeply entwined with gravity that the two are one. Kleist's puppets submit to the law of gravity but the puppet is graceful because it does not think. Our way back to Eden is barred by the angel, says Kleist, we cannot undo the Fall into knowledge and self-consciousness, we must go forward into total knowledge, make the journey round the world to see if Paradise is open at the back, as he puts it. Kierkegaard dreamed of a leap of faith which would in one bound set us free from melancholy and suspicion, return us to the lightness of the Greeks but with a new, Christian awareness of our humanity. Hölderlin and Rilke, in their greatest poems, imagine what it would be like to overcome our human condition of doubt and anxiety, our perpetual need to search for our origins and define goals for ourselves. Nietzsche, recognising that 'the trust in life is gone: life itself has become a *problem*', preached, in his more ecstatic moments, what Wallace Stevens called a *gai savoir*, accepting that everything that happens will happen again and again and urging us therefore to accept the moment and live it to the full. Yeats, recognising that we have 'lost the old nonchalance of the hand', that 'we are but critics, or but half create', felt nevertheless that

> surely there are men who have made their art
> Out of no tragic war, lovers of life,
> Impulsive men that look for happiness
> And sing when they have found it.

And post-Modernists from Calvino to Kundera, from Barthes to Lyotard, have sought to return us to a lightness of being, no matter how difficult to bear.

In all these cases, it seems to me, wish has triumphed over reality. All these writers sense that our Romantic melancholy and suspicion is a curse from which we must escape, but none of them quite succeeds in convincing us that such a possibility is more than a dream. There is something willed, desperate even, about Nietzsche's call for 'another kind of art — a mocking, light, fleeting, divinely untroubled, divinely artificial art that, like a pure flame, licks into unclouded skies'. Certainly his own attempts to produce such an art, in *Zarathustra*, are almost embarrassingly banal. Indeed, Auden's clerihew on Kierkegaard could be the epitaph of the whole heroic enterprise:

> Søren Kierkegaard
> Tried awfully hard
> To take The Leap
> But fell in a heap.

The real poise and lightness of *A Midsummer Night's Dream* is nowhere to be found in our post-Romantic world.

It may be different in music and painting. In Stravinsky and Picasso above all, we sense a new and genuine lightness – one has simply to compare Stravinsky's Three Pieces for String Quartet of 1914 with what was being produced at the same time by the Second Viennese School, or Picasso's delightful post-Cubist collages of 1915–16 with the contemporary productions of the *Blaue Reiter* school to see what I mean. A new spirit has indeed entered European art, a spirit which owes much to non-European traditions, to pre- rather than post-Renaissance traditions, and which does seem to herald a genuine renewal, with its emphasis on making, not expressing, on wit, not profundity, on clarity, not suggestiveness. I sometimes wonder what would have happened to European philosophy in this century had Nietzsche heard and been able to meditate on *The Rite of Spring*. After all, that work was first performed in 1913, when Nietzsche, had he lived, would only have been sixty-nine. Surely he would have felt that here at last was the art he had always dreamed about, an elemental yet light art, quite comparable to that of Greek tragedy, whose origins and power he had begun his career by exploring. But of course it was not to be.

Yet even here we have to recognise how much depends on the amazing careers of two men, on the enormous span as well as the constant renewal of those careers. No doubt they showed the way to later artists and helped the likes of Berio and Birtwistle, Bacon and Hockney to find their voices. Nevertheless, what the careers of these later artists show is that Beckett's Spirit of Seriousness will not, cannot be laid to rest. Each new work carries with it the risk of failure, lightness and wit have constantly to be fought for, are never simply given. There are no universal panaceas, no single defining leaps. To imagine that there are is to fall in a heap. (In politics of course that same dream of the single leap has led to many if not all the horrors of our century.) Rather, for the artist, there is a lifetime's struggle and endeavour, and, for us, the need to examine each career on its own terms and to recognise that in every case the dialectic of trust and suspicion which I have been exploring works in slightly different ways. How an artist negotiates that at every stage is, it seems to me, of far deeper and more central significance than the particular school or movement to which he claims he owes allegiance or which claims him retrospectively.

The lesson of Kafka and Beckett is that to accept and repeat the forms and the words that are given is to become complicit with that in which you no longer believe, that which keeps you from seeing how things are, as the aunt's 'They must be' and Belaqua's 'it's a quick death, God help us all' stop them from responding to the lobster's plight. No. Not its plight. That is too abstract a word. Its thirty seconds of agony before its light goes out.

At the same time the lesson of Beckett as of Proust is that to trust the darkness is to find release. This is of course no simple or single thing. In retrospect we can see where Wordsworth and Coleridge misread the signs; in retrospect we can see how Kafka and Beckett came into their own. But for them, at the time, there was only the daily struggle, the daily uncertainty, the daily need for artistic and human choices in a world where there are no longer any guidelines for such choices.

I want to stay with this phenomenon of blockage and release for a little while. With Proust, Kafka and Beckett, we have seen, an acceptance of 'dear incomprehension' leads to a new sense of direction after years of frustration and dissatisfaction. The same pattern, with slightly different emphases, can be found in Eliot's career, from the early poems where the return home, the re-integration into the routines of daily life, is described as 'the last twist of the knife', through the stifling constriction of 'Gerontion' and the desperation of *The Waste Land*, to the growing sense of release in 'Journey of the Magi' and *Ash Wednesday* and up to the poise, the resigned resilience, of the *Four Quartets*. Beckett would not have thanked me for drawing a parallel between his own career and Eliot's, but, again in retrospect, I think there can be no doubt that many of the same patterns of pressure and release are there in the two men. The difference is perhaps that whereas Beckett, like Proust, only really comes into his own in the second half of his career, leaving us with the feeling that, for all its brilliance, there was something profoundly unresolved about the early work, Eliot seems to have been able to find his voice early both in the articulation of blockage and in the articulation of release. Indeed, many readers feel that his greatest poetry was written in the first half of his career.

I want to look at two works, not perhaps central to the canon but wonderful poems nonetheless, one from the first and one from the second half of his life. The first is 'Sweeney Among the Nightingales', the most powerful of his quatrain poems, written between 1917 and 1920, thus just before *The Waste Land*. After the mysterious title comes, as so often in early Eliot, an epigraph in a foreign language and, here, even in a script most of us today are unable to decipher. It comes from Aeschylus' *Agamemnon* and it begins onomatopoeically – a nice irony since we need to know the script to make the sound: '*Ômoi*, I am struck by a fateful blow within!' This is Agamemnon, calling out from within the house as Clytemnestra strikes him down in his bath. Why is it there and how does it relate to the poem that follows?

Kierkegaard's essay on ancient and modern tragedy, which I examined in my second chapter, can help us here. There is a lightness, an insouciance about the Greek tragic hero, says Kierkegaard, for he is enfolded 'in the substantial categories of state, family and destiny. The hero's destruction is, therefore', Kierkegaard goes on, 'not only the result of his own deeds, but is also a suffering.' The fact that the hero's guilt is objective, a pollution, is both terrible to behold and strangely releasing, for it allows him to speak his plight, even if it is only, as in Agamemnon's case, to utter this terrible cry of agony. The modern tragic hero, by contrast, enfolded in no such set of public categories, is thrown back on himself, overcome by guilt, and unable to speak, for he is not even sure what it is he might say or what exactly it is that is happening to him.

In Eliot's poem it is impossible to say whether it is something trivial or momentous that is taking place. On the one hand we seem to be in a low dive where some sort of plot is being hatched against someone, but what and against whom remains concealed. Is Sweeney about to be murdered – as a result of some private feud or perhaps simply for his few possessions – or does he only imagine that this is about to happen, or is it simply we who imagine it while Sweeney, whether out of stupidity, drunkenness or a much more commonsensical view of the situation than ours, remains blithely indifferent? One thing is certain: Sweeney cannot cry out as Agamemnon did, and the poet cannot either. For in a sense it makes no difference if Sweeney is to be murdered or will walk out unscathed. A murder of this kind will be a matter of chance rather than destiny, an end rather than a conclusion. Whether it happens or not, we might say, Sweeney will not change and we, as witnesses to it, will not be changed either. The poet would thus be false both to himself and to the world in which and about which he is writing were he to turn this into a version of the ancient tragedy; but he would be equally false were he to insist that there is no such thing as tragedy today, only meaningless stabbings in back alleys after drunken brawls in bars. For Sweeney, after all, for all his ape neck, is a man like Agamemnon, a sentient being who is perhaps still – even if only vestigially – bound up in a larger world than that of his senses. His tragedy, in fact, is precisely that he cannot utter a cry or reach a conclusion.

This is where the nightingales come in. They are, we are always told, prostitutes, and Eliot was using an Elizabethan term for them. But though Eliot was no doubt delighted to discover the Elizabethan word, to suggest that this is *the* meaning of the word in the poem is to miss its point. The last two stanzas read:

> The host with someone indistinct
> Converses at the door apart,
> The nightingales are singing near
> The Convent of the Sacred Heart,
>
> And sang within the bloody wood
> When Agamemnon cried aloud,
> And let their liquid siftings fall
> To stain the stiff dishonoured shroud.

If Sweeney can no longer die as Agamemnon did, shamefully for a warrior but nevertheless still retaining the ability to cry out and say what is happening to him, there is still a continuity between them: the nightingales sing now as they did then, and Eliot's mastery was never so well displayed as in his manipulation of the tenses here: the nightingales are singing *now*, and sang *then*, but what tense is 'let' in 'And let their liquid siftings fall'? Was it *then* and is the shroud Agamemnon's, or is it *now* and is the shroud Sweeney's? By itself this ambiguity might be simply troubling; but the contrast between the sense and the sounds of the last two lines raises the whole poem to a new height. For though the meaning seems to be that the birds' droppings in some sense shame Agamemnon's corpse, the soft *s*'s act as a gentle binding agent and the staining seems more like a blessing – on Agamemnon, a man after all, despite his killing of his daughter and his commander's arrogance, or Sweeney, apeneck, yet a man too, acting out his destiny as Agamemnon acted out his, still enclosed in the movement of the moon and the stars, still able to hear the song Agamemnon heard so long ago, that song of the nightingales which, since the time of Homer, has been taken by poets as an emblem of their own singing.

So Eliot, instead of simply lamenting the fate of the modern Antigone or Agamemnon, like Kierkegaard, brings it into the orbit of our consciousness, even if only faintly. For the voice is not entirely stifled, it lingers on in a fragment from some older time, in a language we can hardly read, just, faintly, audible. He reminds us that though we may not be able to grasp the meaning of our lives, as we cannot decipher the Greek letters, that does not imply that life has no meaning – the verse from Aeschylus is there for us to read. So, not 'As flies to wanton boys are we to the gods', but 'We that are young / Shall never see so much, nor live so long'.

In the plays he wrote after *King Lear* Shakespeare wrote of the impossible return of lost daughters to grieving fathers, 'murdering impossibility', in the words of *Coriolanus*; and this seems a better model of what I have been trying to describe in the course of this book than does the supremely willed epic of Milton, which is the half-conscious model of the Romantics, or the post-Modern works of player-artists who, accepting that nothing can be said, are content to enjoy their own cleverness. Eliot seems to acknowledge this in the second poem I want to look at, 'Marina', which is at once about Shakespeare, about art, and about his new understanding of how the suspicion that had driven his early works, that sense that Sweeney cannot even utter a cry at the moment of his own death, can be overcome without denying its force:

What seas what shores what grey rocks and what islands
What water lapping the bow
And scent of pine and the woodthrush singing through the fog
What images return
O my daughter . . .

What is this face, less clear and clearer
The pulse in the arm, less strong and stronger –
Given or lent? more distant than stars and nearer than the eye

Whispers and small laughter between leaves and hurrying feet
Under sleep, where all the waters meet.
Bowsprit cracked with ice and paint cracked with heat.
I made this, I have forgotten
And remember.
The rigging weak and the canvas rotten
Between one June and another September.
Made this unknowing, half conscious, unknown, my own.
The garboard strake leaks, the seams need caulking.
                                        . . . let me
Resign my life for this life, my speech for that unspoken,
The awakened, lips parted, the hope, the new ships.

What seas what shores what granite islands towards my timbers
And woodthrush calling through the fog
My daughter.

There is always of course the possibility that this is only a halluci-
nation, as the epigraph from Seneca's *Hercules Furens* acknowledges, but that acknowledgement, far from weakening the poem,
only strengthens it. Now it is the classical hero who is caught up in
the web of privacy and the modern man, Pericles, the poet, who,
accepting the fog as part of his visual field, not something to be
seen through ('dear incomprehension!'), catches a glimpse of the
daughter he hardly knew he had, the poem he has made almost
unknowingly (as always, Eliot responds to boats with an upsurge of
emotion), but which is now present as the voice of the woodthrush is present, calling through the fog to him, to us.

I suggested in the second chapter that Homeric lightness could not
withstand the force of Platonic gravity, and I have been arguing in
later chapters that when Coleridge felt constrained to produce a

magnum opus, to ground his feelings and imagination in a coherent philosophy, he lost his way, and that Proust could only find *his* way when he recognised the error of trying to find 'a subject to which I could impart a philosophical significance of infinite value' and trusted instead to the writing of a narrative of his failures and confusions, the ways of Swann and the Guermantes. This might seem to imply that I am here replaying the old quarrel of literature and philosophy under the new headings of trust and suspicion, lightness and gravity. And in part this is true. But as I hope has become clear in the course of this book I don't believe such a quarrel is necessary, only likely. Here, for example, is the century's greatest philosopher in the Preface to his greatest work:

> It was my intention at first to bring all this together in a book whose form I pictured differently at different times. But the essential thing was that the thoughts should proceed from one subject to another in a natural order and without breaks. After several unsuccessful attempts to weld my results together into such a whole, I realised that I should never succeed. The best that I could write would never be more than philosophical remarks; my thoughts were soon crippled if I tried to force them on in any single direction against their natural inclination. – And this was, of course, connected with the very nature of the investigation. For this compels us to travel over a wide field of thought criss-crossing in every direction . . . I make [it] public with doubtful feelings. It is not impossible that it should fall to the lot of this work, in its poverty and in the darkness of this time, to bring light into one brain or another – but, of course, it is not likely. I should not like my writing to spare other people the trouble of thinking. But, if possible, to stimulate someone to thoughts of his own. I should have liked to produce a good book. This has not come about, but the time is past in which I could improve it.

Wittgenstein is being admirably precise here, in his Preface to the *Philosophical Investigations*, the fruit of his last years and of course not published in his lifetime. And admirably frank. First of all he confesses that this was not the book he had hoped to write, which, presumably, would have been an organic, unified philosophical treatise. And he is not being coy: everything we know about him and his work suggests that he means exactly what he says: 'I realised that I should never succeed.' But then he changes tack and asserts that what he has produced may actually be truer to the nature of the investigation he has undertaken than such an organic, unified treatise would ever have been. The peculiar form – fragmentary, elliptical, non-linear – may not after all be the result of a failure, but rather be 'connected with the very nature of the investigation'. And he insists that it is not meant to be the answer to everything but rather a stimulus to further thought. Thus one part of him wishes to apologise for not having been able to do better while another part is ready to question the entire basis of that 'better' and to insist that *this* is the way it should be. But the doubts have not been fully dissipated, and he ends by ruefully acknowledging that he would have liked to produce a good book but that was not to be, partly because of the 'darkness of this time', and partly because of his own weaknesses.

So the question remains, in his mind and ours, as it does with other modern works, such as *The Waste Land* and Beckett's Trilogy: was this precisely the book he *should* have produced, a book which honestly acknowledges its own lack of authority, its inability to transcend time and human frailty, and, in the process, guides the reader on the way to thought? Or was it a failure, albeit an honourable one ('these fragments have I shored against my ruins')?

It is fascinating to see the extent to which Wittgenstein, one of the most original men of his time, was nevertheless in many ways very much a product of his time. As Ray Monk has shown, he was as influenced by the ideas of Otto Weininger as any other Viennese intellectual at the beginning of the century. Later he would accept uncritically the equally half-baked notions of Oswald Spengler. Both these figures owed their popularity, of course, to the fact that they summed up – and coarsened – many of the issues – on the role of genius, on the difference between culture and civilisation, on the place of the Jews in Western society – which had been debated again and again throughout the nineteenth century. In the notes on these topics which Wittgenstein jotted down during the course of his life and which have been published under the title *Culture and Value* we can see him turning these themes over and over and trying to relate them to himself. In an earlier chapter I quoted some of his remarks on Shakespeare and Beethoven; here he is on the Jewish question: 'It might be said that the Jewish mind does not have the power to produce even the tiniest flower or blade of grass; its way is rather to make a drawing of the flower or blade of grass that has grown in the soil of another's mind and to put it into a comprehensive picture. We aren't pointing to a fault when we say this and everything is all right as long as what is being done is quite clear. It is only when the nature of a Jewish work is confused with that of a non-Jewish work that there is any danger, especially when the author of the Jewish work falls into the confusion himself, as he so easily may. (Doesn't he look as proud as though he had produced the milk himself?)'

Jews cannot create as Gentiles can; they are dry, intellectual, cold, secondary. They have talent but no genius. Genius is 'talent in which character makes itself heard', and it is the preserve of the Gentile. Genius is the flowering of nature, and the man of genius is creative while the man of talent is only critical: 'Even the greatest of Jewish thinkers is no more than talented. (Myself for instance.) . . . I don't believe I have ever *invented* a line of thinking. I have always taken one over from someone else.'

Thus we can see the old Romantic themes revived and re-worked in relation to race: the sense of a lost tradition; of the need now to rely on the self; on the failure of the self to respond and the consequent feeling that we have entered a barren time. As Schiller had drawn the lines between the naive and the sentimental; as Wordsworth had explained his sense of his adult dryness by contrasting it with a benign vision of childhood; so Wittgenstein, in the wake of Weininger and Spengler, draws up the lines between himself, a Jew, and — say — Beethoven, the Gentile creator.

But this was of course before Hitler. It is striking that unlike Pasternak, that other Christianised Jew, who hated what he conceived as Jewishness and went on hammering away at the contrast between (bad) Jew and (good) Christian long after what had happened in Europe between 1933 and 1945 had become general knowledge, Wittgenstein thoroughly re-thought his position in the wake of Hitler's rise to power. Fania Pascal recounts how Wittgenstein in 1937 went round Cambridge actively telling people about his Jewishness, fearing that he had misled them into thinking he was a Gentile. At the same time a profound change was taking place in his thought. This would not lead to any clear resolution, as the preface to the *Investigations* makes clear, but it would lead to a questioning of his earlier certainties. One of the remarks in *Culture and Value* suggests his new attitude: 'When you can't unravel a tangle, the most sensible thing is for you to recognise this; and the most honourable thing, to admit it. (Anti-Semitism.) What you ought to do to remedy the evil is *not* clear. What you must *not* do is clear in particular cases.'

This change of attitude coincided with (and no doubt meshed with in complex ways, rather like Eliot's conversion and change of poetic direction in the 1920s) a new acceptance of his gifts, rather than an attempt to fight them. 'Is what I am doing really worth the effort? Yes, but only if a light shines on it from above. And if that happens — why should I concern myself that the fruits of my labours should not be stolen? If what I am writing really has some value, how could anyone steal the value from me? And if the light from above is lacking, I can't in any case be more than clever.' Perhaps these questions of originality and secondariness don't really matter. Perhaps his inability to create a rich organic work is not his fault – for being who he is, for being a Jew – but is, rather, 'connected with the very nature of the investigation'. And indeed it is possible to see the *Philosophical Investigations* and all Wittgenstein's later philosophy not only as a partial repudiation of his own early work, but as an effort to undermine the platitudes of Weininger and Spengler and their Romantic heritage. It would of course be foolhardy for a non-philosopher to venture into the minefield of what precisely Wittgenstein was up to in his later work and what he achieved, but it is nevertheless striking to what an extent his remarks fit into the subject of this book and how much light he throws on to it. For it seems to me that against the Spenglerian notion of culture as rooted in the soil, as opposed to civilisation, which is merely superficial, Wittgenstein attempts to develop an argument about what I have called craft traditions, and to show that language itself is to be understood as such – not as rooted in nation and soil and not as willed and arbitrary, but rather as a *human practice*.

'Let us now examine the following kind of language-game: when A gives an order B has to write down series of signs according to a certain formation rule. The first of these series is meant to be that of the natural numbers in decimal notation. – How does he get to understand this notation? – First of all series of numbers will be written down for him and he will be required to copy them (. . .) And here already there is a normal and an abnormal learner's reaction. – At first perhaps we guide his hand in writing out the series 0 to 9; but then the *possibility of getting him to understand* will depend on his going on to write it down independently.' (143) He may make a mistake, or he may keep making the same mistake. We will know if he has mastered the rules if he can go on by himself and get it right. 'But how far need he continue the series for us to have the right to say that? Clearly you cannot state a limit here'

(145). It is the same with chess. It is unclear exactly how we master the rules, and certainly true that it is only in the act of playing that we can show how far we have mastered them. 'Where is the connexion effected between the sense of the expression "Let's play a game of chess" and all the rules of the game? – Well, in the list of rules of the game, in the teaching of it, in the day-to-day practice of playing' (197).

Thus we grasp a rule not by interpreting but by doing. ' "Obeying a rule" is a practice. And to *think* one is obeying a rule is not to obey a rule. Hence it is not possible to obey a rule "privately" ' (202). 'How am I able to obey a rule?' he has someone ask. And he answers: 'If this is not a question about causes, then it is about the justification for my following the rule in the way I do. If I have exhausted the justifications I have reached bedrock, and my spade is turned. Then I am inclined to say: "This is simply what I do" ' (217). Wittgenstein is trying to make us understand that speaking a language is not a matter of willing each step: 'When I obey a rule, I do not choose. I obey the rule *blindly*' (219). This may be open to misinterpretation: I obey because it is my duty to do so. But this is not what he means. He means rather that we do not question it the way the craftsman does not question what he does with his hands as he makes a pot or a carpet. What human beings say may be true or false, but they agree in the language they use: 'That is not agreement in opinions but in form of life' (241). Of course when the forms of life cease to be agreed upon that spells the end of the craft tradition. This is clearly what was starting to happen in the Renaissance and the Reformation, and what clearly happened with Romanticism. But Wittgenstein's quarry is not cultural history but the way in which craft tradition still inheres – and must do, so long as it exists – in ordinary language: 'What we are supplying are really remarks on the natural history of human beings' (415).

In order to bring this out he resorts to tactics rather similar to those used by Beckett in relation to fiction and drama: to make us see how things are by suddenly bringing us up against how it would be if they were not. 'I say the sentence: "The weather is fine"; but the words are after all arbitrary signs – so let's put "a b c d" in their place. But now when I read this, I can't connect it straight away with the above sense. – I am not used, I might say, to saying "a" instead of "the", "b" instead of "weather", etc. But I don't mean by that that I am not used to making an immediate association between the word "the" and "a", but that I am not used to using "a" *in the place of* "the" – and therefore in the sense of "the". (I have not mastered this language)' (508). Mastering a language is like mastering a game or a craft. Our problems with language arise when we think of it as like a work of genius, dependent on the inspired choices of the individual; or else, which is simply a mirror image of the first, when we think of it as authoritatively given once and for all. (The affinities between Wittgenstein's emerging concept of language here and Dante's in the *Commedia* are striking.)

I say the words 'Mr Scot is not a Scot'. Do I *mean* the two words differently as I utter them? No, of course not. Meaning does not turn on the intention of the speaker but on the language-game being played. (II.ii) Again, one doesn't take what one knows to be cutlery *for* cutlery when one sits down to eat, 'any more than one ordinarily tries to move ones mouth as one eats, or aims at moving it' (II.xi, p. 195). One just knows how to use a knife and fork through force of habit and, if they are provided, one uses them. And when we look and speak we don't form hypotheses which may perhaps prove to be false: 'Do not think you knew in advance what the "state of seeing" means ... Let the use *teach* you the meaning. (p. 212) The use is what he calls the language-game or the form of life and what I have called the craft tradition. To understand how language, the language we use every day, is a form of life, is to grasp that 'If a lion could talk we could not understand him' (p. 223).

Wittgenstein's aim, as he puts it, is, in examples like these, to substitute patent nonsense for hidden nonsense, which again is not far from what Beckett was up to in his early work and what Kierkegaard felt he had to do when he remarked that 'to find the conclusion it is necessary first of all to observe that it is lacking, and then in turn to feel quite vividly the lack of it'. Wittgenstein is as inventive as Kierkegaard in thinking up images for this state of lack. Do not imagine you are swimming, says Kierkegaard, when you are trussed up in a harness and raised from the floor and make swimming motions with your arms. 'Philosophical problems arise', says Wittgenstein, 'when language *goes on holiday*' (38). Example: ' "A new-born child has no teeth." – "A goose has no teeth." "A rose has no teeth." – This last at any rate – one would like to say –·is obviously true! It is even surer than that a goose has none. – And yet it is none so clear. For where should a rose's teeth have been?' (II.xi, p. 221). 'The confusions which occupy us arise when language is like an engine idling, not when it is doing work' (132). As with Kierkegaard, Wittgenstein is no detached observer: he has too often been the victim of language going on holiday while he is struggling with philosophical issues not to feel desperately the need for it to be properly at work. 'What would you be missing', he asks, 'if you did not understand the request to pronounce the word "till" and to mean it as a verb, – or if you did not feel that a word lost its meaning and became a mere sound if it were repeated ten times over?' (II.xi, p. 214). *He* has clearly often felt this, and felt it to be wrong. That is why he is so insistent: 'We have got on to slippery ice where there is no friction and so in a certain sense the conditions are ideal, but also, just because of that, we are unable to walk. We want to walk: so we need *friction*. Back to the rough ground!' (107). Like Proust and Eliot, Kafka and Beckett, he desperately wants to walk and at the same time knows how easy it is simply to *imagine* that you are walking. Somehow we need to find a way of creating friction, of feeling the ground beneath our feet.

But that is only so as to arrive at the point where you can be understood when you say you have reached bedrock and your spade is turned; when you say, not 'I do this because', but 'This is simply what I do'. 'Doubting', as he puts it, 'has an end' (II.v). The full implications of this, however, are worked out not in the *Investigations* but in the collection of remarks which have been published under the title *On Certainty*. It could equally well have been called *On Trust*, since its central argument is that there is a point at which suspicion has to end, at which the striving for certainty has to be replaced by action: 'How does someone judge which is his right and which his left hand? How do I know that my judgement will agree with someone else's? How do I know that this colour is blue? If I don't trust *myself* here, why should I trust anyone else's judgement? Is there a why? Must I not begin to trust somewhere? That is to say: somewhere I must begin with not-doubting; and that is not, so to speak, hasty but excusable; it is part of judging' (150).

What Wittgenstein is insisting on is that we have to trust not in the truth of certain propositions, as Descartes thought, but in the responsiveness of the world to our agency: 'Giving grounds, however, justifying the evidence, comes to an end; − but the end is not certain propositions striking us immediately as true, i.e. it is not a kind of *seeing* on our part; it is our *acting*, which lies at the bottom of the language-game' (204).

There are no foundational truths; but it is not a question simply of following our own whims. Rather, we have to trust in time as we advance by a process of trial and error, intuition and correction, responsive to the world at every step, confident that out of error and confusion we will arrive at something true, we will cease to slither on the ice of self-delusion and reach that solid ground on which we can advance. Wittgenstein wants to make us grasp that we are born into a world which is already filled with language and cultural practices and have to make do with that world. The notion, common to Plato and Descartes, that we can escape from tradition and start afresh is a mirage, born of unease with what they have come to feel as 'mere' conventions, 'mere' traditions. It is also of course an absurd overestimation of what individuals can do. This is a potent myth, but instead of helping us to function better it in fact leads to error and misery. In the case of the Spenglerian myths of race and decline it can, of course, lead to something much worse, as our century has unfortunately witnessed. Though language may be arbitrary in the sense that it is not linked irrefragably to the world, it is arbitrary only as the game of chess or the diverse craft traditions are arbitrary, and by learning to speak and to write we can grow into ourselves, fulfil our potential. Language is not something to be mastered or dismissed or treated as our plaything, but rather to be recognised as in a sense our partner in a voyage of discovery.

This emphasis on trust as part of what it means to be human, brought to our notice by startling examples of what happens when trust falters, finds interesting corroboration from quite a different quarter, the work of the neurologist Oliver Sacks. In his studies of the neurologically impaired Sacks makes frequent use of a concept he derives from his mentor, the great Russian neuro-surgeon, A. R. Luria. This is the notion of kinetic melody. To simplify: we do not walk by carefully putting one foot in front of the other, nor do we read by carefully deciphering each letter of a text. Faced with patients whose impairment led to their trying to do precisely this, Sacks realised that what was important was to get them to treat walking not as a series of separate operations, and reading not as decipherment, but somehow to give them enough confidence in their own abilities, in the firmness of the ground on which they trod, as it were, to allow them to plunge in and find their own rhythms. Music helped, but it was an inner music, he realised, that he needed to help them to discover. 'Kinetic melody', the melody of movement and melody in movement, seems to me a beautiful term and one which all of us who are fortunate enough to be able to walk and read without effort have experienced when we have felt ourselves to be walking or reading particularly well. Yet what Sacks brings out is that, like the old notion of the music of the spheres, it is always there, though so much a part of what we ordinarily do that we cannot hear it. Those for whom doing the ordinary thing is not possible can help the rest of us to see what a miracle the ordinary existence of human beings really is. And they can help us to see that in the rather different area of artistic creation the discovery by each artist of kinetic melody is the way to overcome the debilitating effects of the disappearance of craft traditions and the rise of suspicion.

Now that we are approaching the end let me try to sum up the main lines of my argument. I won't succeed, but let me try.

For those living and working within 'the substantial categories of state, family and destiny', both life and art are carefree, though that does not of course mean free of sorrow. But, trusting in those categories, the individual is freed of the burden of choice at every stage of his life and thus of an abiding sense of frustration and guilt; trusting in a craft tradition the artist thinks of himself as a maker, not a creator; as a supplier of something that is needed by the community, not as the unacknowledged legislator of mankind. When that trust goes, eroded by suspicion about those substantial categories of state, family and destiny, and, eventually, about the craft tradition in which the artist is working, for the citizen as for the artist the options seem to be either to rely on his own will and subjectivity or to obey the laws unquestioningly. But out of the Enlightenment and Romantic crisis there emerges a new understanding of the fundamental nature of trust, which is revealed as nothing less than our grounding in the world and in language. Trust now becomes something which has to be discovered, or acknowledged or yielded to, and this is never easy and takes different forms for each of us. But what the art and thought of the past two hundred years teaches us is not the lesson the deconstructionists and post-Modernists would draw from it, a lesson of our freedom to live as we want, to choose the stories and traditions we want to live by, the lesson of the hopeless entanglement of all culture and language in hidden struggles for power; it is, rather, that it is not possible to exist without trusting, that to walk and talk and, *a fortiori*, to write and paint and compose is only possible because of trust. When we grasp this we grasp too that denying trust is denying life itself as something that has to be lived in time and in the world of others, the world into which we have been born and in which we will die.

I want to end with two brief points, one about the reading of books and one about writing today.

What a reading of the later Wittgenstein and of Sacks suggests is that reading itself is always an act of trust. That is why it seems to me that the premise of an Adorno, a Leavis, a de Man, that we must at all times be on our guard lest we be taken in, is not a very good educational precept. This is not to advocate a return to the gushing enthusiasm of a certain type of Edwardian critic. As I hope I have sufficiently indicated, this is not what I would want at all. But suspicion has to follow trust, not precede it; it is only by opening ourselves up to the literature of the past and the present that we can begin to see what works and authors are meaningful to us and why in some cases we feel that the trust we initially invested in them has been betrayed. To begin with suspicion is to condemn ourselves to solipsism, as Iago and Goneril are condemned.

And so, finally, to writing. I began this book with the obscure sense that I wanted to explore certain problems which troubled my own writing. I am not sure now, having come to the end, that I have succeeded in shedding light for myself on what it means to feel the need to write today in a world bereft of craft traditions, in a 'dürftiger Zeit', a time of spiritual poverty, as Hölderlin put it, in 'der Finsternis dieser Zeit', the darkness of these times, as Wittgenstein would have it. Except to see that no amount of critical and intellectual examination of these issues really helps when one is faced by the blank page and decisions are required about whether to write 'He said' or 'He said firmly', about whether to describe a house in a phrase, a paragraph, a page or not at all. What happens then is that a form and a style have to be found that will satisfy not because suspicion has been momentarily lulled to sleep but because the means have been found to overcome it.

Of course I know, as Yeats knew, that we have 'lost the old nonchalance of the hand' and that our temptation is to substitute for it 'the gentle sensitive mind' or the dirty realism that is merely its flip side. And I know that it is folly to imagine that any political or philosophical or artistic *progamme* can take the burden of choice from my shoulders. And I know that the solutions of a Dante, a Shakespeare, a Proust, a Kafka, a Beckett, are solutions for them only, and that

> last year's words belong to last year's language
> And next year's words await another voice.

But I know too that if these writers are no help to others in the practical day-to-day choices we all have to make, they are nonetheless models and guides, who can give us courage in our darkest hours simply by having done what they did, having been what they were. And so, as Eliot enjoins us elsewhere in the *Four Quartets*,

> Not fare well,
> But fare forward, voyagers.

Notes

p. 4, 'last year's words' – 'Little Gidding', *Four Quartets*, London: Faber and Faber, 1970.

p. 6, epigraph – Franz Kafka, *Letters to Friends, Family and Editors*, tr. Richard and Clara Winston, London: John Calder, 1978, 70.

p. 6, 'L'Ère du Soupçon' – in Nathalie Sarraute, *L'Ère du Soupçon: Essais sur le roman*, Paris: Gallimard, 1959.

p. 6, Theodor Adorno – *Minima Moralia: Reflections from a Damaged Life*, tr. E. F. N. Jephcott, London: New Left Books, 1974, 25; 34; 63.

p. 7, a remark of Stendhal's – *Souvenirs d'égotisme*, ed. Henri Martineau, Paris: Le Divan, 1950, 7.

p. 7, 'Health and Spirits' – *The Letters of John Keats*, ed. M. B. Forman, London: Oxford University Press, 1952, 57.

p. 8, Adorno himself was later to write – 'Parataxis: On Hölderlin's Later Poetry', in *Notes to Literature*, ed. Rolf Tierman, tr. S. W. Nicholsen, New York: Columbia University Press, 1992, vol. II, 109–49 (143).

p. 8, described by Paul Ricoeur – See *Freud and Philosophy: An Essay in Interpretation*, tr. Denis Savage, New Haven: Yale University Press, 1970, and 'Psychoanalysis and the Movement of Contemporary Culture', in *The Conflict of Interpretations: Essays in Hermeneutics*, ed. Don Ihde, Evanston: Northwestern University Press, 1974, 121–59.

p. 8, 'Consider the cattle' – Friedrich Nietzsche, 'On the Use and Abuse of History', or, as the title is more clumsily rendered in the standard English translation, 'On the Use and Disadvantage of History for Life', in *Untimely Meditations*, tr. R. J. Hollingdale, Cambridge: Cambridge University Press, 1983, 60–1.

p. 9, 'These men' – Friedrich Nietzsche, *The Genealogy of Morals*, tr. Francis Golffing, New York: Doubleday, 1956, 287; 288–9.

p. 10, 'It is not improbable' – Søren Kierkegaard, *On Authority and Revelation: The Book on Adler*, tr. Walter Lowrie, London: Everyman's Library, 1994, 113–14.

p. 13, 'The finality common to both' – Roland Barthes, *Le Degré zéro de l'écriture*, Paris: Seuil, 1974, 32 (this and the following Barthes translations are my own).

p. 13, 'the discontinuous' – Barthes, 'Littérature et discontinu', in *Essais critiques*, Paris: Seuil, 1964, 175–87 (185).

p. 14, 'Pensive, the marquise' – Barthes, *S/Z*, Paris: Seuil, 1976, 222–4.

p. 15, 'Re-reading' – *ibid.*, 22–3.

p. 15, 'Today's writing' – Michel Foucault, 'What is an Author?', tr. Josue Harari, in *The Foucault Reader*, ed. Paul Rabinow, Harmondsworth: Penguin Books, 1991, pp. 101–20 (102).

p. 17, 'Among so-called negative thinkers' – Søren Kierkegaard, *Concluding Unscientific Postscript*, tr. D. F. Swenson and Walter Lowrie, Princeton: Princeton University Press, 1968, 76.

p. 17, 'All men are bores' – Kierkegaard, *Either/Or*, tr. D. F. and L. M. Swenson, New York: Anchor Books, 1959, vol. I, 284; 285; 295.

p. 21, 'I haven't written a single line' – Kafka, *Letters to Friends*, 70.

p. 23, a matter of temperament or circumstance – This is not rhetorical. Duchamp and Kundera, for example, seem to me to have a genuinely cold and ironic temperament which I respect and even admire in certain instances, though I cannot identify with it.

p. 23, 'What tedium!' – Beckett, *Malone Dies*, London: John Calder, 1966, 195.

p. 25, epigraph – Kierkegaard, 'The Ancient Tragical Motif as Reflected in the Modern', in *Either/Or*, I, 143.

p. 25, Thomas Mann – quoted in Julius A. Elias's introduction to his translation of *On Naive and Sentimental Poetry*, New York: Frederick Unger, 1966, 1.

p. 25, 'with free resignation' – *ibid.*, 101.

p. 26, 'One finds' – *ibid.*, 102.

p. 26, 'Nature seems' – *ibid.*

p. 26, 'The poet' – *ibid.*, 106.

p. 26, 'misled by acquaintance' – *ibid.*, 107.

p. 27, 'This touching depiction' – *ibid.*

p. 28, 'the more' . . . 'which will not be absorbed' – Kierkegaard, 'The Ancient Tragical Motif as Reflected in the Modern', in *Either/Or*, I, 141.

p. 28, 'even if the individual' – *ibid.*, 141.

p. 28, 'his whole life' – *ibid.*, 142.

p. 28, 'when the age' – *ibid.*, 143.

p. 28, 'lives as carefree' – *ibid.*, 153.

p. 28, 'If this is dark' – *ibid.*, 154.

p. 29, 'If this is seen' – *ibid.*

p. 29, 'My Antigone' – *ibid.*, 160–2.

p. 30, 'The Greeks' – Friedrich Nietzsche, Preface to *The Gay Science*, tr. Walter Kaufman, New York: Vintage Books, 1974, and Epilogue to *Nietzsche contra Wagner*, *The Portable Nietzsche*, New York: Viking, 1979, 661–83.

p. 30, 'I recognised Socrates' – *Twilight of the Idols*, tr. R. J. Hollingdale, Harmondsworth: Penguin Books, 1968, 29.

p. 30, 'Ultimately my mistrust' – *ibid.*, 106.

p. 31, the realism of Thucydides – *ibid.*, 107.

p. 31, John Jones . . . – John Jones, *On Aristotle and Greek Tragedy*, London: Chatto & Windus, 1964; Bernard Williams, *Shame and Necessity*, Berkeley: University of California Press, 1993; Martha Nussbaum, *The Fragility of Goodness*, Cambridge: Cambridge University Press, 1986; Colin McLeod, Introduction to *Iliad XXIV*, Cambridge: Cambridge University Press, 1986; Jasper Griffin, *Homer on*

Life and Death, Oxford: Oxford University Press, 1980; Oliver Taplin, *Homeric Soundings*, Oxford: Clarendon Press, 1992; Eric Havelock, *Preface to Plato*, Oxford: Oxford University Press, 1963; Gregory Nagy, *The Best of the Achaians*, Baltimore: Johns Hopkins University Press, 1979, and *Poetry as Performance*, Cambridge: Cambridge University Press, 1996.

p. 31, 'And now all the rest' – There are many good modern translations of Homer, in both verse and prose, but I have chosen to give the Loeb translations of A. T. Murray, which have a Victorian ring to them, because I feel they maintain the right balance between the archaic and the contemporary – since even when it was first sung Homen's poetry, we must assume, had an 'archaic' feel to it. The whole question of how best to translate Homer has of course been fiercely debated, but I feel that a fine contemporary translation like Martin Hammond's, which Taplin, for example, uses in his book on the *Iliad*, reads almost too naturally.

p. 32, *Hymn to Demeter* – Again, I use the Loeb translation, by Hugh G. Evelyn-White.

p. 33, and late Shakespeare – but see the excursus to chapter 4 below.

p. 36, 'The Greeks' – Jones, *On Aristotle*, 54.

p. 36, 'For the society' – *ibid.*, 168–9.

p. 36, 'the moment when a man' – *ibid.*, 170.

p. 37, 'My children' – *ibid.*, 234.

p. 37, Lawrence Langer – Lawrence L. Langer, *Admitting the Holocaust*, Oxford: Oxford University Press, 1995, 58.

p. 39, Martha Nussbaum – *The Fragility of Goodness, passim.*

p. 39, 'Plato suggested' – *ibid.*, 342.

p. 41, When Homer became – see Nagy, *Poetry as Performance*, Part II.

p. 42, my own book – *The Book of God*, London: Yale University Press, 1988.

p. 43, Umberto Cassuto – *The Documentary Hypothesis*, tr. Israel Abrahams, Jerusalem: The Magnes, Press, 1961.

p. 45, that fatal need to clarify – see Williams, *Shame and Necessity*, 43; 186 n. 5.

p. 45, 'knowing when to stop' – see chapter 9 below.

p. 52, Robert Alter – *Genesis: Translation and Commentary*, New York: Norton, 1996, 128.

p. 52, Bernard Williams and Martha Nussbaum – *Shame and Necessity: The Fragility of Goodness.*

p. 53, John Winkler – *The Constraints of Desire*, London: Routledge, 1990, 136–7.

p. 54, whether his bad luck – this is the subject of Bernard Williams's influential paper, 'Moral Luck', reprinted in Williams, *Moral Luck: Philosophical Papers 1973–1980*, Cambridge: Cambridge University Press, 1981, 20–39.

p. 55, *The Merchant of Venice* – see the note on Shakespeare references to p. 93 below.

p. 58, 'the famished brother' – Alter, *Genesis*, 129.

p. 59, 'This crucial verb' – *ibid.*, 140.

p. 59, 'At birth, Jacob's name' – *ibid.*, 142.

p. 62, Rashi – quoted *ibid.*, 182.

p. 62, Meir Shalev – unpublished lecture.

p. 62, my book on the Bible – *The Book of God.*

p. 64, 'Jacob's somber summary' – Alter, *Genesis*, 281.

p. 67, epigraph – Dante, *Paradiso*, XXVI. 130–31.

p. 67, 'What meaning' – *The Diaries of Franz Kafka, 1910–1923*, ed. Max Brod, Harmondsworth: Penguin Books, 1964, 400.

p. 68, Jacques le Goff – *La Civilisation de l'Occident médiévale*, Paris: Arthaud, 1972, 342.

p. 68, 'Ma per chiare parole' – I use the edition and translation of the *Commedia* by Charles Singleton, Princeton: Princeton University Press, 1970.

p. 70, 'cast forth' – I use the Temple Classics edition of the *Convivio*, ed. and tr. Philip H. Wicksteed, London, 1903.

p. 73, 'the supreme standards' – I use the Temple Classics edition of the *De vulgari eloquentia*, ed. and tr. A. G. Ferrers Howell, London, 1905.

p. 76, John Freccero – 'The Significance of Terza Rima', in John Freccero, *Dante: The Poetics of Conversion*, ed. Rachel Jacoff, Cambridge, Mass.: Harvard University Press, 1986, pp. 258–71; Teodolinda Barolini, *The Undivine Comedy*,

Princeton: Princeton University Press, 1992, 24–5. On pp. 25–6 she makes the further point that the *ri* in *mi ritrovai* is another example of spiralling motion, one step backwards to two steps forwards, so to speak.

p. 76, Freccero – 'The Prologue Scene', *Dante*, 1–28.

p. 80, the Romantic Bloomian notion – Harold Bloom, *The Anxiety of Influence*, New York: Oxford University Press, 1973.

p. 81, Here Dante and Virgil – I develop this in 'Eating Your Words: Dante as Modernist', reprinted in Gabriel Josipovici, *Text and Voice: Essays 1981–1991*, Manchester: Carcanet, 1992, 32–47.

p. 82, Giuseppe Mazzotto – *Dante's Vision and the Circle of Knowledge*, Princeton: Princeton University Press, 1993, 51.

p. 83, the childish babble – I am indebted here to Robert Hollander, *Allegory in Dante's 'Commedia'*, Princeton: Princeton University Press, 1969, chapter 3.

p. 88, Peter Hawkins – 'Dido, Beatrice and the Sirens of Ancient Love', in *The Poetry of Allusion*, ed. Rachel Jacoff and Jeffrey T. Schnapp, Stanford: Stanford University Press, 1991, 113–30 (122).

p. 90, Douglas Biow – 'From Ignorance to Knowledge: The Marvelous in *Inf.* 13', in *The Poetry of Allusion*, ed. Jacoff and Schnapp, 45–61; 58–9; 61.

p. 93, epigraph – Shakespeare, *King Lear*, I. iv. 319. This and all other references to Shakespeare are to *William Shakespeare: The Complete Works*, general editor Alfred Harbage, New York: Viking Press, 1977.

p. 96, Peter Brown – 'Society and the Supernatural: A Medieval Change', in *Society and the Holy in Late Antiquity*, London: Faber and Faber, 1982, 302–32 (307; 311).

p. 96, 'The hand' – *ibid.*, 312.

p. 96, 'when the traitor' – *ibid.*

p. 96, 'it is not a judgement' – *ibid.*, 313.

p. 97, Tony Nuttall – 'Shallow's Orchard, Adam's Garden', in *The Stoic in Love*, London: Harvester, 1989, 49–55.

p. 98, 'which had tended to be treated' – Brown, 'Society and the Supernatural', 325.

p. 98, 'for appeal to reason' – *ibid.*, 324.

p. 98, 'The same Lateran Council' – *ibid.*, 326–7.

p. 101, Emrys Jones – *The Origins of Shakespeare*, Oxford: Clarendon Press, 1977, chapter 1.

p. 102, Wittgenstein – *Culture and Value*, tr. Peter Winch, Oxford: Basil Blackwell, 1980, 84–5.

p. 103, 'What is Shakespearean' – Jones, *The Origins of Shakespeare*, 21.

p. 103, W. D. Snodgrass – 'Moonshine and Sunny Beams: Ruminations on *A Midsummer Night's Dream*', in *Radical Pursuit*, New York: Harper Books, 1975, 203–40/

p. 105, 'He wants to play' – *ibid.*, 226.

p. 105, Patricia Parker – 'Rude Mechanicals', in *Subject and Object in Renaissance Culture*, ed. Margreta de Grazia, Peter Stallybrass and Maureen Quilligan, Cambridge: Cambridge University Press, 43–82 (52; 53).

p. 109, Wittgenstein – *Philosophical Investigations*, tr. G. E. M. Anscombe, Oxford: Basil Blackwell, 1963, para. 20; see chapter 9 below.

p. 124, Stanley Cavell – 'Recounting Gains, Showing Losses: Reading *The Winter's Tale*', in *Disowning Knowledge in Six Plays of Shakespeare*, Cambridge: Cambridge University Press, 1987, 193–221.

p. 126, Cavell's fantasies – *ibid.*

P. 145, epigraph – *Collected Letters of Samuel Taylor Coleridge*, ed. F. L. Griggs, Oxford: Clarendon Press, 1956, vol. I, 656.

p. 145, 'Il est amer et doux' – Charles Baudelaire, 'La Cloche fêlée', *Œuvres Complètes de Baudelaire*, ed. Y.-G. le Dantec et Claude Pichois, Paris: Gallimard, Edition de la Pléiade, 1961, 68.

p. 147, '*Sapere aude!*' – in *The Portable Enlightenment Reader*, ed. Isaac Kramnick, Harmondsworth: Penguin, 1995, I.

p. 147, 'Bliss was it' – *The Prelude*, *The Poetical Works of Wordsworth*, ed. Thomas Hutchinson, revised by Ernest de Selincourt, London: Oxford University Press, 1969, 570 (Book XI, l. 108, 1850 edn).

p. 147, 'We poets in our youth' – 'Resolution and Independence', *ibid.*, 156.

p. 147, 'Holy Vessels are the poets' – 'Buonaparte', *Hölderlin*, tr. Michael Hamburger, London: Harvill, 1952, 6.

p. 147, 'But, my friends' – 'Bread and Wine', *ibid.*, 151–3.

p. 148, 'There was a time' – 'Ode on Intimations of Immortality', *Works*, 460.

p. 148, 'As to Poetry' – *Letters*, I, 656.

p. 149, Descartes – *Discourse on Method*, tr. Arthur Wollaston, Harmondsworth: Penguin Books, 1960, 44.

p. 152, Isaiah Berlin – 'The *Naiveté* of Verdi', in *Against the Current: Essays in the History of Ideas*, London: Hogarth Press, 1979, 287–95.

p. 153, 'Kohlhaas, striding up' – Heinrich von Kleist, 'Michael Kohlhaas', in *The Marquise of O – and Other Stories*, tr. Martin Greenberg, New York: Frederick Ungar, 1960, 182.

p. 154, 'as innocent as a newborn' – 'The Duel', *ibid.*, 310–11.

p. 155, 'wherever it was assumed' – *ibid.*, 318.

p. 155, Stanley Cavell – see especially *The Claim of Reason*, Oxford: Oxford University Press, 1979; *In Quest of the Ordinary*, Chicago: Chicago University Press, 1988.

p. 155, Richard Sennett – *The Fall of Public Man*, London, 1986.

p. 156, Goethe himself – quoted in G. F. Parker, *Johnson's Shakespeare*, Oxford: Clarendon Press, 1989, 13.

p. 157, 'Falstaff is a character' – quoted *ibid.*, 48.

p. 157, 'admires Falstaff's real abilities' – *ibid.*, 49.

p. 157, 'Falstaff is the most agreeable' – quoted *ibid.*, 85.

p. 158, 'something too horrible to be read' – quoted *ibid.*, 177; 184.

p. 158, 'For Coleridge' – *ibid.*, 150.

p. 159, 'The old religion' – quoted *ibid.*, 67.

p. 160, 'we see not Lear' – quoted *ibid.*, 95.

p. 161, Roland Bainton – Roland H. Bainton, 'The Bible in the Reformation', in *The Cambridge History of the Bible*, Cambridge: Cambridge University Press, 1963, vol. III, 1–37.

p. 161, 'how his neighbours' – *ibid.*, 23.

p. 162, 'This relation' – Johnson, *The Life of Richard Savage*, in *The Lives of the English Poets*, Everyman's Library, London, 1925, vol. II, 142.

p. 162, 'Is it, at the very last' – Richard Holmes, *Dr Johnson and Mr Savage*, London: Flamingo, 1994, 227. It was Rachel Trickett who first alerted me to the relevance of Holmes's book to my argument.

p. 163, 'I believe' – *ibid.*, 230.

p. 163, 'In Johnson's hands' – *ibid.*, 230–1.

p. 163, 'As honours are paid' – Samuel Johnson, 'An Essay on Epitaphs', in *Samuel Johnson: A Critical Edition of the Major Works*, ed. Donald Greene, Oxford: Oxford University Press, 1984, 97.

p. 165, 'There was a roaring' – 'Resolution and Independence', *Works*, 155–7.

p. 167, 'You are sad' – Lewis Carroll, *Alice in Wonderland and Through the Looking-Glass*, London: Collins, n.d., 284–90.

p. 169, 'Animal Tranquillity and Decay' – *Works*, 448.

p. 170, 'imagined as an inevitable knowledge' – Wallace Stevens, *Collected Poems*, London: Faber and Faber, 1955, 503.

p. 171, 'A more absolute climax' – Thomas McFarland, *Romanticism and the Forms of Ruin*, Princeton: Princeton University Press, 1981, 234.

p. 171, Gregory Nagy – *Poetry as Performance, passim*.

p. 173, epigraph – Proust, *A la Recherche du temps perdu*, II, 350 / III, 48. I have used the latest revision of Scott-Moncrieff's translation; though not the handiest, in six volumes, it is by and large the best. This and following quotes are followed by reference to the four-volume Pléiade edition, General Editor Jean-Yves Tadié, Paris: Gallimard, 1987, then to *In Search of Lost Time*, tr. C. K. Scott-Moncrieff and Terence Kilmartin, rev. D. J. Enright, London: Chatto & Windus, 1992.

p. 173, Paul de Man – 'Reading (Proust)', in *Allegories of Reading*, New Haven and London: Yale University Press, 57–78.

p. 174, 'The burden of the text' – *ibid.*, 64.

p. 174, 'In a passage that abounds' – *ibid.*, 67.

p. 174, 'The disjunction' – *ibid.*, 72.

p. 175, 'but . . . in allegory' – *ibid.*, 74–7.

p. 176, '*A la Recherche*' – *ibid.*, 78.

p. 176, 'By suggesting' – *ibid.*, 65.

p. 181, Rosamond Tuve – *A Reading of George Herbert*, Chicago: University of Chicago Press, 1952; *Images and Themes in Five Poems by Milton*, Cambridge,

Mass.: Harvard University Press, 1957; *Allegorical Imagery: Some Medieval Books and their Posterity*, Princeton: Princeton University Press, 1966.

p. 182, Erich Auerbach – see *Dante: Poet of the Secular World*, Chicago: University of Chicago Press, 1961.

p. 198, epigraph – Franz Kafka, *Collected Stories*, ed. Gabriel Josipovici, London: Everyman's Library, 1993, 195.

p. 198, 'A stair' – Franz Kafka, *The Collected Aphorisms*, tr. Malcolm Pasley, Harmondsworth: Penguin Books, 1994, 14.

p. 198, 'Nothing is granted to me' – *Letters to Milena*, ed. Willy Haas, tr. Tania and James Stern, New York: Schocken Books, 1953, 219.

p. 199, 'He remembers a picture' – *Collected Aphorisms*, 37–9.

p. 201, 'Once when I was a child' – *Collected Stories*, 279. The Sterns' translation, used in the Everyman edition, and the Muirs' earlier translation, are both unsatisfactory here, so I give my own version. See Franz Kafka, *Sämtliche Erzählungen*, ed. Her. von Paul Raabe, Frankfort: Fischer Verlag, 1982, 218.

p. 202, 'I was, after all' – 'Letter to his Father', in *Wedding Preparations in the Country*, tr. Ernst Kaiser and Eithne Wilkins, London: Secker & Warburg, 1954, 163.

p. 203, 'Marrying, founding a family' – *ibid.*, 204.

p. 204, 'the plans to marry' – *ibid.*, 202.

p. 204, 'The sight' – *The Diaries of Franz Kafka, 1910–23*, ed. Max Brod, Penguin Books, 1964, 371.

p. 205, 'It is easy' – *ibid.*, 163.

p. 206, 'If he should' – *ibid.*, 9.

p. 206, 'I live only here' – *ibid.*, 51.

p. 206, 'when I arbitrarily' – *ibid.*, 38.

p. 206, 'The tremendous world' – *ibid.*, 222.

p. 206, 'I can't write' – *Letters to Friends, Family and Editors*, 70.

p. 206, 'How is it possible' – *Letters to Felice*, ed. Erich Heller and Jürgen Born, tr. James Stern and Elisabeth Duckworth, New York: Schocken Books, 1973, 259.

p. 207, 'a description' – *Diaries*, 36.

p. 207, 'Wrote badly' – *ibid.*, 80.

p. 207, 'It is so easy' – *Letters to Friends*, 16.

p. 208, 'Childish games' – *Diaries*, 405.

p. 208, 'Szafransky, a disciple' – *ibid.*, 58.

p. 208, 'The disordered sentences' – *ibid.*, 104–5.

p. 209, 'He seduced a girl' – *ibid.*, 192–3.

p. 210, 'Once I projected' – *ibid.*, 37.

p. 212, 'In high spirits' – *ibid.*, 221.

p. 212, 'Dear Fraulein Bauer' – *Letters to Felice*, 5.

p. 213, 'This story' – *Diaries*, 212–13.

p. 214, 'An innocent child' – *Collected Stories*, 38.

p. 214, 'At this moment' – *ibid.*, 39.

p. 216, 'We have a new advocate' – *ibid.*, 163.

p. 218, 'I could never' – *ibid.*, 195.

p. 218, 'when I come home' – *ibid.*, 204.

p. 219, 'I was in great perplexity' – *ibid.*, 164.

p. 219, 'In his right side' – *ibid.*, 167–8.

p. 220, 'Strip his clothes' – *ibid.*, 168.

p. 220, ' "Do you know" ' – *ibid.*, 169.

p. 221, 'Like old men' *ibid.*, 169–70.

pp. 221–2, 'No fixed abode' – *ibid.*, 184.

p. 223, 'proof that inadequate' – *ibid.*, 398.

p. 223, 'Ulysses, it is said' – *ibid.*, 399.

p. 224, 'Last night as I lay sleepless' – *Letters to Friends*, 333–4.

p. 226, 'In 1846 the prolific painter' – See Alethea Hayter, *A Sultry Month*, London: Faber and Faber, 1965, for a detailed account of Haydon's last days.

p. 227, 'I always wanted' – *Collected Stories*, 231–2.

p. 229, epigraph – Samuel Beckett, *L'Innomable*, London: John Calder, 1966, repr. 1994, 7.

p. 230, 'Monologue? What's that?' – Samuel Beckett, *Dream of Fair to Middling Women*, London: John Calder, 1993, 25.

p. 231, 'The end is terrific!' *Endgame*, London: Faber and Faber, 1964, 34.

p. 231, 'What's happening?' *ibid.*, 17.

p. 232, 'Let us call it' – 'Dante and the Lobster', in *More Pricks Than Kicks*, London: Picador, 1974, 18.

p. 232, 'a fine girl' – *Watt*, London: John Calder, 1963, 100.

p. 233, 'Mr. Bagby was quite right' – quoted in Christopher Ricks, *Beckett's Dying Words*, Oxford: Clarendon Press, 1993, 168.

p. 234, 'They assured me' – 'Dante and the Lobster', 18–19.

p. 236, 'A plug of moustache' – *More Pricks Than Kicks*, 109.

p. 236, 'The sun shone' – *Murphy*, London: Calder and Boyars, 1969, 5.

p. 237, 'Spiritually a year' – *Krapp's Last Tape*, London: Faber and Faber, 1959, 15–16.

p. 237, 'dark he had struggled' – Deirdre Bair, *Samuel Beckett: A Biography*, London: Jonathan Cape, 1978, 312.

p. 238, 'I see a little more clearly' – *ibid.*, 317.

p. 239, 'Je suis dans la chambre' – references to the Trilogy follow the quotes. French references are to the Gallimard edition of the novels, *Molloy*, 1951, *Malone Meurt*, 1951, *L'Innommable*, 1953; English references to the one-volume Calder edition, 1966, 1994 reprint.

p. 249, 'There is no longer' – 'Trying to Understand *Endgame*', in Adorno, *Notes to Literature*, I, 241–75 (242).

p. 250, 'Moment upon moment' – *Endgame*, 45; 35.

p. 250, 'dire stroms of silence' – *Dream*, 139 (of Beethoven).

p. 250, 'A voice comes' – *Company*, London: John Calder, 1980, 7.

p. 250, 'Use of the second person' – *ibid.*, 9.

p. 251, 'What an addition' – *ibid.*, 20–1.

p. 251, 'Devised deviser' – *ibid.*, 64.

p. 251, 'Huddled thus' – *ibid.*, 86–7.

p. 252, 'Pacing: starting with right foot' – *Footfalls*, in *Collected Shorter Plays of Samuel Beckett*, London: Faber and Faber, 1984, 238–43 (239).

p. 252, 'Amy' – *ibid.*, 241.

p. 253, 'After the leaves' – 'The Plain Sense of Things', in *Collected Poems*, 502.

p. 254, epigraph – Ludwig Wittgenstein, *On Certainty*, tr. Denis Paul and G. E. M. Anscombe, Oxford: Basil Blackwell, 1979, paragraph 204.

p. 254, Kleist's puppets – 'On the Puppet Theatre', in *An Abyss Deep Enough: Letters of Heinrich von Kleist, with a Selection of Essays and Anccdotes*, ed. and tr. Philip B. Miller, New York, E. P. Dutton, 1982, 211–16.

p. 254, Nietzsche – *The Gay Science*, 37.

p. 254, Yeats – 'Ego Dominus Tuus' – *Collected Poems*, London: Macmillan, 1958, 180–3.

p. 254, epigraph – Ludwig Wittgenstein, *On Certainty*, 204.

p. 255, 'another kind of art' – *The Gay Science*, 37.

p. 255, Auden's clerihew – *Academic Graffiti*, London: Faber and Faber, 1971, 29.

p. 258, '*Ômoi*' – 'Sweeney Among the Nightingales', T. S. Eliot, *Collected Poems 1909–1935*, London: Faber and Faber, 1963, 57–8.

p. 261, 'what seas' – 'Marina', *ibid.*, 115.

p. 263, 'It was my intention' – Wittgenstein, *Philosophical Investigations*, ix–x.

p. 264, Ray Monk – *Ludwig Wittgenstein: The Duty of Genius*, London: Jonathan Cape, 1990.

p. 265, 'It might be said' – *Culture and Value*, 18–19.

p. 265, See on all this the suggestive essay by Yuval Lurie, 'Jews as a Metaphysical Species', *Philosophy*, 64:249 (July 1989), 323–47.

p. 266, unlike Pasternak – see my review essay, 'A Mistaken Position', *Times Literary Supplement*, 9 February 1990, 135–6, and the subsequent correspondence.

p. 266, Fania Pascal – 'Wittgenstein: A Personal Memoir', in *Ludwig Wittgenstein: Personal Recollections*, ed. Rush Rhees, Oxford: Basil Blackwell, 1981, 26–62.

p. 266, 'Is what I am doing' – *Culture and Value*, 57–8.

p. 267, 'Let us now examine' – *Philosophical Investigations*. I give the paragraph number after each quote, except for the quotes from II.xi, where I follow that by the page, as the section is so long.

p. 270, Do not imagine – Søren Kierkegaard, *Fear and Trembling*, tr. H. V. Hong and E. H. Hong, Princeton: Princeton University Press, 1983, 37–8.

p. 271, 'How does someone' – *On Certainty*, I give the paragraph number.

p. 272, Oliver Sacks – *A Leg to Stand On*, London: Picador, 1991.

Index